C000072481

INCOMPETENCE, CONFUSION AND LIES.

BENEATH THE BLUSTER

A DIARY OF DESPAIR

THE CONSERVATIVE GOVERNMENT 2019 - 2021

SUE WOOD

First published in Great Britain as a softback original in 2021

Copyright © Sue Wood

The moral right of this author has been asserted.

All rights reserved.

No part of this publication may be reproduced, stored in a retrieval system, or transmitted, in any form or by any means, without the prior permission in writing of the publisher, nor be otherwise circulated in any form of binding or cover other than that in which it is published and without a similar condition including this condition being imposed on the subsequent purchaser.

Typeset in TheAntiquaB

Editing, design, typesetting and publishing by UK Book Publishing

www.ukbookpublishing.com

ISBN: 978-1-914195-78-5

I dedicate this book to my family and friends who are as angry and despairing of the present government as I am. To those of you who think that this government is doing a good job in difficult circumstances I just ask you to read the following pages with an open mind. Thank you.

CONTENTS

PREFACE

SIX IMPOSSIBLE THINGS BEFORE BREAKFAST

This book started out as a dossier on what I perceived to be the shortcomings of this government. But as I woke up each day and found more and more to write about, it has become a book which I hope gives a voice to those in our society who are not being heard. So many lives have been affected by the two tsunamis that have swept this country, Brexit and the pandemic, that it is important to remember exactly how it came to be. The final decisions on Brexit were enacted by politicians, and the pandemic has needed a government of wisdom, competence, compassion and transparency. As you browse through the following pages, I think you will find, like I did, that this has not been the case.

Much has already been written about the last couple of years, but I obviously write from a woman's point of view. Although written first as a diary, I have gathered the different topics into individual chapters on women, our children, asylum seekers, the homeless, poverty, housing, the NHS, foreign aid, worker's rights, Nazanin Zaghari-Ratcliffe and much more. Then of course there is a chapter called 'Contracts, Transparency, 'Chumocracy' and the Ministerial Code'.

This book shines the spotlight on to a period of governance which will prove to be one of the most shameful in our history. It has become a

1

litany of the inadequacies of our present government and their self-serving policies which have caused so much damage and upset to so many people. This Prime Minister and his cabinet have a complete disregard for all regulations, rules and the law, and do not hesitate to try to change the law if it doesn't suit them.

Every day I have been upset, shocked and angry in equal measure at the stories I have written about. So hold tight, fasten your seat belts; it is a bumpy ride!

****

THE FIRST FEW MONTHS: BE CAREFUL WHAT YOU WISH FOR.

2019

JULY 24TH
Boris Johnson becomes Prime Minister and achieves his lifelong ambition.

****

AUGUST 28TH
The PM asks the Queen to **prorogue parliament** from the 9th September until 14th October.

****

SEPTEMBER 3RD
The PM removes the whip from 21 senior Conservative MPs after he lost the first round of a 48-hour Brexit battle against a hardliner Remainer alliance. **Sam Gyimah, David Gauke, Alistair Burt, Philip Hammond, Guto Bebb, Steve Brine, Caroline Nokes, Justine Greening, Sir Nicholas Soames, Anne Milton, Rory Stewart, Ed Vaizey, Margot James, Stephen Hammond, Ken Clarke, Richard**

Harrington, Sir Oliver Letwin, Richard Benyon, Dominic Grieve, Antoinette Sandbach, Greg Clark.

Some of these people had been MPs for a long time and had many years of experience. Indeed, there is Winston Churchill's grandson there. Ken Clarke, the Father of the House, was dismissed, as was the former Chancellor and the former Minister of Justice. So now we have a Brexit Cabinet and we hope that they are up to the tasks that lie ahead.

****

SEPTEMBER 28TH

All 11 judges in the Supreme Court decide unanimously that the **prorogation is unlawful** and parliament resumes on the 25th September. So although Boris Johnson had asked the Queen to do something unlawful, he refuses to resign.

****

DECEMBER 12TH

This was the general election when Boris Johnson won with what he called a 'stonking' majority of 80. He broke the so-called Red Wall in the North and promised them he would make "**levelling up" his top priority.**

****

And then the beginnings of the pandemic started to appear.

****

2020

JANUARY

The first reported cases of coronavirus in Europe were in late December 2019 and the first recorded case of the coronavirus in the UK was on the 29th January 2020 in York.

****

The PM missed **five Cobra meetings** at the beginning of the year. Boris Johnson was in Westminster for most of them but decided he had other things to do. But for one of them he was on **holiday in Mustique** with his fiancée Carrie Symonds.

****

FEBRUARY

The total number of cases in the UK had risen to 13 after four cruise ship passengers, flown back to Britain, tested positive for the virus. A government spokesperson said, "**We are well prepared for UK cases**, we are using tried and tested procedures to prevent further spread and the **NHS is extremely well prepared** and used to managing infections."

The PM was **shaking hands** in hospitals and on television and boasting about it.

****

MARCH

On March 1st the UK total of coronavirus cases climbs to 36 after 12 new patients are identified in England, and Scotland reports its first case.

****

The **Cheltenham races** took place on Tuesday 10th March and the four-day event saw 250,000 people attending. Also, the **Liverpool football match** took place on March 11th when 3,000 fans from Madrid flew in to join the 52,000 Liverpool fans and that was the very day that the WHO officially declared coronavirus a pandemic. But Boris Johnson was saying it was still OK to go about your business as usual.

****

But then, nearly a year later, we hear all of this.

2021

FEBRUARY 24TH

Four days ago in the Saturday *Guardian*, John Vidal wrote an article about the **Cheltenham races** which were allowed to go ahead last March, 2020. OK, it is easy to be wise after the event but even so...It is a long and detailed article but I really need to quote parts of it! On the 9th March the PM said, "As things stand...the best thing we can all do is to wash our hands for 20 seconds with soap and water." On the 13th March **Sir Patrick Vallance** told the BBC that he was opposed to further restrictions and that, "our aim is to ... build up some kind of herd immunity." That advice was to change dramatically in the days that followed. The behaviour of the crowds that were there (65,000) was described as sheer lunacy. Sports writer Alan Tyers recalls that, "people were rammed six deep at the bars, there was drunken shouting and singing. If you were going to design a virus dispersion hub, you could do worse than the indoor bits of a packed racecourse".

Racing is the second biggest sport after football, worth hundreds of million pounds a year in tax revenue. No sport had more powerful political patrons. One of the seven Jockey Club directors was **Dido Harding,** a close friend of **David Cameron** and the person who made such a hash of test and trace (see below). It is just interesting to note also that **Matt Hancock's links with the racing world** run deep. His West Suffolk constituency includes Newmarket, home to the Jockey Club. He was also a trained jockey, winning a charity race at Newmarket aged 33! And investigations by *The Guardian*, *The Mirror* and others have shown how Hancock's office has benefited from around £350,000 in political donations from wealthy figures linked to Cheltenham since becoming Newmarket's MP in 2010!

So, it was made absolutely clear by the government that the races should go ahead. Interestingly though, of the 20 members of the SAGE committee who attended most meetings in the five weeks before Cheltenham, none were employed by the NHS. And on the 5th March **Sage** noted, **"There is no evidence to suggest banning very large gatherings would reduce transmissions."**

NHS data analysts Edge Heath have calculated the impact of the Cheltenham Festival and the two big football matches played that same week resulted in **more than 100 deaths, 500 hospitalisations and 17,000 infections.** Nearly a year later we remain the country with the **highest number of Covid cases and deaths in Europe and the fifth worst-affected country in the world.** Sir David King, *The Independent* Sage founder says, "I believe they did not appreciate the severity of the disease. I don't believe anyone who did understand its severity would have allowed them to go ahead."

Geoff Bodman a 56 year old painter and decorator from Cardiff had gone to the races and now nearly a year on after contracting Covid-19 last March, he is still recovering. His breathing is difficult and he has had to learn to walk again. "I think it was the money that persuaded them to let Cheltenham go ahead," he said. "Whatever it was it should never have happened."

****

And so Boris Johnson begins to deal with the beginnings of a pandemic on top of having to cope with the results of his Brexit. 'Get Brexit Done' was his slogan and he thinks it will be done once the transition period ends on December 31st, 2019. But as you will see, Brexit does not 'get done'. It goes on and on and on. I ask again: Is this government up to the challenges that lie ahead? And is Boris Johnson going to be the leader of authority, wisdom and vison that we will undoubtedly need?

****

LOCKDOWN

So the word 'lockdown' was being bandied about and we all wondered exactly what that would mean. Well **Lockdown** didn't come till **23rd March 2020,** which everyone was saying was much too late. The scientific advice was saying on March 16th that without some form of lockdown 250,000 people could die of Covid-19 in the UK. Although social distancing and hand washing was recommended, there was no enforcement. Eventually the Prime Minister bowed to pressure, but it was the first example of dither and delay which certainly cost many lives.

We then found out very quickly what it meant! This first lockdown went on until...July 4th... Fortunately the weather was sunny and warm so we could get out for our daily walks, but apart from buying food and attending medical appointments there was little else we were allowed to do. Absolutely everywhere was closed including, of course, schools.

****

2020

APRIL 12TH
Dominic Cummings took a trip north whilst we were all locked down. Everyone will remember this! However (January 2021) Durham police

have not ruled out charging Cummings for perverting the course of justice. **A senior investigating officer has been appointed.**

****

Then at the beginning of **September 2020** Boris Johnson is urged by the Labour Party and others to have **a circuit-breaking lockdown** for two or three weeks, including half term. Again he refuses to do this and delays and delays, but brings in a three tier lockdown system instead.

****

NOVEMBER 14TH

Dominic Cummings has left Downing Street and he is now apparently set to accuse Boris Johnson of being prepared to put lives at risk by refusing to impose this second lockdown. Allies of Cummings have claimed he has a number of documents that could be damaging to the Prime Minister. It has been claimed that Johnson was strongly against **imposing another lockdown** in England last year, despite the advice from scientists at the time. He is said to have faced pressure from Michael Gove and Health Secretary Matt Hancock over the need for more Covid restrictions, with critics stating that the January lockdown could have been avoided had the November measures been more stringent.

The PM allegedly raged in response: "No more f***ing lockdowns – let the bodies pile high in their thousands." Downing Street has strongly denied that Johnson made the comment. Mr Cummings is reported to have a 'treasure trove' of internal memos and emails from the height of the pandemic that could paint the Government in a bad light. Well, at the moment, we have no evidence that Johnson said that awful sentence but the very fact that some believe he did is damning enough. And he certainly dithered and delayed about the second lockdown, ignoring advice. **Everyone was trying to persuade him to have a circuit break, which he refused to do until the 5th November.**

****

This lockdown was lifted on the **2nd December.** Hooray, we could all make plans for Christmas and look forward to meeting our families again.

And then...the country was given six hours' notice of the **South east and London going into Tier 4,** in spite of advice yet again having been to do this much earlier. This happens five days before Christmas. We and many others have mountains of food because we were expecting the family to be here.

****

2021

Then the inevitable happened and we were all put into lockdown once again on **5th January 2021**... This lockdown was really hard. The weather was cold and wet, and the days were short. It went on and on and on and we all seemed to get lockdown fatigue.

****

Then on the **22nd February** a four-step roadmap with dates was set out for the easing of the lockdown. But, at the time, all the dates seemed so far away.

****

MARCH 8TH

Schools are able to go back and Care home residents can have one regular visitor so long as they wear PPE equipment etc. We can have a coffee with one person outside.

****

APRIL 12TH

Hairdressers open!! This was such a special date for so many of us. Other retail outlets open, with zoos and leisure centres and self-catering cottages. The roadmap of the easing of the lockdown is now going really well.

****

MAY 16TH

And so tomorrow we are at stage 3 of the current road map out of lockdown. We will be able to meet up to six people or two households inside and pubs and hospitality generally can open their doors once again.

But wait a minute, what is this? An Indian variant has raised its ugly head and is spreading like wildfire and threatening not only this easing of the lockdown but the final one promised on the 21st June.

****

JUNE 9TH

And so, as predicted, stage 4 of the lockdown road map is 'hanging by a thread'. **Michael Gove** says today he would put his money on restrictions ending on the 21st June. **Other ministers** believe that the government should wait a little longer to assess the data and to ensure that more over 50s are vaccinated. And last night it was reported that **Rishi Sunak** was open to a delay of up to a month to ensure that the lifting of the lockdown was 'irreversible'. Then we have **Andrew Lloyd Webber**, all set to open his theatres this month, having spent a fortune on getting them Covid-safe, saying he is going ahead, come what may, and if the government does not like it he will say to them 'come to the theatre and arrest us'. That could be well over 1,000 people!

****

So again, uncertainty, no clarity, and a lot of confusion.

JUNE 12TH

Well, the papers are all saying that the easing of the lockdown will be extended for another four weeks to the end of July in order for more people to be vaccinated.

****

JUNE 15TH

Yesterday the Prime Minister announced that the final easing of the lockdown on the 21st June would be **delayed by 4 weeks** (probably) because of the spread of the Delta (Indian) variant. At least 20,000 people flew into the UK from India before the border was closed and PHE data has revealed at least 122 people brought the Indian variant to Britain from New Dehli and Mumbai between late March and the end of April. He was so sorry because he knew it was all his fault as he did not close the borders with India as soon as he realised that the Indian variant was entering the UK, and he kept them open for at least three weeks when they should have been shut. OK, OK, I made that last bit up! All true, of course, but obviously there are no apologies forthcoming.

We need transparency and honesty and someone with the ability to make the tough decisions.

****

So, this Indian variant in particular reached our shores because of the **problems with our borders and we see the general story in the following chapter.**

****

TRAVEL AND BORDERS

2020

APRIL 10TH

At a press briefing Matt Hancock the health secretary was asked **why our borders were still remaining open**. He said that the UK is "following the science". And he added: "we follow the science in terms of international travel all along and we saw right at the start of this pandemic that the two countries who brought in the draconian travel restrictions – the US and Italy – both of them have got serious problems themselves so I think that the science which we followed on international travel has been borne out by events." And then Professor Van-Tam discussed the reasons for not closing the borders more in-depth. He said: **"Our scientists have been very clear from the outset that that would not work as a measure to prevent the ingress of coronavirus into the UK. Coronavirus is now in the UK and transmitting very widely."**

****

MAY 7TH

Despite strict rules on the movement of people within the UK, there are still **no limitations on passengers** arriving from outside.

****

2021

FEBRUARY

Such a mix up about our borders. Some borders are closed which should have been done months ago. This was going to happen on Friday January 15th, but was delayed until Monday 18th 2021 because the tests hadn't been verified. Priti Patel is on record as saying that they should have been closed last March. But there are still 10,000 people arriving at UK airports every day. Who are they and where are they coming from? Now it is being said that they all need to quarantine in hotels on arrival. But still now at the beginning of February only people from certain hotspots are being told to isolate. **As Keir Starmer says, the schools are closed but the borders are open.**

****

The PM gave parliament the **wrong number** of countries that will be expected to quarantine at airport hotels on arrival in this country. He said it was 22 yesterday when in actual fact it is 30. Just a small mistake but it would be so good to be accurate.

****

FEBRUARY 11TH

People will have to **quarantine in hotels** for 10 days after they have arrived at airports from certain other red spot countries, it was announced. They will have to pay for their accommodation. There will be security guards and if they lie on their form about where they have been they will be fined £10,000 and sent to prison for 10 years. This, of course, is **complete and utter nonsense**. And when people went on-line to book in for a hotel the IT website crashed.

****

FEBRUARY 12TH

Apparently, the only airports where this quarantine applies are Heathrow, Gatwick, London City and Birmingham. Manchester, the third busiest airport in the UK, is not affected. Also, staff at the hotels will not get free regular tests.

****

FEBRUARY 13TH

New quarantine laws are said to be a complete shambles. Airports said the policy is not ready to launch with less than 48 hours to go. Border officials have not even been told how the system will work.

****

Reports of the South African variant are circulating in some areas and so everyone in certain postcodes will be tested whether they have symptoms or not. But SAGE were advising the government a week ago to make it mandatory that all people arriving from abroad should be quarantined in hotels. Matt Hancock and Priti Patel were also asking for this, but they were over-ruled by Johnson.

****

MARCH 1ST

Six cases of the **Brazil variant** of the coronavirus have been discovered, three in Scotland and three in England. Five have been contacted, the sixth is being looked for. It looks as though the border controls are not working properly.

****

APRIL 6TH

There has been a lot in the news about the **borders still being too open** for people entering the country. We are told they have to have negative tests and they have to isolate for 10 or 14 days, but it still seems incredible that despite the ban, Border Force staff say roughly

20,000 people are arriving in the UK each day, of which around 40 per cent are **tourists – around 8,000 people**. One tourist was said to have been granted a visa despite writing on their application form that the purpose of their trip was to "visit Big Ben"! Apparently as many as **90% of arrivals at Gatwick** are tourists. However, the immigration minister Kevin Foster said "we do not recognise these figures" and that "tough health measures" were in force even for those arriving in the UK "on a visitor visa for legitimate reasons". Nevertheless, that does not stop us all from being very concerned and worried about this apparent blatant disregard of the restrictions.

****

APRIL 20TH

Well, the Prime Minister has cancelled his **trip to India** at the end of this month. He was being urged to do that at least three weeks ago. Also, India has just been put on the red list of countries which imposes a travel ban on countries with high levels of Covid infection. But three weeks ago, Bangladesh and Pakistan were put on the red list and people were surprised that India wasn't. It has been revealed that thousands of people have arrived here from India since a new variant emerged. Again, the government has been accused of acting too slowly and shutting the stable door after the horse has bolted. This ban will not be enacted until 4 am on Friday. (Today is Tuesday.) At least 16 more flights will have arrived from India by then. There are at least **250,000 new cases a day** in India at the present time.

****

MAY 3RD

"**Utter Confusion.**" In *The Times* yesterday these were the first words in the **travel section** by Ben Clatworthy. He was talking about **the international tourist industry.** And he goes on to say that the words 'total disarray' would be appropriate as well. He writes about the appalling level of bureaucracy which as he says sucks the fun out of travelling. Ten forms to fill in, long queues to stand in, tests and more tests which can be expensive if done privately and having to take ages to try to find the results certificates, and the passenger location form with questions that need re-reading multiple times in order to be understood. "For Britons," he says, "**much of the stress is caused by our government** and it doesn't have to be this way. If the government maintains its requirements that UK border force officials check all arrivals' documents then they need to have the resources to be able to do so. This needs to include the technology to reopen e-passenger gates to prevent huge queues." I would not have thought that this was rocket science, so let's hope the government is reading and learning.

****

MAY 6TH
India is reporting more than 400,000 new Covid cases every day. A delegation from India has recently arrived in the UK for a G7 conference and two members have just tested positive. **So the whole Indian delegation is isolating**. Was it really a good idea to come?

****

Ten hour queues at airports have been forecast for people planning to go abroad this summer. Border Forces have warned there is "no way around delays" as they face checks on Covid tests, vaccine certificates and documents on every passenger. It sounds absolutely awful, as they say that people from all round the world will be mixing inside for hours as everything is checked for every passenger. The main thing that people appear to be concerned about at the moment, according to the media, is when can they get away for the summer holidays. Understandable, I suppose, but it really doesn't sound worth it to me.

****

MAY 14TH
It has been reported today that **Spanish and Italians** who are arriving at Heathrow Airport for **legitimate work in the UK** are being arrested by border staff and taken to a detention centre if their paperwork is not completely in order. **They are being taken to Colnbrook**

Immigration removal centre where some are held for up to five days before being removed from the UK. And like most detention centres, Colnbrook is surrounded by barbed wire fences. Some cells are reportedly windowless, and what windows there are have bars on them. It has been described as "a prison" by one detainee. Mobile phones are seized on entry to prevent people taking photos or videos – although they are later allowed to use phones without cameras. Also reported by La Repubblica, an Italian newspaper, arrivals are repeatedly searched and have their belongings confiscated – including suitcases, wallets and money.

Boris Johnson's official spokesman defended the removals, but while he insisted **EU citizens were "our friends and neighbours",** he refused to comment on "individual cases".

So, this is how we treat our friends. Is this government unaware or are they really this callous?

****

MAY 16TH

The third step of the road map is due tomorrow and even that has been causing concern amongst the scientists because of the spread of the Indian variant. A report by Public Health England said that more than 3,345 people arrived in the UK from India between the **25th March and the 7th April;** 4.8% tested positive for Covid when for those in England it was 0.1%. India was eventually put on the **red list for travellers on the 23rd April. But again, it was much, much too late.** To quote Jonathan Calvert and George Arbuthnott in *The Sunday Times* today, they say that "Britain's borders with India remained open for weeks as the PM prepared for a trip to the country in April where he planned to discuss a huge post-Brexit trade deal. The variant had first been detected in late February as the virus was fast becoming out of control in India. But hundreds of people were being allowed to fly into the UK each day for more than two months before Johnson abandoned his trip and put India on the red list". Now these are the two journalists who wrote the book 'Failure of State' which is a brilliant read and a well-researched account of the failures of this government over the pandemic.

However, at the press announcement two days ago, and from MPs on the radio today, we hear them all saying that no it wasn't too late, everyone had to take tests and quarantine, all is fine, black is white and the pigs are flying. And also, that the final date of easing the lockdown on June 21st is now definitely 'hanging in the balance'.

****

MAY 17TH

In a story that we hear about this morning there are apparently **special exemptions when quarantining in hotels for people with psychological or physical disabilities**. Obviously forms have to be filled in and if there is clear medical evidence then special arrangements can be made. However, the father of a boy with such difficulties was saying that they were treated appallingly when trying to quarantine at Heathrow. There was no indication that anyone with medical qualifications had read their forms and they were forced into a basic hotel where there was no food, where they had to be in a separate room from their son, where every time they tried to visit his room they were questioned by security staff in the corridors, and where they were only allowed out for a very short time for any fresh air. This has done untold damage to their son and a lawyer was saying that there would appear to be many others in a similar situation. He said that the department of health and the health secretary need to sort themselves out. There is a route whereby this can all be resolved but at the moment it is being ignored.

****

MAY 19TH

There is so much **confusion around travel** and about which countries people can now visit. There is now a traffic light system with green, amber and red lists for international travel, but politicians have offered differing advice over where the public are permitted to travel abroad. On Monday, Mr Johnson said: "I think it's very important for people to grasp what an amber list country is: it is not somewhere where you should be going on holiday, let me be very clear about that." Then a health minister appeared to **contradict official advice** over travel following the relaxing of restrictions by saying all international trips were "dangerous". But Environment Secretary George Eustice said people can travel to amber list countries if they quarantined when they returned. Health Minister Lord Bethell also added to the confusion after indicating in the House of Lords that people should not travel abroad, full stop.

****

MAY 20TH

Dr Gabriel Scalley, an independent member of SAGE, has criticised the government's handling of **the Indian variant**. He told LBC today that he was "amazed" that they are "getting it so wrong again": 110 direct flights from India have landed in the UK in the three and a half weeks since it was put on the red list.

****

MAY 24TH

All still seems to be confusion and chaos at our airports. Uncertainty and incompetence are the order of the day.

****

MAY 30TH

In the news today is the fact that the **Indian variant** was known about by the government on April 1st but we were not told until the 15th. And of course it was another eight days before it was put the red list. We will be informed on the 14th June whether or not the lockdown will be over on the 21st. I am not sure how Boris Johnson will be able to give us bad news for which he will be directly responsible.

****

JUNE 3RD

This evening it has just been announced that **Portugal** has been moved from the green list to the amber list. Apparently, cases of the coronavirus have been increasing in Portugal all of a sudden.

****

JUNE 4TH

Well, everyone is furious today! All the headlines are about holidays being cancelled, the travel industry worrying about jobs and consumer confidence, the boss at Heathrow saying that the airline sector faces another lost summer and Portugal saying that it can't understand the logic of the move as they have clear rules for the safety of those who live there and those who visit. So, when the government does for once act quickly it still looks rather incompetent.

The amber rule for Portugal comes into effect on Tuesday the 8th at 4am so everyone is scrambling to get home by then in order to beat the need to self-isolate for 10 days.

For we need to remember that it was only last week when the cup final between Chelsea and Manchester City was played in Portugal. Thousands of fans flew over to watch the match, returning the same day. Some have already been alerted by the health app, that they have been in contact with someone with the virus.

****

JUNE 7TH

There are photographs everywhere today of the chaos at airports in Portugal as everyone rushes to get home by 4am tomorrow.

Tim Alderslade, of Airlines UK, criticised the move, labelling the Government's traffic light method a "pretend traffic light system".

He told *The Times*: "They have ignored their own recommendations and led an entire industry down the garden path."

And Paul Charles, chief executive of the PC agency, a travel consultancy, said that the traffic light system for foreign travel is 'dead'.

****

JUNE 9TH

And now some ministers are saying just don't go abroad at all, which is making the entire travel industry furious. Today the Foreign Office was still advising people that Portugal was safe for travel. Complete incompetence once again.

****

JUNE 10TH

Theresa May attacks the government today and accuses their approach to foreign travel as being absolutely "chaotic". She said: 'One year on, we are no further forward – indeed, what we have is a devastated industry, jobs lost and Global Britain shut for business. More than not being any further forward, we've gone backwards.

'We now have over 50 per cent of the adult population vaccinated – a wonderful programme – yet we're more restricted on travel than we were last year. In 2020, I went to Switzerland in August, South Korea in September, there was no vaccine and travel was possible – this year there is a vaccine, travel is not possible. I really don't understand the stance the Government is taking.

'Of course it is permissible to travel to countries on the amber list provided it is practicable for you to quarantine when you come back but Government ministers tell people that they mustn't travel, they can't go on holiday to places on the amber list. The messaging is mixed and the system chaotic.'

She went on to say that 'Portugal was put on the green list, people went to the football, then Portugal was put on the amber list – leaving holidaymakers scrambling for flights and devastated families having to cancel their plans, not to mention the impact on the airlines, travel agents here, and on the travel industry and tourist industry in our longest-standing trading partner in Europe.

'Variants will keep on coming. There will be new variants every year. If the Government's position is that we cannot open up travel until there are no new variants elsewhere in the world, then we will never be able to travel abroad ever again.'

She also said that, 'Sadly, people will die from Covid here in the UK in the future, as 10,000 to 20,000 people do every year from flu.'

Well that just about sums it all up perfectly.

****

JUNE 13TH
The leader in *The Sunday Times* today says what I have been saying all along. "It is possible to be critical of a Prime Minister who failed to shut down travel from India quickly enough, probably because he didn't want to jeopardise trade talks with his Indian counterpart. This allowed the Delta variant (as it is now called), now responsible for more than 90% of new UK cases, according to the health secretary, to seed itself in this country."

****

And of course, especially when travelling, but also for work and for when people are beginning to attend huge events, they have to get tested numerous times and this can be expensive. Indeed, one of the most important tasks for any government is a really efficient track, test and trace programme. So how is it going, I wonder?

****

TEST AND TRACE PROGRAMME

2020

A test and trace app was outlined on the **23rd April 2020**. This, said the PM, would be **"world beating"** and would be ready by mid-May. It was delayed until June and then it was abandoned in favour of a different system. It became properly active to the public in September but is still not quite reaching its target in 2021. Baroness Harding, chum of David Cameron, was appointed to run the test and trace, and was a disaster. Questioned by Jeremy Hunt, chair of the health committee, she was unable to answer his questions or to give crucial details of the scheme, despite having had sight of the questions before the meeting. Contract consultants were hired at cost to the taxpayer of between £1,000 and £7,000 a day. Questioned as to why it couldn't be done locally, they said these people were needed because speed was of the essence. They are still being paid these amounts today (January 2021) and it is still not working efficiently. So it looks as though the government went into panic mode when **what was needed were cool heads, a measured approach and value for money.**

****

But read the following personal story. It is anonymous: "When I got polio on a farm in the middle of the Irish countryside in 1956, an Irish

Health Ministry official visited our nearest neighbour, a farmer called Dick Cunningham, the next day. He told him what had happened and advised him to keep his children at home. Other farmers in the area, none of whom had a phone, received similar visits and advice. All epidemics are by their nature local events. A certain person at a certain address catches polio, TB or coronavirus. Such diseases can only be contained locally by well-organised and well-informed people able to respond at speed to identify, isolate and trace the contacts of the infected person. Those going into voluntary self-isolation will have their lives severely disrupted so they should be told to do so by somebody with real authority and credibility and not by a voice from a call centre. We see that the centralised body charged with doing so, headed by Baroness Dido Harding of Winscombe, works less well than the ill-resourced health officials in impoverished rural Ireland more than half a century ago. Yet finding, testing, isolating and immediately tracing the contacts of anybody who has Covid-19 should be at the heart of any campaign to combat the pandemic. **It would have made so much more sense to have enabled local authorities to have organised it."**

****

2021

MARCH 10TH

MPs are warning that the impact of **NHS Test and Trace** is still unclear – despite the UK government setting aside **£37bn** for it over two years. Committee chairwoman of the Commons spending watchdog, Meg Hillier, said it was hard to point to a "measurable difference" the test-and-trace system had made. "The promise on which this huge expense was justified – avoiding another lockdown – has been broken, twice," she said. And the strange thing is that most of its contact tracers spent last year sitting idle. A third of its capacity is now going unused but still more than £2.7 million of taxpayers' money is spent a day on 2,500 management consultants. They are still being paid over **£6000**

a day!! Questions are being asked as to why these consultants still need to be there and how it could surely be run locally by now. I first mentioned this in April last year when the PM first announced this scheme and said it would be "world beating". I itemised the problems which followed." And **Baroness Harding, chum of David Cameron, is still in charge.**

****

MAY 20TH

It has just been reported by Public Health England that the **surge in the Indian Covid**-19 variant was fuelled by **failures in England's test-and-trace system**. Eight local authorities did not have access to the full data on positive tests in their areas **for three weeks** in April and May, it says. The number of missing cases was highest in Blackburn with Darwen, in Lancashire – where a recent surge in infections was linked to the Indian variant. The other areas affected by the apparent technical glitch were Blackpool, York, Bath and North-East Somerset, Bristol, North Somerset, Southend-on-Sea and Thurrock, the BBC revealed. Heads should roll.

****

JUNE 12TH

An American company called Innova Medical Group, who have sent the UK more than a billion lateral flow type tests, have told people to throw them away over concerns about their accuracy. They are being used at the moment on school children and for mass asymptomatic testing. They have also been used for large events including the pilot scheme of 180,000 spectators for the test match between England and New Zealand at Edgbaston this week. "This requires a seriously prompt response in the UK," a senior fellow of the Royal Statistical Society said. "The Medicines and Healthcare Products and Regulatory Agency is aware of these concerns and are reviewing all available information and are working closely with the NHS test and Trace programme."

It just shows how careful we need to be. Apparently, the US Food and Drug Administration said that this test had not been approved for commercial distribution or use in the USA, and Americans had been advised to throw them away or send them back.

****

And even as the Test and Trace system was, we thought, getting underway, we were all being told that it was essential that the NHS should not be over-run. We must **stay at home, protect the NHS and save lives.** And by and large this is what most of us did.

****

THE NHS AND
SOCIAL CARE

It was indeed one of the main concerns of all of us that the NHS should function well during this dreadful time. But years of underfunding by successive governments prior to the pandemic meant that it was already struggling before the pandemic took hold. However, as a result of the delay in lockdown, the inpatient numbers started to rise inordinately, medical staff were called on to abandon their speciality lists to work on the Covid wards, and actually hospitals were very quickly becoming overwhelmed.

In March 2020, shortly after the first lockdown was announced, it was discovered that agency staff moved between homes, and patients were being discharged from hospital into care homes without being tested. This went on until the middle of April, thus causing many unnecessary deaths in care homes and leading them to be virtually locked up and barred from having any sort of visiting for over a year.

****

I have also just discovered that critically ill Covid patients were being transferred from overstretched hospitals to other hospitals sometimes **more than 300 miles away** in order to free up ICU beds for new patients. Critically ill patients were being transferred from Ashford, Kent to Plymouth; from London to Newcastle and Sheffield; and from Sussex to Northampton. Dr Claudia Paoloni, president of the Hospital Consultants and Specialists Association, said this showed that the NHS was "on the ropes" after years of underfunding. This is an NHS that was definitely overwhelmed. "No one would consider doing this unless the situation was exceptionally bad, usually because specialist treatment is unavailable or staffed critical care beds had run out," she said. "This reflects the unprecedented gravity of the situation facing our NHS." But still we were being told to "Stay home, Protect the NHS, Save Lives". I think we all thought that the NHS was just about coping. But it obviously wasn't, and we continued to have the highest death rate in Europe. So, still no transparency, no honesty, more incompetence and more criminal (to my mind) negligence.

****

And again I read the book 'Failures of State' by Jonathan Calvert and George Arbuthnott. The authors tell us about what really happened behind the scenes and the **lies and incompetence** are terrifying. I just quote one comment from a hospital doctor who wrote to the Doctor's Association UK in March 2020 as the PM was still prevaricating: **"Too few ICU beds; too few hospital beds; poor staffing and resourcing; crushing underestimation of the potential impact on the part of the Secretary of State for Health and the PM."** And I keep thinking that if I had been admitted to hospital in the early days of the pandemic **I would have been left to die** in a general ward as I was over 70. The medical staff had been instructed to save the few ICU beds for younger, potentially fitter patients. But also, a document was distributed by Buckinghamshire NHS Trust asking all clinicians and GPs to urgently **'identify all patients who are frail or in the latter stages of life and score them based on their level of frailty'**. It made clear that the move was necessary because intensive care was 'expected to far outweigh capacity by several thousand beds in the south-east region due to Covid-19 and there was a limited staff base to look after sick patients in our hospitals'. This approach was being adopted all across England (page 267 in 'Failures of State').

No wonder the PM does not want an inquiry. So as we were being told to **"Stay at Home, Protect the NHS, Save Lives"**, I think the reality would have been **"Do your Duty, Protect the NHS, Die at Home"**.

****

But after a dreadful year there came some good news. On the **9th December** the first person in the world was given a vaccination in Coventry.

****

2021

JANUARY
The vaccination roll-out proceeds at a rather slow pace.

Still a slow roll-out of vaccines...**11th January.**

****

JANUARY 26TH
Boris Johnson has been condemned by a prominent nursing union after he made an "inaccurate" claim that nurses have been given a 12.8% pay rise over three years. At today's Downing Street press conference, the prime minister declined to give NHS staff in England a financial bonus as a gesture of support, after health and social care staff in Scotland got a £500 payment.

****

MARCH 5TH
Labour has accused Boris Johnson of lying to MPs after he wrongly claimed Sir Keir Starmer had voted against a pay-rise for NHS workers in England.

The party is calling on the PM to "correct the record" after he said Labour had voted against a 2.1% rise.

The 2.1% proposal – which has since been scrapped in favour of 1% – was approved **without a vote** in 2020.

Downing Street said the mistake had been clarified and there was no need for the PM to apologise. **If MPs knowingly lie to parliament then they are expected to resign**. In the final chapter of 'The Assault of Truth' by Peter Oborne it is suggested that if we hear of a lie in parliament we should write to the Speaker and to our MP. So that is precisely what I am about to do.

****

MARCH 18TH

It has been revealed that more than 500 people may have had their human rights breached over **'do not resuscitate'** decisions made at the beginning of the pandemic. Some families, it says, were not properly involved and others totally unaware that decisions had been made. The Care Quality Commission was asked by the Department of Health and Social Care to conduct a rapid review of how these decisions were used at the start of the coronavirus pandemic. It followed concerns that decisions were being made without the involvement of patients or relatives, and that they were being applied in a **blanket way to particular groups, for example people with learning disabilities**. Some families are threatening to take legal action against the government.

****

MARCH 24TH

Well how did I miss this? Buried in the budget by Rishi Sunak on the 3rd March was the withdrawing of a planned increase **of £30 billion in day- to-day spending** at the department for **Health and Social Care** from April this year. It came as the head of *The Independent* spending watchdog revealed that the Budget offered **no cash past the end of the 2021-22 financial year to deal with the legacy of the pandemic**. Yes, the government has put in a lot of extra funding because of the pandemic, but the legacy of the pandemic is going to be an enormous strain on the NHS. So, the additional funding will stop and there will be nothing extra for all the delayed operations, the annual vaccination programme, an on-going test and trace capacity and no help for the 4.5 million people on the waiting lists. The NHS was under-resourced at the start of this pandemic. Doctors and nurses and all those working in our hospitals and with the NHS at the moment are burnt-out, exhausted and traumatised. This latest cut beggars belief. The NHS is under-staffed and so many medics are threatening to leave. Why are our government so blind? These are the people who have saved so many lives, including that of the Prime Minister.

****

Scottish nurses are to be offered a pay rise of at least 4% in a deal from the Scottish Government. It will actually benefit nurses, paramedics and allied health professionals, as well as domestic, healthcare support staff, porters and other frontline health workers. It will also mean that staff on the lowest pay point will get a 5.4% increase. It will be backdated from December, meaning all those covered by the deal will receive an extra benefit. Just saying.

****

All Nightingale hospitals to close on April 1st. Seven Nightingale hospitals were built in England, starting in April 2020 with the 4,000-bed facility at London's ExCel centre. Another was set up in Belfast, while Scotland and Wales had their own temporary hospitals. These were hailed as a brilliant exercise and a wonderful answer to the overwhelmed hospitals. But they were never used on a large scale, because the NHS did not have enough trained staff to fill the Nightingales as well as the permanent hospitals. The Royal College of Nursing said the government had been misguided in believing that spending on beds and buildings would increase the NHS's treatment capacity. "Increasing capacity doesn't just mean providing more equipment; it means providing the trained staff to operate it and provide high quality care," said Jude Diggins, the RCN's interim director of nursing, policy and public affairs. "We entered this pandemic with **almost 40,000 nursing vacancies in the NHS in England alone so it would have been difficult to fully staff these facilities safely."**

So why did the government think that they could staff these hospitals when the NHS was already so short of staff? Surely anyone with half a brain could figure that one out. It was a massive publicity venture which became a massive white elephant.

****

Only three of the seven Nightingale hospitals in England have ever been used to treat Covid patients – despite costing the taxpayer more than **£500m** to set-up and keep on standby.

The Birmingham Nightingale hospital was built from scratch in just two weeks by more than 400 workers, supported by 60 Ghurkhas from the British Army. It was officially opened by Prince William. **It has not treated a single patient.**

The Yorkshire Nightingale in Harrogate has **not treated a single virus patient** during the pandemic. However, it was used for non-virus diagnostic tests and outpatient appointments. As I write, contractors have started removing medical equipment from the venue.

The Nightingales at Sunderland and Bristol have **never been used for any Covid inpatient** care despite thousands of beds being available for this purpose.

Manchester and Exeter treated just over 100 patients each.

****

APRIL 1ST
All Nightingale hospitals close today.

****

APRIL 20TH

The national midwife shortage continues, with the NHS in England short of the equivalent of almost **2,500 full-time midwives**. That is according to the latest Royal College of Midwives analysis of birth figures published earlier this month by the Office for National Statistics. Services are already stretched almost to breaking point, with 42% reporting that half of shifts are understaffed, and a third saying there are very significant gaps in most shifts. These shortages are taking their toll on midwives and maternity support workers, with morale at rock-bottom. Seven out of 10 have considered leaving the profession, while more than a third are seriously thinking about it.

Gill Walton, Chief Executive of the Royal College of Midwives, said: "Maternity staff are exhausted, they're demoralised and some of them are looking for the door. For the safety of every pregnant woman and every baby, this cannot be allowed to continue."

Targets set in 2010 by Prime Minister David Cameron to increase the number of midwives by 3,000 have failed to materialise 10 years on.

Gill Walton added: "Midwives and maternity support workers are incredibly resilient, and it saddens and angers me to see the system crushing that indomitable spirit. They come into the profession to support women and families through a life-changing time in their lives. They aim to provide safe, high quality care. The legacy of under-funding and under-investment is robbing them of that – and worse still, it's putting those women and families at risk. It shouldn't have taken a global pandemic to shine a light on these issues. We are saying to policy-makers, stop kicking the can down the road. **Fund maternity services now**, fund them properly, and give staff the resources and support they need before we lose more of them, cutting even deeper into the ability of maternity and the NHS to ensure safe services and the best care."

So, in the light of all this it is sadly no surprise to hear that Councillors in Birmingham have now agreed a goal to halve the area's rate of infant mortality after being shown that **100 babies die in the city every year before their first birthday.** But a letter in *The Times* today also makes very interesting but shocking reading. Dr Peter Green, who is chairman of the National Network of Designated Healthcare Professionals for Children, writes that, "if all the infants born in the UK in 2017 had been born in Finland as **many as 1,500 more would have survived**". He says that "when assessed over the past decade, the statistics indicate **well over 10,000 excess UK infant deaths in that time**". And he goes on to say that "reversing the state of infant mortality should not be for Birmingham alone but should be a paramount concern for all of us".

I cannot begin to tell you how distressing I find this story.

****

MAY 5TH
And now MPs have urged the Government to change the law to ensure an end to the **blanket ban on care home visits**. Government guidance makes clear that care home providers should not impose blanket bans on care home visits, but should instead conduct **individualised risk assessments** for each resident. However, a report published today by the Joint Committee on Human Rights argues that this guidance should be **underpinned by law**. The committee chair, Harriet Harman, said that "The Government has listened to recommendations from this committee and others that restrictions on visiting rights must only be implemented on the basis of an individualised risk assessment which takes into account the risks to the resident's physical and mental wellbeing of not having visits". However, she added: "By not underpinning this guidance in law, care homes have not felt bound by it and important rights have therefore not been respected." Responding to the report, the minister for care, Helen Whately, said, "We recognise that every care home has a unique layout, physical environment and facilities, and residents have their

own individual health and wellbeing needs, which is why **care homes themselves are best placed to decide how to enable visiting safely."**

This makes perfect sense, but it is far too late for so many families who were unable to visit loved ones as they were nearing the end of their lives.

****

It is anticipated that **social care reforms and funding** will be delayed and not announced in the Queen's Speech on 11th May. We will see. But when Johnson came to power he promised to "fix the crisis in social care once and for all". Last month he said it was "highly likely" that his plan would be in the Queen's Speech.

****

MAY 7TH
Adding 1p to income tax, national insurance and VAT would allow the government to properly fund the NHS and tackle the social care crisis, experts have said in *The Lancet* today. Reporting, after three years, the London School of Economics and Political science –Lancet Commission on the future of the NHS describes how although the NHS is internationally held up as a leading example of universal health care, the health of the UK population lags behind that of other high-income countries.

The authors highlight the **comparatively low funding** for the health service, as well as the long-standing impact of poorly resourced social care and public health programmes on the health of the nation and its role in driving inequalities. They say **that decades of costly re-organisations, years of austerity, extreme cuts in funding to social care and an expansion of public health capacity have widened inequality and left the NHS under-resourced**. They go on to say that social care and public health should each receive a spending injection of £3.2billion in 2018/2019 terms.

But as Polly Toynbee says in *The Guardian* today, "Don't hold your breath for genuine social care reform. Expect only bungs to stop councils collapsing under the strain in this autumn's comprehensive spending review. The Institute for Fiscal Studies says the last budget delivered 8% cuts to most departments: **councils yet again will be forced to wield the Treasury's axe.**"

****

MAY 11TH

Well she is absolutely right. There was nothing in the Queen's Speech today about social care reform, just as we expected. Just one sentence saying plans will be ongoing. So, nothing delivered on that then.

****

Anaesthetists out of jobs.

And also in the media today there is an item which reports that apparently **hundreds of doctors** working on the front line during the Covid pandemic have been told they **won't have jobs** in the NHS training scheme from August, despite the health service being dependent on them to tackle surgical backlogs.

The Independent reports that almost **700 anaesthetists** – who had key roles caring for critically ill patients struggling to breathe during the Covid surges – have been dropped from the NHS training scheme and are unable to progress in their careers because of a **shortage in places**. They go on to say "One junior doctor listed 40 jobs across the country that he would have considered moving to, but had been rejected for every single one, despite ranking in the top third of candidates nationally."

On top of all this from next year, the RCOA is also adding an extra year before registrar training starts and so as doctors try to avoid the changes the bottleneck gets worse. Dr Helgi Johannsson, from the RCOA, said the number of doctors being trained was not enough to meet the demands of the NHS. He said: "These people have already been through one extremely competitive recruitment round and then to be rejected at the second one is going to be psychologically crushing, especially in a year where their training has been disrupted enormously by Covid.

"These are doctors who've been absolutely frontline in the fight against coronavirus. This could dissuade some trainees from pursuing their career in anaesthesia, which would be a great tragedy."

He added: "The number of anaesthetists being trained does not match the capacity need at the moment and certainly not in the near future while we try and get the elective operating capacity back up, to provide the public with the surgical and anaesthetic service they need."

There are now a record 4.7 million patients waiting for routine hospital treatment, including more than 350,000 who have waited more than a year.

So, if you are ever called in for your long awaited surgery, check that they have got an anaesthetist lined up. Alternatively, **write to your MP NOW** and ask what on earth is going on.

****

Health worries in Prisons.

Early release schemes have been recommended by the World Health Organization as one way of getting prisoners with health vulnerabilities out of harm's way. The government announced such a scheme for England and Wales early on in the pandemic. A mere 316 prisoners were released under the scheme before it was discontinued last year. To put this in perspective, Northern Ireland, with a fraction of the prison population of England and Wales, has to date released 335 prisoners. Prioritising prison staff and prisoners for vaccination is another policy the government could pursue, but have so far declined to do so. Earlier this week, the Bishop of Gloucester, who is also the

Bishop to prisons, was the latest parliamentarian to call for such an approach.

****

The Centre for Crime and Justice Studies has just sent me a copy of a new report from the government's scientific advisors on **COVID-19 in prison**. The treatment of prisoners is a cause close to my heart and this report is very clear. This is part of their email:

*"Prisons are highly vulnerable to COVID-19 outbreaks, with rates of infection and hospitalisation higher than in the general population, the report from the government's SAGE committee, **Covid-19 Transmission In Prison Settings**, points out. Even as rates of infection in the wider community decline, prisons remain at high risk of outbreaks. Controlling the transmission of COVID into and out of prison will prove to be more and more challenging, the scientists argue, as activity in the courts and the wider criminal justice system returns to pre-COVID levels. Unsurprisingly, the scientists behind the report argue in favour of **early vaccination** of staff and prisoners. "**Increasing early vaccination of all prisoners and staff**", the report points out, "would allow faster lifting of severe restrictions, reduce outbreaks and decrease mortality, and benefit the wider control of Covid-19". Since the start of lockdown just over a year ago, 143 prisoners have died as a result of COVID 19. The SAGE report, and the grim death toll in our prisons, should be more than enough to prompt the kind of proactive vaccination programme that many, including the Centre for Crime and Justice Studies, have been advocating for some time.*

*Appearing before members of parliament last week, the Justice Secretary **Robert Buckland** declared himself **"quite worked up"** about the SAGE report. Unfortunately, he was agitated by the awkward challenge it posed to his policies, not seized by the opportunity it presented to do something to better protect the lives of prisoners and prison staff. "I think it's wrong, I think it's based upon misconceptions, **I reject it", he said.***

*Having **failed** previously to implement an **early release programme**
to get as many prisoners as possible out of harm's way, the Justice
Secretary now appears more interested in trashing serious-minded
scientific analysis than in being guided by its insights. In the fight
against COVID in prisons, we can only hope that science and reason
will, at some point, triumph over base political calculation."*

How can anything even begin to improve if our ministers just
reject the experts and talk rubbish like that? But we know that this
government does not see vulnerable people as human beings to be
treated with fairness and compassion. Yes, of course, some prisoners
and some asylum seekers are difficult to deal with, but to treat them
all as though they are sub-human is despicable.

****

Yes, the vaccine programme has been a success for most people,
largely due, I have to say, to Kate Bingham, her team and the scientists,
but there has been no real discussion as to who should be vaccinated
and in what order. Not an easy decision by any means, but police,
teachers, and those in prison could, I think, have come after the
elderly. But anyway as you get your vaccine just be glad you are not
in prison. Always, always ignored.

****

MAY 17TH

And there is a letter in *The Times* this morning from Juliet Lyon,
chairwoman of *The Independent* Advisory Panel on Deaths in Custody
and two others, about the urgent need **to vaccinate all prison staff
and prisoners,** more so now especially since the Indian virus. She
writes that increased early vaccination of all those who live and work
in prisons would, Sage says, "allow faster lifting of severe restrictions,
reduce outbreaks and decrease mortality, and benefit the wider
control of Covid-19".

****

MAY 19TH

A nurse who cared for Boris Johnson when he was in hospital with Covid-19 has decided to quit the nursing profession in this country because of the lack of respect by this government for health care workers and because of the bad handling of the pandemic by them. The latest pay review was the last straw. She was asked to join in a clap for carers photoshoot with the PM but refused to do so. "I wanted to stay out of it," she said. "Lots of nurses felt that the government hadn't led very effectively—the indecisiveness, so many mixed messages. It was very upsetting."

****

A programme on television last night about the Coventry University Hospital just highlighted some of the problems facing the NHS at the moment. Because so many of our lovely European nurses have returned to Europe and because we are not training nearly enough of our own nurses, they are 'importing' nurses from India. About 300 of them have come to Coventry and are being trained up. After three years they will then be able to bring their families over here. Now of course the Indian variant has put a stop to that for the moment. And of course, India needs nurses more than ever. It is absolutely immoral to take nurses away from India.

****

MAY 27TH

At last the Government has just announced that **care home residents** will be able to leave for 'low risk' visits without having to self-isolate for 14 days when they get back. The rule change comes after the government was **threatened with legal action**, by family members who said that the government was causing care homes to act unlawfully by imprisoning residents in their homes, and they called the existing regime 'barbaric'. From Tuesday (tomorrow) residents leaving their home for a walk or to visit a friend's or family's garden will no longer have to isolate for two weeks on their return. But they must be accompanied by either a member of staff or one of their two nominated visitors, and stick to social distancing rules throughout. They will not be allowed to go indoors, except to **use the toilet** or, listen to this, **to cast a vote** in the upcoming local elections on the 6th. Well, well, very timely. They should also avoid public transport where possible. It is understood a resident would be able to eat outside at a restaurant or cafe with their care worker or nominated visitor if they agree this with the care home in advance. However, those leaving for medical appointments and for overnight visits will still be required to self-isolate for 14 days as before. But the story of one woman was that she had had a hospital appointment once a week for the last five or six months, so had spent all that time in her room. Also, there are many **younger people in residential homes** for health reasons and they feel victimised as well. The charity **John's Campaign** had threatened to issue legal proceedings next week unless the blanket self-isolation requirements were dropped. The charity's fellow co-founder Julia Jones said: "It should never have been considered permissible to confine adult members of society, without their consent (or those who speak for them) merely because their address happens to be that of a care home."

One woman was talking about her mother who is suffering from dementia. On going outside for a walk for the first time in months she said the **light had come back to her eyes.** Outrageous that there was no way they could get out for a walk like the rest of us before now.

****

MAY 27TH

But today Matt Hancock is in trouble trying to defend the decision to send people out of hospital into care homes **without testing them first**. Dominic Cummings has **accused him of lying.** What Hancock says he said at the time, though, was that he was setting up a system of testing but it wasn't ready straight away and there was not enough capacity initially. Of course, they were desperate to free up beds but testing didn't actually happen until the middle of April. And of course, many care homes were unable to isolate residents, workers were moving between homes and some staff were not being paid sick leave so had to keep working whilst ill. But Boris Johnson was claiming that he had put a "protective ring around care homes" which Helen Wildbore of the Relatives and Residents Association says is a "complete nonsense". She says that "people using care were failed by the very systems designed to protect them including the government and the regulator. To hear this confirmed after 14 long months and so much unnecessary loss is devastating".

Why is it impossible for the government and in particular the Prime Minister to say "sorry, we got it wrong"?

****

MAY 30TH

And today in the news the accusations and retributions go on. Sam Monaghon, chief executive of MHA, the largest charitable provider of care homes in the UK said, "On **12th March (2020)** there was a meeting of a large number of care home providers with the department (of health) to talk about the pressures the NHS could come under and whether or not we could facilitate and support the NHS. We made it very, very clear right from the get-go that we couldn't take people unless they were tested." He goes on to say that "on the 2nd April (2020) rules on discharge to care homes from hospitals clarified that negative tests were not required before discharge. By that time," he says that "nobody was talking to us. Some of our managers have described it as feeling abandoned by everyone around them." And last night it was revealed that Hancock was sent an email on 26th March (2020) from social care leaders specifically warning him that care homes were being "pressured" to take patients who had not been tested and who had symptoms of coronavirus. This email was also sent as a letter to the Prime Minister. And the government's official guidance was not updated until 15th April (2020).

There seems to be no doubt that this practice cost many lives in our care homes, and it would appear that panic and incompetence was at the heart of government at this time. Yes, it was an unprecedented and alarming situation, so maybe we can understand that to a certain degree, but what I, for one, cannot condone is the lack of honesty or as the shadow social care minister Liz Kendall said, the rewriting of history to avoid responsibility. We all know that the NHS needs a massive increase in funding and staff and training, and to glibly say that there are going to be 40 new hospitals in their manifesto is just dishonest and ignorant.

****

JUNE 4TH

Now you do really need to be aware of this one. The government is proposing a scheme whereby the NHS will upload the records of every person registered with a GP surgery in England to a **central database** without their explicit consent. All details about your health will be available to academic and commercial third parties. A lot of people are unhappy about this and David Davis (Conservative MP), together with a group of doctors and campaigners, is **threatening to sue the government about this.** The information will be anonymous so maybe you are not too worried. But it was tried and discarded as a bad idea about eight years ago. Some people think that it is being processed too quickly and that it is not a good idea to do it in the middle of a pandemic. They are saying that maybe it is being done now because not many people will notice! Can you believe that?

Sone GPs have said that they will refuse to hand over the data. You have until 23rd June to opt out, but I am afraid that this book won't be published by then. But at least you will know what has been happening.

****

JUNE 7TH

Apparently, **Dido Harding** (remember her?) is thinking about applying for the post as the next head of the NHS. Well, I am not sure that she would be the best person for the job. As reported in *The Times* today her allies say that she has built up from scratch a system capable of administering millions of tests every week and monitoring Covid levels across the nation. But a recent report claimed that failures in Test and Trace might have contributed to a **surge in the Indian variant**. And Sage said last year that the system had had **"minimal impact on transmission"**. Well, that is a damning indictment on the scheme which as we remember cost up to **£37billion** with no questions asked.

****

JUNE 8TH

A highly critical report has come out this morning from the Health and Social Care committee and it calls for immediate action to support our exhausted hospital staff who have worked throughout the pandemic. It also points out though, that even before Covid-19 there were 50,000 nursing vacancies in the UK. The Royal College of Psychiatrists has said a lack of staff is one of the biggest causes of workforce burnout in mental health services. And we already know about the shortage of midwives and the dreadful effect this is having on our maternity services.

Tory MP and former health secretary, Jeremy Hunt, who is chairman of the committee, said: "Workforce burnout across the NHS and care systems now presents an extraordinarily dangerous risk to the future functioning of both services.

"An absence of proper, detailed workforce planning has contributed to this, and was exposed by the pandemic with its many demands on staff.

"Failure to address this will lead to not just more burnout but more expenditure on locum doctors and agency nurses."

There just does not appear to be any long term planning for what has been an extremely long term problem. I do not understand how we allow this scale of incompetence.

****

JUNE 9TH

The government have just said they will extend the time needed for people to opt out of the NHS digital plan for patients, to September 1st.

****

JUNE 10TH

Matt Hancock spoke to a liaison committee today for four and a half hours defending the actions he and the government took over the pandemic. He never mentioned Cummings by name but said that the workings of the government have been better over the last six months...in other words since Cummings left in November. He said that the government was now better prepared to handle another pandemic.

Ben Wright, political correspondent of the BBC, said: "It had better be, because Mr Hancock's testimony added to the picture of a government stunned, sometimes inert and often overwhelmed as the Covid crisis engulfed it at the start of last year".

And families of the bereaved, especially of those in care homes, are not convinced and will be expecting further answers.

****

This is a litany of negligence and dishonesty, underfunding and false promises. The future of our NHS does not look safe in the hands of this present government.

****

But the one encouraging thing about this pandemic is that it doesn't appear to affect young children very much and so few young people ended up in hospital. So let us now look at how our children fared generally throughout this pandemic.

****

OUR CHILDREN

In fact, our young people from pre-school to university **have been amongst those who have had the most difficult time.**

2020

20th March. All schools close except for vulnerable children and children of key workers.

****

JUNE 1ST
After the long lockdown, some **primary schools** and nurseries re-open in England for children in nursery and years 1 and 6.

****

JUNE 9TH
Then Gavin Williamson, the Education Secretary, scrapped plans to bring primary children back before the summer holidays so schools close again after just nine days. Families, especially mothers, are tearing their hair out as having returned to work they now have to stop again, or search for some appropriate childcare, or work from home whilst trying to home-school.

****

JUNE 15TH

Then there is a scandal over **free school meals,** which is highlighted by the footballer Marcus Rashford.

Marcus Rashford has vowed not to give up after Boris Johnson rejected a plea from the Manchester United and England striker to reconsider the government's decision not to extend its free school meals voucher system for low-income families over the **summer holiday period**. Rashford tweeted on Monday afternoon: "We aren't beaten yet, stand strong for the 200,000 children who haven't had a meal to eat today." He asks people to keep retweeting his post. That post had been retweeted 13,000 times within an hour of going up with his initial letter being liked by more than 170,000 people. However, Downing Street has confirmed the scheme will end when the school term ends. The prime minister's official spokesman said: "The PM understands the issues facing families across the UK, which is why last week the government announced an additional £63m for local authorities to benefit families who are struggling to afford food and other basic essentials." They went on to say that "**The PM will respond to Marcus Rashford's letter as soon as he can** – he has been using his profile in a positive way to highlight some very important issues." Rashford responded, "I encourage you to hear their pleas and find your humanity. Please reconsider the decision to cancel the food voucher scheme over the summer holiday period and guarantee the extension. This is England in 2020 and this is an issue that needs urgent assistance. Please, while the eyes of the nation are on you, make the U-turn and make protecting the lives of some of our most vulnerable a top priority." And, as I report in a further chapter, at about this time gourmet food hampers were being delivered to the back door of Downing Street.

****

JUNE 16TH

And then Boris Johnson does a **U-turn** on his decision not to award free school meal vouchers over the summer holidays in England. The Prime Minister's official spokesperson said on Tuesday: "Owing to the coronavirus pandemic, the prime minister fully understands that children and parents face an entirely unprecedented situation over the summer. To reflect this, we will be providing a Covid summer food fund, and this will provide food vouchers over the six-week summer holiday period. This is a specific measure to reflect the unique circumstances of the pandemic. The scheme will not continue beyond the summer."

Why are they so uncaring? I just don't understand.

****

JULY 17TH

I write a **letter to *The Times*** which is published on 18th July.

Sir, The lack of women at the heart of government is indeed a disgrace (Alice Thomson 15th July). A top priority for Mr. Sunak should be free child-care for all children from the age of one. This would unleash a huge number of women into the work-force at a stroke. I very much doubt, however, that it has even been discussed. The complete debacle around school attendance and about home-schooling would indicate that the well-being of children and their mothers is never thought about by this male-dominated government.

****

AUGUST

A level and GCSE debacle. The exam results were produced using an algorithm. There was no proper preparation or transparency, and the algorithm did not work. There was no consultation with teachers and there was a massive **U-turn**. The Prime Minister has blamed a "mutant algorithm" for this summer's exam results fiasco. "I am afraid your grades were almost derailed by a mutant algorithm and I know how stressful that must have been," he told pupils at a school. The National Education Union called Mr Johnson's comments "brazen" and accused him of trying to "idly shrug away a disaster that his own government created". The prime minister had previously defended the controversial exam results as a "robust set of grades". So it was decided to use predicted grades from teachers instead.

****

Education Secretary **Gavin Williamson** has faced calls to resign, but Number 10 said it had full confidence in him. However, the chief **civil servant** at the Department for Education has **been sacked** following the row over A-level and GCSE results in England. The general secretary of the FDA union, Dave Penman, criticised the decision to sack Jonathan Slater. He said: "If it wasn't clear before, then it certainly is now – **this administration will throw civil service leaders under a bus without a moment's hesitation to shield ministers from any kind of accountability**." He accused the government of "scapegoating" civil servants and claimed trust between ministers and civil servants was "at an all-time low". **Mr Slater is the fifth permanent secretary to leave his post in six months.** Again, there are further details of these civil servants in chapter 16.

****

SEPTEMBER 8TH
There is an article in *The Times* by Janice Turner about **affordability of childcare. So again I write to *The Times*.** It was published on the 7th September.

Sir, What a brilliant and pertinent article from Janice Turner in today's Times (September 5th). Of course this male dominated cabinet has not given child-care a thought. It will certainly be easier and cheaper for many mothers to continue to work from home if they possibly can.

Obviously things are a bit different now due to Covid but it is quite astonishing to me that secondary schools finish the school day at 3pm. I think that they should be kept open until at least 6pm with sports and clubs and supper available, plus quiet areas where the pupils could do 'homework' or rather 'independent' work. The resources are all there and at the moment going to waste. Obviously teachers could complete their contact teaching at say 4pm but then sports coaches, music teachers, club leaders and others could be employed for the next 2 hours. This will still leave time for the school to be cleaned etc. Yes it will cost money, but it will give employment to many, allow parents to do a full day's work without worry, and it is actually about time that we put children first.

****

OCTOBER 16TH

Boris Johnson has defended his **refusal to extend free school meals** yet again for children in England over the October half-term holiday, saying he was "very proud" of the government's support so far. "I totally understand the issue of holiday hunger," he said. "The debate is, how do you deal with it." He said the government will "do everything in our power to make sure that no kid, no child goes hungry". Pressure has risen on the PM, including from his own MPs, to rethink the issue. Mr Johnson also said he had not spoken to Manchester United footballer Marcus Rashford – who has been leading a high-profile campaign to extend free school meals into the holidays – since the summer. He has also included the Christmas holidays in this refusal.

But despite Mr Johnson's Government rejecting the plans, local councils, businesses and other organisations nationwide stepped in to offer children in need food during the October half-term.

****

NOVEMBER 8TH

Then we read that disadvantaged children **will** be given free school meals over the Christmas holidays, in **yet another major Government U-turn** that has delighted campaigning England footballer **Marcus Rashford**. The Prime Minister finally caved in to pressure on the issue after facing a barrage of criticism for blocking an extension of the scheme over October half term.

Labour's shadow education secretary Kate Green accused the Government of "incompetence and intransigence" in waiting until after the autumn half-term to make the announcement, and said ministers had "created needless and avoidable hardship for families across the country".

Why do they keep doing this? How can they learn from their mistakes if they don't think they have made any?

****

2021

JANUARY 5TH

Such a dreadful school fiasco at the beginning of the spring term. On Monday am 4th January the PM said yes schools will go ahead and open tomorrow as planned. At 8pm that evening they were told no, they will be shut from tomorrow, Tuesday. Others were starting on Tuesday so children went to bed on Monday thinking they were going to school on Tuesday only to find when they woke up that they were not. Some schools had gone back on the Monday so had one day at school. **Chaos and confusion yet again.**

****

Cannabis medication for children with epilepsy is not getting through to the UK. Earlier this month, the families spoke of their anger and despair because they felt the Department of Health had dismissed concerns about accessing the life-changing treatment which helps limit seizures. There has been no response to a letter written by a worried mother from either Boris Johnson or Dominic Raab. However, the families of more than 40 children with severe epilepsy, fighting to maintain a supply of cannabis medication from the Netherlands, have just won a six-month reprieve from rules that will stop the export of the drug. The children's parents have been told by the Department of Health that the Dutch government has agreed to allow the continued supply of Bedrocan oil against UK prescriptions for existing patients until 1st July. The DHSC added that it will use the time between now and July to come up with a more permanent solution.

****

JANUARY 13TH

The Government has come under severe fire for **outsourcing food for children** eligible for Free School Meals to a private catering company, with pictures showing pathetic amounts of food delivered to England's most vulnerable children during a time of unprecedented national crisis. Cheap and insubstantial food parcels were sent out to families in need. Parcels of food costing £5 were sent out to feed a family for 10 days instead of £30 vouchers. Chartwells, the food company responsible, said they would investigate.

****

JANUARY 25TH

And **still not enough computers for children** to be home-schooled. One in three families have no computers. Ofcom estimated last year there were 1.78 million children in the UK without access to a device for online learning. Since then, the Government has ordered 1.3 million laptops. So far, 800,000 have been delivered, leaving almost one million children without a device.

****

FEBRUARY 3RD

It has been announced today that there will be a **review on lockdown on the 22nd February** when hopefully schools will be told they can open on the 8th March.

****

FEBRUARY 4TH

Sir Kevan Collins has been appointed as the government's school catch-up tsar. This is wonderful news as he is saying the school day should be extended by a couple of hours for things like sport, music, drama and general health and well-being. Teachers need not be involved but volunteers and club leaders etc can be brought in. The facilities are there and should be used. In fact maybe he read my letter to *The Times* on the 7th September!! But Robert Halfon MP who is chair of the Education Select Committee is also saying the same thing. At last some excellent news for our children and their education.

****

Also today, Labour and others, including me, are saying how important it is to **vaccinate teachers**. If a teacher is ill then children are sent home once again. And today there is a letter in *The Times* from 130 head teachers and teachers saying they should be vaccinated sooner rather than later. But obviously it is a matter of opinion and I think the government will carry on with their plan of going down through the ages.

****

FEBRUARY 14TH

And yet again there are no plans in place for free school meals over February 2021 half-term. I really cannot believe that I am writing this again! Guidance from the Department of Education says "Schools do not need to provide lunch parcels or vouchers during the February half-term." Instead, the government has said there is already wider financial available to help families and children outside of term-time through the Covid Winter Grant Scheme and so will be provided by local authorities. Kevin Courtney, joint general secretary of the NEU, warned of potential disruption to free school meals provision during the break. He said: "Suggesting that local councils will be able to recreate a brand new system of supplying free school meals for the week of half-term using the Covid Winter Grant Scheme is an unnecessary logistical nightmare, and the **confusion and chaos** this could cause will put millions of children at risk."

On the provision of free school meals during the half-term, the Prime Minister's official spokesman said: "My understanding is they will continue during the February half-term, as they were over Christmas." So at the time of writing no-one is quite sure. **Is this another U-turn**?

****

FEBRUARY 18TH

The court of Appeal has upheld a decision that the Home Office's high **registration fees for child citizenship is unlawful**. The Home Office charges £1,012 for a child to register for British citizenship. A high court judge said this fee prevented many children from being able to register for citizenship, leaving them feeling 'alienated, second-best and not fully assimilated into the culture and social fabric of the UK'.

How can the Home Office charge such fees? Oh, of course, it is Priti Patel.

****

MARCH 12TH

If you read nothing else ever again you need to read this. It is 25 years since **16 primary children and their teacher were killed** during a PE lesson in Dunblane. The perpetrator then turned the gun on himself. The outcry that followed led to the parents and others, including the then opposition leader Tony Blair, to call for a complete ban on handguns which was introduced 18 months later after Blair became Prime Minister. This ban has now made us one of the safest countries in the world when it comes to gun crime.

However, Boris Johnson was a journalist at that time for The Daily Telegraph. Some of the articles he wrote then have just resurfaced and are being commented on in the press today. I warn you. It makes shocking reading.

He pushed back against the regulation and described it as part of a "knee-jerk legislation" that had led to "an enormous erosion of individual liberty, swept away, very often, in a tide of public panic". He said, "There will always be those who say we must do more. 'We must tighten again,' they say". He adds that, "they say, 'If one child's life is saved it will have been worth it'. Never mind that this has been the argument of authoritarians down the ages, those who would tap telephones and break down doors in the middle of the night in the name of that single notional child. The central point is that knee-jerk reaction does not work." He added that he found the Conservative Party's "continual ratcheting of protective legislation" to be "dismaying".

Mick North, a retired academic who lost his five year old daughter at Dunblane, said today that his pain had been compounded by the likes of Boris Johnson who had painted the response of grieving families as an over-reaction. "What always struck me," he said, "was just his callous disregard for others. This was a week after my daughter had died – just a week – and he was writing columns that were essentially demeaning us."

And in a later Telegraph article in 1997 as guns were being handed in following the introduction of the ban, Boris Johnson wrote that, "nanny is confiscating their toys". **This is the man who is now running our country.**

And I have just discovered that Mick North was at secondary school with a friend of mine. My friend says that tragically his wife had died of cancer a year earlier and not surprisingly he sank into a deep depression and couldn't work for several years. Did you know that, Mr Johnson, when you wrote those articles?

MARCH 29TH
Well today we can meet up to five other people outside. Fantastic. However, for some children as young as 12 that will not be the case. The following is an email I have just sent to the editorial department of *The Times*.

I am appalled at the layout of your paper today on pages 4 and 5.

*On page 5 there is a half- page spread with three photos of dogs going blind because of inbreeding. On page 4 there is a tiny paragraph of 11 short lines of text in the quick news column about conditions at **Rainsbrook secure training centre** in Warwickshire where children as young as 12 are being kept in their cells for 23 and a half hours a day.*

This is not a new story. 9 recommendations were made in April 2020 and when inspected last October none of these had been implemented and it was ordered again to improve. When inspected un-announced in December nothing had changed and Robert Buckland was delivered an 'urgent notification' to reply. A new report came out today and Buckland, who awarded this contract to a private American Company, at a cost of £5.4 million is being told to abort the contract and put it back into the hands of the state. However after their 5 year contract is completed in May he has awarded it a further extension of another 2 years. This whole story is absolutely dreadful and I would encourage one of your excellent columnists to write about it in detail. All the information is on the following website:-

https://publications.parliament.uk/pa/cm5801/cmselect/cmjust/1266/126607.htm

I pick up this story because I am a member of the Howard League for Penal Reform but I doubt that many will see it as they will be too busy reading about dogs. This treatment of our most vulnerable children would be seen as a form of torture in a civilised country. It is not even newsworthy here.

I have also written to Oliver Dowden, who is my MP, and The Howard League. But why have I not heard about this before? The contract was awarded in 2016.

Please don't be a vulnerable child in the UK today. It is worth recording that the criminal age of responsibility in England is 10 years old. This is the youngest in Europe. For most European countries it is 14.

****

MARCH

But now for some **good news**. For after that we really need to know about the amazing people full of compassion and commitment who are going above and beyond the already difficult things they are being asked to do. An inner-city primary school has decided to open the school on **Saturday mornings** after the Easter holidays for sport, music, art and fun. So many of the children have no gardens and the head decided that there was no point in waiting to open a summer school if they could help to improve the children's welfare now. The children are on course to carry on with the three Rs but have missed out on the three Fs...**fitness, friendship and fun.** The wonderful thing is that all the teachers have agreed to go in, as have almost all the pupils. The head says it is primarily for the children but also for the parents as well. "We want to say a big thank you," he says, "for all the home schooling and we want to give you three hours or so in which you can relax and have rest and respite at home." What an amazing head and his name is Rob Driscoll. He deserves a medal. However (there always seems to be a however), the government is only **funding secondary schools to set** up **summer schools and not primaries**, would you believe? Hopes of recouping the substantial cost of Saturday openings to his school from council or government has not been realised. So, he says, "We basically decided to **fund it ourselves**. The financial cost is massively outweighed by the social advantages for the children." **The photograph in *The Times* today of these children looking so happy is a testament to the kindness, thoughtfulness, caring attitude, professionalism and dedication of Mr Driscoll and his staff.**

****

One of Boris Johnson's ministers has been accused of a "pathetic" attempt to **re-write history**, after claiming the decision to extend free school meals had nothing to do with pressure from Marcus Rashford. Children's minister Vicky Ford **denied a high-profile push** by the Manchester United footballer and campaigner was behind the U-turns on meals provided to some of England's poorest families during an interview on **Thursday 25th March**. Appearing on *Good Morning Britain*, the minister suggested the government had decided to "extend" the eligibility of a food voucher scheme before Mr Rashford's intervention. But she was one of 321 Conservative MPs who **voted against a Labour motion for free school meals during the October half term! How can they lie so blatantly?**

Labour MP David Lammy accused the minister of attempting to "re-write history" on the government's free school meals "fiasco". The shadow justice secretary said: "No one will believe this dismissal of Marcus Rashford's campaign. Arrogant and delusional."

Rashford has since called for an urgent review of the government's policy in the wake of the coronavirus pandemic, along with so many others.

****

So we see how our young people are not being taken care of by this government in spite of their grand words. Plans for a **summer of play after lockdown are in jeopardy** as budget cuts see parks and playgrounds neglected. So parents and play experts are having to turn to **crowdfunding** to rebuild and maintain playgrounds as cash-strapped local authorities cut their budgets across England. In Coggeshall, Essex, Jemma Green and her neighbours got the idea for crowdfunding their playground from others. "It's incredibly common now. We have got £110,000 and nearly all of that has come from fundraising. The parish council saved for two years to give us £30,000 – we are lucky they could do that. And we had £25,000 from Enovert, a local landfill company. But all our other grant applications were turned down."

In parliament last month, the Housing Minister Luke Hall confirmed parks and green spaces received £16m between 2017 and 2019. But Anita Grant, head of the charity Play England points out how little this is. "£16m over three years on 27,000 parks is £200 per park. The abysmal funding of parks right now means the degradation of the play areas will continue and get worse. What we really need is long-term investment for staff and maintenance."

The Association of Play Industries (API) has warned of a continued decline in the funding of park playgrounds. Using freedom of information requests, it found that since 2014, 347 playgrounds have been shut down across England. For those that survive, the API estimates there will be a decrease in spending of over £13m a year on average. Mark Hardy, who chairs the API, says: "The steady decline in funding started during austerity but what is worrying now is that in the last 18 months or so funding is not going back to normal. Play is not a statutory provision and local authorities have a lot of priorities." He says that while larger "destination" playgrounds do sometimes still get funding, many local spaces are in effect abandoned. "Neighbourhood playgrounds are becoming rather sad things. We need doorstep play, particularly in deprived areas."

But I thought this government has said that **children are our top priority**. Or is that yet **another lie?** Once again parents step in to try to save children from the government's incompetence.

****

APRIL 12TH

And it is not just young children who are ignored. **University students** are displaying real stress as they struggle to cope with the uncertainty they are facing about a return date. Universities still haven't been told when the government will allow them to return to face-to-face teaching, although it will probably be sometime in May. Professor Julia Buckingham, vice-chancellor of Brunel University and president of Universities UK, which represents university vice-chancellors, said students who have been learning remotely are being treated "very unfairly" compared with other groups of young people who have been allowed to resume face-to-face learning. "Our students seem to have been left out," she said. "We're very concerned about how this is impacting on their mental health and wellbeing. We know many are struggling with financial hardship, because of course there aren't the part-time jobs they normally have. And there is good evidence that their feelings of isolation and loneliness have increased. This is obviously contributing to their anxiety levels, at this very tense time of year, when everyone's worried about exams. I feel desperately sorry for students right now." She goes on to say that "Students do need warning if they're going to come back to campus – they have to book travel arrangements. Staff need warning too. The longer we wait, the more challenging this is for everyone and the less opportunity there will be for students to get the support they need". *The Observer* thinks the government will make a decision by the end of next week.

Julia Buckingham urged the government to allow students to return. "Please bring back students," she said. "Please recognise the very, very difficult time they're having and please support them. They have responded to extraordinary challenges over the past 12 months and I think they have been remarkable. I think the government owes it to them, now, to support them in the best way possible – and that is to allow them to come back to campus and get on with their learning." Students are saying that they see no logic in the fact that children are back at school, all shops are open including gyms, hairdressers and swimming pools, and yet they seem to be ignored. So let us see what next week brings. Let us find out who, in the government, is listening to the needs of our young people.

****

But there are yet **more young people** who need an understanding and compassionate ear. There is a disturbing article by Sonia Sodha in *The Observer* about children born to EU parents who have settled here or who have lived the first 10 years of their life here and therefore have the right to register for British citizenship. She tells the story of a young boy who was born in the UK and taken into care as a baby. As he was told that he didn't have enough information about the status of his estranged mother his application was rejected three times and the Home Office threatened to deport him to Jamaica. It was only when the Windrush scandal was in the news that his case became newsworthy and he was able to get a passport. She goes on to say, "There can be no greater symbol of **the rotten sickness that Conservative prime ministers have introduced into our immigration system through the 'hostile environment.**"

But all these children must apply for citizenship before they turn 18 and because of Brexit thousands of young people are at risk because many are not even aware that this is what they have to do. And local authorities have to pay over £1,000 to register a child in their care for citizenship. But if you check my entry on February 18th The Court of Appeal has ruled that these high rates charged by the Home Office for child citizenship applications are unlawful. So are they or are they not still being applied?

The dead line for these applications is now less than three months away.

****

APRIL 13TH
I was shocked to hear today that one in eight primary schools have no library provision. Some will have a few books in the classrooms and many of the books will be in a poor condition. And so I hear of a brilliant new scheme by Waterstones whereby six primary schools across the country will receive a new library. It is being started by Waterstones children's Laureate, Cressida Cowell, and it is called her Life Changing Libraries Campaign. She says that "All of the head teachers have commented about the **lack of books in their pupils' homes** and the **lack of opportunity to access local libraries**. One of the head teachers said 'I have had various conversations with parents where they'll see a book and say "ooh it's lovely" and it really brings it home that they don't have books at home'."

Cressida Cowell has written an open letter to the Prime Minister and I quote a small fraction.

*I have visited primary schools across the country over my 20-year career as a children's author-illustrator and it is heart-breaking to see just how unevenly this fundamental opportunity is distributed. So often the children who need books the most are in schools that cannot provide them with even an **adequate** school library, let alone a good one. Worse still schools with a higher proportion of children on free school meals were more than twice as likely not to have access to a designated library space.*

Over time, £100m a year would enable every primary school in England to invest in the key areas of library excellence – books, expertise, space – that their pupils so urgently need. The gap in educational attainment and opportunity remains stark, worrying and urgent. I urge you to take this positive step to invest in our children's and our country's future.

Put simply Libraries change lives. Literacy changes lives.

As a retired primary school teacher I cannot believe that there are so many primary schools still without a library. But then again when I look at the statistics from the Reading Agency maybe I can. They say that one in five children in England **cannot read well by the age of 11**. They also say that only 35% of 10 year olds in England report that they like reading 'very much'. This is shocking. Prime Minister, do you have the smallest clue as to what is needed for our children today? Gavin Williamson, Education Minister, what are you doing? **School libraries should be your top priority**.

****

Well actually we know what Gavin Williamson is doing. He is talking about **discipline in schools** and saying that children have lacked "discipline and order" during lockdown. He is talking about silence in corridors and banning all mobile phones. He wants 'behaviour hubs' to teach other schools how to keep order.

Well, there has been a huge backlash from headteachers saying that actually children returning to school after lockdown have been "calm and considerate and well behaved". So no, Mr Williamson, you need properly paid, dedicated teachers, an extended and varied curriculum which includes music, dance, sport, drama, design technology, art, natural history, fewer tests and exams, and decent **well stocked school libraries**. This, in other words is what used to be called an all-round education. But no, as Polly Toynbee said in *The Guardian* in an excellent article recently, Gavin Williamson is "a planet away" from anything like this.

****

APRIL 15TH

Rainsbrook detention centre This is a dreadful story in the news today and this is my reply to Oliver Dowden to an email which he had sent to me. It is self- explanatory.

Dear Oliver,

I really appreciate your reply to my email about the Rainsbrook Secure Training centre in Warwickshire. And of course you feel that the government is committed to ensuring that secure training centres are safe for children and staff and are at the standard you would rightly expect. However I understand that you will be extremely busy at the moment and therefore have had no time to read the recent House of Commons report. I have therefore highlighted some of the most important points that it makes, in what is a very comprehensive statement. As you will see it makes very disturbing reading.

"House of Commons Justice Committee Rainsbrook Secure Training Centre Seventeenth Report of Session 2019–21 Report, together with formal minutes relating to the report Ordered by the House of Commons to be printed 23 March 2021

"In the six months before the inspection, in October, 2020 there had been 587 violent incidents at the unit, which houses about 65 boys and girls aged 12-18.

The inspectors judged Rainsbrook as 'Requires improvement to be good'—exactly the same judgment made at the previous three inspections in October 2018, June 2017 and October 2016. The inspectorates made 19 recommendations in April 2020; nine to be actioned immediately and 10 within three months. As will be seen, these were largely ignored.

"Six months on, between 26 and 29 October 2020, Ofsted, CQC and HMIP returned to Rainsbrook and found new and serious concerns. Most alarmingly, for their first 14 days at the centre, children were allowed out of their rooms for only 30 minutes a day, spending the remaining 23 and a half hours locked inside. The inspectors noted that there was "no rationale to support this practice", which was "tantamount to solitary confinement" and "highly likely to be damaging to children's emotional and physical well-being".

The joint inspectors notified senior managers in the Ministry of Justice (MoJ) and on 16 December 2020 they invoked the Urgent Notification (UN) process.

They write:

"We took evidence on 9 March 2021. We were shocked and appalled by what we heard and are deeply concerned about MTC's ability to manage the Rainsbrook contract. The failures identified over five years are not, though, the responsibility only of the provider, MTC. The Youth Custody Service and Ministry of Justice, as the contracting authority, have a responsibility to ensure that the contracts they let are delivered effectively and to prevent such situations from occurring. They have, in this case, failed to exercise their responsibilities as a contracting authority, and we consider that departmental oversight has been inadequate, contributing to the appalling and consistent failures at Rainsbrook. We recognise that all prisons and other custodial institutions face additional pressures during the current covid-19 pandemic, but we do not consider those to be justification or excuse for the continued poor conditions at Rainsbrook and the repeated absence of effective action to remedy them by staff employed by MTC at Rainsbrook and senior staff at the Ministry of Justice and Youth Custody Service.

"We are not confident in MTC's ability to deliver the action required by recommendations repeatedly made over a period of years by the three inspectorates. We recommend that MTC and the Youth Custody Service report to us by June 2021, setting out in detail what progress has been made against the action plan now developed. MTC should also set out what impact changes made have had on children at the centre. If no substantial improvement is then apparent, the Ministry should consider taking Rainsbrook back in house. It is clear that further work is needed.

"Early in 2020, the MoJ granted the maximum possible two-year extension to the contract, taking the end date to May 2023. Given that concerns already existed by then about MTC's performance and sanctions were already in place, this decision looks misjudged. Given what has happened since, it looks like a serious error of judgment.

"We asked the Secretary of State whether consideration had been given to taking Rainsbrook back in-house on the basis that the failures were so gross that MTC could not be trusted to safely carry out its contractual responsibilities.

"Robert Buckland QC MP, Lord Chancellor and secretary of State for Justice told us: 'I will not make glib remarks about last chance saloons or people being on probation, but it is very clear to me that, as a result of the incidents that we are dealing with and your Committee is seized of, MTC have frankly a lot to demonstrate to make me satisfied that the future at Rainsbrook can be one that we can be confident about. But they have that contract. They need to get on with the job and demonstrate that they can deliver. As I have said, that particular consideration is very much in my mind in the months ahead.'

"We are concerned that Ministry of Justice awarded MTC the maximum possible contract extension. Based on the evidence heard on 9 March, coupled with the inspectorates' findings, it is clear that MTC have failed to fulfil a number of contractual obligations. The company clearly did not fulfil the requirement to 'deliver a service that places Young People at its heart and considers their needs, wants and wishes at all stages of their stay at the STC.' While the difficulties of re-letting a contract and potentially changing a Secure Training Centre provider during the covid-19 pandemic may be considerable, there can be little justification for retaining the services of a badly under-performing contractor, and even less for giving them two more years of that contract. Notwithstanding the complications of letting a contract during a pandemic period, no one's needs, and in particular the needs of some of our society's most vulnerable children, should be placed second to administrative considerations. We seek a clear explanation of why the Ministry of Justice chose to extend MTC's contract by two years when the contractor's ability to deliver was already in question, and we ask what ministerial involvement there was in making that decision and, in signing it off.

"Consistently sub-standard performance of a contract does not merit renewal in any circumstances. We recommend that the Secretary of State urgently reviews whether his Ministry plans to renew any other contract or any contractor whose performance is similarly consistently poor."

Frances Crook, Chief executive of the Howard League for Penal Reform, said: "Children should only be placed in settings where they are safe and where they can flourish. Once again, inspectors have found that Rainsbrook fails this test. The safety of children should never arise as a question; it should be a given. And yet, more than a year after Her Majesty's Chief Inspector of Prisons declared that there was not a single jail in the country that was safe for a child and almost three years after a Panorama investigation exposed abuse in another training centre, we continue to see a report such as this. It is disgraceful that, after all that has been said and done, the youth courts and the Ministry of Justice are still placing children in institutions where they are not safe.

"The Howard League opposed the creation of secure training centres in the 1990s and warned that children would be damaged and hurt in these institutions. A long line of inspection reports has underlined that this is a failed model of detention. After 30 years of children being mistreated, it is time to put an end to this."

I think it is time to treat this account with the seriousness it deserves. We really do not want meaningless platitudes any more. We want action. You must agree that this is appalling. It really does amount to the torture of young children as this report says. I have written to the Ministry of Justice but they take 4 weeks to reply.

****

I did eventually get a reply from the Ministry of Justice but it was not enough for me, so I wrote again on the **29th April** copying this letter, at the beginning of which I wrote:-

I ask you one question. Are children still being held in their cells for 23 1/2 hours a day?

Well skipping ahead, today, **21st May 2021**, I get a reply from HM the Prisons and Probation Service and **I get an answer to my question!** It would appear that children are no longer held in their cells on arrival as changes have been made. However, after the inspection on the 10th December and because of the serious shortfalls that were found then, no children have been placed in the detention centre since December. So basically this ruling of a 23 and a half hour day in solitary confinement has not needed to be applied! This inspection was unannounced and was in response to an urgent notification process after the inspection in December.

However, during this visit, **some early signs of improvement** were seen, which is good, but the report says that much of the action plan has yet to be implemented. Some actions that have been completed have not yet been embedded, or are yet to show a demonstrable positive impact on children's lives. But the children's living units have begun to be redecorated and everywhere looked clean and tidy.

Children told inspectors that they have been consulted about how the communal areas should be furnished, and new furniture and paint have been ordered. Children can personalise their rooms with photographs and pictures. There was a lot of activity at the centre at the time of the visit, with a sense of positivity about the refreshment programme and the impact an improved environment could have on children and staff. However, arrangements for **education during the COVID-19 pandemic are ineffective**. Children told inspectors that education work packs are not 'stretching' them in terms of their learning, and work is not marked. While children receive some direct teaching sessions delivered by teachers on the living units, this is not an environment conducive to effective learning. Centre staff try to stand in for teachers by doing schoolwork with children, which is admirable but is not an appropriate substitute for learning delivered by teachers.

Additional resources at management level and additional scrutiny as a result of the urgent notification process have increased both oversight and support provided to the centre. However, the director fully acknowledges that, while inspectors saw some improvements in practice at this visit, **there is still much work to be done to implement, and fully embed, best practice and cultural change within the centre**. The urgent notification action plan is comprehensive, but it is in the very early stages of its implementation.

But it is disturbing to note that **violence and self-harm within the centre had increased over the three months prior to this visit**. The centre's attempts to manage the safety of children during the Covid-19 outbreak, by separating children into 'bubbles' of those who had tested positive and those who had tested negative for Covid-19, resulted in issues with children's compatibility and an increase in both peer-on-peer violence and assaults on staff. The director has taken action to address this, but it is too soon to know whether this action will be effective in reducing these incidents.

The email to me ended by saying that:-

"You may be interested to know that we will be responding to the Justice Select Committee (JSC) shortly where we will be providing a full response to their recommendations.

As mentioned in my previous response, the Youth Custody Service will continue to monitor progress very closely and the Lord Chancellor will not hesitate to take appropriate action should necessary improvements not be forthcoming.

****

So obviously I will keep a look out for that. But what an appalling indictment in the way we treat children in this country in the 21st century.

****

Well, well, we skip ahead again to **June 17th** and I read that the Ministry Of Justice is removing all children from the Rainsbrook Training Centre amid serious concerns for their safety. The centre is being 'mothballed'. **After five years** of appalling inspection reports and repeated assurances by the Ministry of Justice and my MP that all is well, decisive action is taken. No wonder I call this book a diary of despair.

****

APRIL 16TH
Money for students is unequal in the UK. Eleanor Langford writes in an article for *PoliticsHome* that Paul Blomfield, chair of the All-Party Parliamentary Group for Students, has told ministers he has "serious concerns" about levels of hardship funding on offer to

students in England. It follows the announcement this week that all students yet to return to in-person teaching would be able to return to campus from 17th May, at the earliest, in line with Step 3 of the government's roadmap. An additional £15 million in hardship funding was also confirmed to help students who may be struggling to pay accommodation costs or other study-related expenses amid the pandemic. However, in a letter seen by *PoliticsHome*, Blomfield branded the offering "frankly insulting", as it represented **"between a half and a tenth" of the funding available in Scotland, Wales and Northern Ireland**.

Writing to universities minister Michelle Donelan, he said: "I had hoped that your further reflection on the issues raised in our APPG for Students report would lead to significant improvements on student hardship. But your announcement of £15 million additional hardship funds, or £7.70 per student in England, is frankly insulting, while students in the devolved nations continue to receive far more generous support through this difficult time."

Blomfield added that students have faced "substantial financial pressure through the pandemic" as many have suffered "a loss of income from retail and hospitality jobs. It is therefore unacceptable that the government is supporting students at English Higher Education Institutions with between a half and a tenth of the support given in any of the Devolved Administrations to students studying in those areas". He continued, "This generation, with those in schools, will be affected over their lives by the pandemic more than any other, and will be paying for the national debt longer than anyone else. We must equip them with the resources they need now to overcome the challenges of Covid-19 and succeed in the future."

****

APRIL 20TH
I read in a very small paragraph in *The Times* today that The Medicines and Healthcare Products Regulatory Agency is investigating how **millions of children were given the wrong instructions for lateral**

flow tests. The kits came with an outdated government leaflet saying they should be used for symptomatic cases, and a note from the Chinese manufacturer that said the tests were for people suspected by healthcare staff of having the coronavirus. In fact, lateral flow tests are only for people without symptoms and all positive results should be confirmed by a more accurate PCR test.

I am at a loss to know what to say about this except that together with all the other accusations I lay at this government's door I have to add "dangerous and negligent".

****

APRIL 28TH

Gavin Williamson, has announced that he wants all schools in England to **become academies.** What on earth is he talking about? His party's 2019 manifesto promised to ensure "every school is a great school". It said nothing about forcing existing schools out of local control and into that of multi-academy trusts. Academies are not the be-all and end-all of educational reform, and some of them are not satisfactory at all. As reported in *The Guardian* today, in 2019 the Department for Education wrote to 94 trusts asking them to justify **high pay for executives and head-teachers**. Also, Academies have lost proportionally more pupils than maintained schools to the practice known as "off-rolling", whereby children leave schools without being formally excluded. On exclusions too, some chains have a shocking record. In 2016-17, nine schools run by Outwood Grange Academies Trust in Yorkshire **excluded at least 20% of their pupils**. This is appalling and indicates unprofessional standards and procedures. **What schools need, Mr Williamson**, as I keep trying to say, is first and foremost professionally qualified teachers who are properly rewarded financially and who are enthusiastic and committed to the welfare of the children in their care. All schools need to be fully resourced and maintained to a high standard. Why are you not talking about school libraries, music and drama in schools, school playing fields and school science labs? How about class sizes, IT equipment and extra-curricular activities? How do you account for the lack of teachers in qualifications such as Maths and physics and how do you account for the fact that so many teachers leave the profession after only five years? Mr Williamson, have you ever been inside a school since you became an adult? Do you actually ever speak to teachers and find out what they want? Or do you just sit in your Westminster bubble and think about ridiculous soundbites? Teachers' morale is at an all-time low and yet they have been working throughout the pandemic both in schools and organizing home schooling, which of course has been very difficult for many children because they never got a promised computer. You should now be concentrating on summer schools and how the school day will function next term. Leave schools with local authorities and do not talk about more red tape and re-organisation.

****

APRIL 30TH

We are responsible. A British girl who was **trafficked to Syria at the age of 12** and then raped by an Islamic state fighter is among 50 women and children who are stranded in refugee camps. A report from the campaign group Reprieve says that many were under 18 when they travelled to Isis territory and have suffered years of exploitation including forced marriage, rape and domestic servitude. The Home Office has brought back a small number of orphans of British citizens from camps but have refused repatriating those accompanied by their families. The government's approach is at odds with that of the United States which has called on Western countries to take responsibility for their citizens and bring them home, warning that the squalid camps are spawning a new generation of extremists. Reprieve's report says: "The UK government claims to be leading the global fight against human trafficking and modern slavery, yet... it is systematically failing trafficking victims." Maya Foa, the director of Reprieve who has visited the camps, says **"these are victims who have been abandoned. I find it cruel, callous and cynical. It is not lawful, not humane and not in our security interests. On every level it is counter-productive"**. And I would add to this the case of Shamima Begum. As Anthony Law writes in *The Times* "she is not a threat. She's totally broken. She needs help". But as we see, this government does not have a reputation of helping vulnerable children.

****

MAY 5TH

England's state nursery schools are being driven towards extinction by budget pressures and uncertainty over future government funding, according to a survey of the sector's financial position.

During lockdown, **state nursery schools** were treated as other schools in England, having to remain open for the children of critical workers or vulnerable children, but were **not given any of the extra funding that primary or secondary schools received.** They also were not eligible for the tax rebates or interest-free loans available to private daycare providers. A survey of the sector's financial position says England's remaining state nursery schools are being driven towards extinction by budget pressures and uncertainty over the future government funding. Beatrice Merrick, the chief executive of Early Education, which represents the sector, says, "Instead of this lifeline being supported, it is being put at risk by government failure to address their routine funding needs." Nursery schools were losing an average of £76,000 in annual income and having to spend an extra £8,000 in costs directly related to Covid-19. "Many maintained nursery schools were in a perilous financial position even before the pandemic but the last year has only deepened that crisis and they have now been pushed to the very brink," said Paul Whiteman, the general secretary of the National Association of Head Teachers. "If we are to avoid widespread nursery closures, the government must urgently come forward with a long-term solution."

****

JUNE 3RD

The national tutoring programme set up to help children catch up after lockdown is **reaching only 1% of pupils** according to figures seen by *The Times* today. The National Association of Head Teachers said the scheme was too restrictive, with schools struggling to access tutors recognised by the programme.

****

MAY 5TH

Still about Children

And now I just have to divert a little to a cause which is close to my heart. On Woman's Hour this morning there was an interview with **Camila Batmanghelidjh**. For those of you who have read my book "Beyond Belief", I mention her on page 65 in my talk on the Howard League, and I talk about the amazing charity she started in London called Kids Company. This charity supported hundreds of disadvantaged and very disturbed children who would otherwise end up in a Young Offenders Institution or in social care. This charity had a phenomenal success rate with these youngsters and between 80 and 90% went back to education, further education or employment, with an 89% reduction in reoffending. The statistics spoke for themselves. But six years ago on the **5th August 2015** the charity was forced to close because there were accusations of alleged misconduct of public finances. There were also allegations of sexual misconduct which meant that donors started to withhold their money.

However, in a ruling on **February 12th this year**, Mrs Justice Falk rejected the case of financial mismanagement and sexual misconduct, and praised the "enormous dedication" the founder had showed vulnerable young people. She ruled: "The public need no protection from these trustees. On the contrary, this is a group of highly impressive and dedicated individuals who selflessly gave enormous amounts of their time to what was clearly a highly challenging trusteeship." On Woman's Hour this morning, Camila Batmanghelidjh said the now Chancellor of the Duchy of Lancaster, Michael Gove, had initially supported the charity's work and handed her a CBE in 2014 when he was in the Department for Education. "But," she said, "by 2015 he was saying he never wanted Kids Co funded, you know, and I find it very difficult when people change colours."

She also said on Woman's Hour: "I personally think it was a smear campaign and I think there were two targets. One is, I believe, David Cameron, because he was seen to have chosen us as Big Society and I think the Brexit team wanted to discredit him, because I don't understand why Dominic Cummings, whom we had never met, was briefing against us in 2015. And I think another bit was campaigning for child protection issues and I think the country has no capacity to address its child protection problems."

A statement issued on behalf of the former trustees said: "Kids Company was forced to close in August 2015 following what the judge records as 'unfounded allegations' of child abuse, which made fundraising from private and government sources impossible. We are pleased that finally the facts have been gathered and assessed in a court of law, and that Mrs Justice Falk has exonerated both the trustees and the founder of Kids Company and said that there was no allegation of dishonesty, bad faith or personal gain."

And let us be quite clear here. These disgusting and life changing accusations were made against a successful charity run by a successful person. This brilliant, highly intelligent, compassionate person happened to be a woman. She was also larger than life and wore highly colourful long robes with amazing turbans. And she was from Iran. The children loved her. But after the charity was closed she had a lot of verbal abuse and was told to go back to where she came from, and even people in the government couldn't believe that she was in fact highly intelligent. And so misogyny and racism raise their ugly heads once more.

But the real question is of course: **What has happened to the thousands of children who were being helped by Kids Company and who would have been helped by Kids Company during these last six years?**

Answers there will be none.

****

But today **May 28th 2021** the full reports of the investigation are in the news and it is being reported that taxpayers face a legal bill for at least **£8m** as a result of the official receiver's disastrous attempt to ban the Kids Company founder Camila Batmanghelidjh and seven fellow charity trustees from holding senior jobs. It is being said that the official receiver hoped that the trial would result in lengthy bans for the charity board. Instead, the judge praised Batmanghelidjh and the trustees as **"a group of highly impressive and dedicated individuals"**, adding: "The public needs no protection from these trustees." Mrs Justice Falk was also scathing of the official receiver's handling of the case, criticising the lack of balance and objectivity in its presentation, and condemning the costly and "oppressive" deployment of thousands of pages of evidence, **much of which was irrelevant and never used in the investigation.**

She concluded that had the unfounded sexual assault allegations not made it impossible for Kids Company to continue to raise funds from philanthropists, it is likely that the charity would have succeeded in its restructuring plans and survived. The report in *The Guardian* today goes on to quote Rupert Butler of Leverets, the barrister who represented Batmanghelidjh, who said that while it was right for the official receiver to investigate the charity, it had failed to change tack when it became clear that there was no serious case to answer. "The impression was left that he had to justify the expense of the investigation by pursuing the directors." Butler accused the official receiver of buying into a "lazy, baseless, caricature – a cartoon-image of Camila and this charity as a feckless joyride for the undeserving poor – that he should have realised ... was categorically untrue". He called for the National Audit Office to investigate the government's handling of the case.

And so that is how this brilliant charity was brought down and how the lives of thousands of children remained in shatters and uncared for. This cannot be laid at the door of Johnson, but we see the names of Gove and Cameron and Cummings up there. They need to talk, explain and apologise.

****

MAY 14TH 2021

Teachers talking on the radio this morning are still very concerned about the assessments process for exams this summer. They are said to be highly stressed about the **overwhelming extra work involved.** One teacher said that "in seven weeks we are expected to catch up students, teach new course content, administer assessments, mark and then quality assure those assessments before attributing a holistic best-fit grade. Not only is this an overwhelming amount of work to expect from class teachers (some of whom have 70+ exam students), the impact on the pupils is unacceptable". Basically she said they are exams by another name and more consultation would have been appreciated. One teacher said the exam grading process had made this term – the first time since Christmas that their pupils have been allowed to return, full time, for face to face teaching – unacceptably stressful for teenagers in exam years at an already difficult time. And there is continuing uncertainty about the next school year also.

****

MAY 16TH

A report in *The Observer* today states that children with **special educational needs** are facing a shortfall of more than half a million pounds because local authorities are having to try to clear historical deficits and the government is stopping them from using other reserves to help with this funding. A council spokesperson said, "Our funding is not sufficient to adequately match the increase in demand."

****

More money is needed for the catch up education programme. Sir Kevan Collins, the education recovery commissioner, has submitted a report to the government calling for **£15 billion** to be spent over three years on measures including extra tutoring, longer school days and more money for teachers. Downing Street is apparently supporting this package, but it is the Chancellor who is dragging his heels. He dislikes the fact that it is a multi-year plan and thinks it should be dealt with in the wider spending review. Well, the Treasury says that negotiations are ongoing and an announcement will be made as soon as a deal is reached. "Sir Kevan is asking for rather more money than the chancellor had in mind," a source said.

****

Gavin Williamson once again shows **how ignorant he is** about the meaning of the word 'education'. The government has just launched a consultation that has put forward plans to **halve a subsidy given to universities for some arts subjects, such as performing arts and archaeology.** The National Union of Students have criticised him for making 'galling' remarks about dead-end subjects which leave students with nothing but debt.

You might well agree that some degrees sound a little off-beat but as Ms Gyebi-Ababio, the NUS vice president for higher education, told *The Independent,* Mr Williamson's comments come after "a year where we have all relied heavily on creative talent, literature and entertainment to ensure our own wellbeing". The body – which represents 140 institutions in the UK – said in a statement: "Increasing funding for high-cost courses such as medicine is vital but the proposed changes to funding for arts subjects is gravely concerning. Cuts to subjects including drama, music, performing and creative arts could mean a reduction in the number of courses offered." The proposals also sparked alarm amongst musicians, who warned that the cut to this channel of funding would be "catastrophic" for most higher education music teaching. Universities UK told *The Independent:* "It is essential that the public has full confidence in the value and quality of a university degree, and the overwhelming majority of courses are high quality and offer good value for students."

So, education under this Minister is becoming more and more under-funded and under-valued.

****

MAY 17TH

And today university students can go back to face-to-face teaching. However many universities have said they will continue online learning until September, and some of them even beyond that, much to the disappointment of many students.

****

MAY 20TH

A report by the Education Policy Institute has criticised the government's approach **to teachers' pay in England as outdated and inflexible.** Although there has been a surge in new recruits since the pandemic, an economic recovery could mean a large proportion leaving for higher paid jobs. Top-up payments were introduced in 2019 for recruits in shortage subjects. An increase in applications since March 2020 led to recruitment targets being met for the first time in eight years and so the retention payments were cut! Paul Whiteman, general secretary of the National Association of Head Teachers, said, **"After the financial crisis new entrants soon melted away; government should learn from this experience."** Well yes, that is what we all keep hoping for over and over again.

****

MAY 23RD

There is a lot of discussion going on about school exams. There is a letter in *The Sunday Times* today from more than 60 headteachers and teachers calling for SATs exams to be put on hold for at least another year. I would say for ever actually.

****

So many teachers are saying that there needs to be **strong reform on all exams** and how it is that tests can restrict the creativity and individual thinking of children. Teaching to the test is counter-productive and we too easily forget about the third of pupils who fail at GCSE level and so think of themselves as failures.

****

MAY 26TH

The public accounts committee has today produced a report which says that the **Department for Education was unprepared for the pandemic and reluctant to learn lessons from the experience**. They had "no plan" in spite of having been involved in a 2016 pandemic exercise. Meg Hillier, chairwoman of the committee, said, "The DfE shows little energy and determination to ensure that its catch-up offer is sufficient to undo the damage of the past 14 months."

We have the worst Minister of Education that I can ever remember.

****

MAY 28TH

Such a disturbing report out today about **child sexual exploitation**. *The Times* has to be congratulated on its investigations on this subject. It was the first to reveal the scale of abuse in Rotherham about a decade ago and it has now unearthed an ongoing scandal based on freedom of information submitted to 45 of the country's police forces which reveal that **children as young as 11 have gone missing 55,000 times in the past three years**. There are so many disturbing cases, but I will write about just one: A teenager with learning disabilities was filmed being abused by a group of men but police initially took no action because she claimed it was consensual. Actually, it makes me feel sick. And internal police reports include a finding that there is "little evidence of the exploiters being investigated" and child protection experts wrongly regarded victims who went missing repeatedly as lost causes. Several forces did not comply with requests from journalists to disclose internal reports on their policing of sexual abuse cases. South Yorkshire cited "highly sensitive information" in its refusal to co-operate. Many reports were heavily redacted. But when fully disclosed, Maurice Frankel, of the Campaign for Freedom of Information said: "The accidentally disclosed material shows that redactions have often been used to conceal police short-comings rather than protect information that could damage law enforcement."

Home Secretary after Home Secretary has pledged to do more. In 2015 Theresa May announced that child sex abuse would be prioritised as a national threat akin to serious and organised crime. Amber Rudd also introduced a fresh set of measures. And apparently it remains high on Priti Patel's agenda. Combating child sex abuse is exceedingly complex, I am sure, and I do not doubt that it is high on everyone's agenda but for goodness sake these are our children, in England, in the 21st century and it needs to get off the agenda and into these children's lives.

****

MAY 30TH

Parents are still incredibly worried about this year's summer A-levels which will be teacher assessed and they are already contacting lawyers about how to appeal against their children's grades. And Headteachers are very frustrated that the appeals process remains unclear. Geoff Barton, general secretary of The Association of School and College Leaders, said, "We really didn't have to be here. Teachers, parents and students still don't know what the appeal process will look like. We tried to help the government get on the front foot. Here we are on the back foot again."

****

A week ago, *The Times* Education Commission was launched and is being chaired by Rachel Sylvester. Never has there been a greater need for a commission about the educational requirements of our children. We have some of the finest teachers, but they are at breaking point. I hope that this commission will produce some lasting and fine results. **The future of our children depends upon it.**

But Mr Gavin Williamson, are you still there? **We are watching and waiting** to see what exactly you and your department are planning to do for our children over the summer. What, Mr Williamson, are you doing?

****

JUNE 3RD

Well, we have just found out what Gavin Williamson and the PM and the Treasury have been doing and I am in shock. On the news at 5.30pm this evening we hear that **Sir Kevan Collins has resigned**. When offered £1.4 billion over three years instead of the £15 billion he asked for, he was appalled. In his letter of resignation, he says that "a half-hearted approach risks failing hundreds of thousands of pupils". This offer means that "the average primary school will receive just £22 per child per year". So to compare that with other countries, the Netherlands have announced a recovery plan worth £2,500 per child and the USA has announced an amount equal to £1,600. Sir Kevan says, "Above all, I am concerned that the package that was announced betrays an undervaluation of the importance of education."

I am so angry that I dash off three emails: one to my MP, one to Rachel Sylvester and one to *The Times*.

****

JUNE 4TH

And today my letter is published in *The Times*.

Sir, The appointment of Sir Kevan Collins as the new education tsar was absolutely brilliant. His ideas were exciting and innovative and much needed for a reform of our education system today. In order to achieve this he asked the government for £15 billion over the next three years. To be offered just £1.4 billion with no information about any further funds was like a slap in the face. So after just 4 months in the job he has resigned.

The Prime Minister keeps saying that children are his top priority. This is obviously not true and the weasel words he constantly utters are an insult to our children, their teachers and their parents. Once again this government, and in particular the Treasury, show that our children, who have suffered so much during this pandemic, are at the bottom of the pile and of no concern.

****

JUNE 8TH

So, we rely on some heart-warming and brilliant charities. In a report by Emma Yeomans in today's *Times* she writes about the **West London Zone Charity** who work in an area of London where they estimate that about 12,000 young people need extra support, and they are working in 29 schools in order to help them. They are funded by local authorities, charities and the Bank of America. Based on a child's progress, children are connected to a link worker who helps them to find the best academic and emotional support and makes sure they turn up to receive it. I have just looked at their website and it is inspirational.

****

Also today, Lord Adonis, education minister from 2005 to 2008, writes in the Thunderer in *The Times* today and says, "The government's rejection of Kevan Collins' education catch up package was a mistake." He goes on to say that there needs to be an "Education 2030 Plan setting out ambitions for change funded by a restoration of the investment levels of the 2000s".

He ends by quoting the philosopher RH Tawney who said, **"What the wise parent would wish for their child, so the state must wish for all children."**

I find it inordinately distressing that this government treats our children with such disdain, neglect and disinterest.

****

JUNE 17TH

But so it goes on. An article in *The Times* today shocks and upsets me in equal measure. Billy Kenber, an investigative reporter for *The Times*, writes about **children's care homes**. Apparently private firms rushed to set up children's homes at the beginning of the pandemic and of course many were not able to be physically inspected but had to be done remotely. Ofsted suspended routine inspections in mid-March 2020 and over the next five and a half months made on-site visits to only 29 homes at which there were serious concerns. *The Times* report says that the homes were being paid tens of millions of pounds of taxpayers' money despite many being deemed 'downright dangerous'. Some homes with especially difficult children were being paid up **to £10,000 a week** to look after **a single child**.

And what were these children able to do? They were able to access drugs and knives, to go out at night under the influence of drugs and weave in and out of traffic, and children who had been victims of sexual and criminal exploitation to continue to be exploited.

The staff at the homes often lacked the skills, qualifications and experience to keep the children safe and meet their needs and had no training in first aid, managing self-harm or other key areas. Support workers at Capital Children Care Ltd home in Braintree, for example, had very long shifts with one working 72 hours without leaving the home and another doing 14 consecutive nights.

So, the average cost of one child for one week in a privately run children's home is £4,130. The average cost for one prisoner a week is £858, and for one person a week in a privately run residential care home is £712.

(These figures are from Revolution Consulting. Ministry of Defence, PSSRU.)

Local authorities are legally responsible for children in care and often rely on private providers because of a shortage of places and budget cuts.

This year a report from the Local Government Association found that the six largest private providers were making combined annual profits of more than £200 million.

Some of these homes are now closed. But who was responsible? Who allowed these homes to be opened without proper checks? No wonder there is no money for education, the NHS or foreign aid. Children's Care Homes? What a misnomer that is. These homes are Children's We Don't Care Homes.

****

On March 25th 2020, Boris Johnson said: "As a society, and as a country, we are doing quite an extraordinary thing, which is for the first time in our history, to get through this crisis, **we are putting our arms as a country, around every single worker, every single employee in this country.**" Well there are an awful lot of people that have been left out as I think you will agree. And in the next chapter we hear about some more.

****

POVERTY AND UNIVERSAL CREDIT

2021

JANUARY

The government is saying that it will be **stopping the increase in universal benefit** in April 2021. £20 a week was added to universal credit payments at the beginning of the pandemic, and it was only meant to be for a year so is due to stop in April 2021. However, there is a backlash from MPs and others saying that it mustn't be dropped. They say the drop will see 700,000 more people pushed into poverty, including some 300,000 children. A further 500,000 in poverty will be plunged into "deep poverty", says the Joseph Rowntree Foundation. Boris Johnson has accused Keir Starmer of getting all of the Momentum trolls to support him and "of playing politics and inciting the worst kind of hatred and bullying (of a kind seen sadly across the Atlantic)", referring to the insurrection like that in the USA when Trump's tribes stormed Capitol Hill. There is a backlash from backbenchers and a debate is being called for by the Opposition on January 18th.

****

JANUARY 18TH

Well, the result of the vote was 278 ayes and 0 noes. All except six Conservative MPs abstained. Not a binding vote but we **expect another U-turn shortly. And I write to *The Times* once more!** This was published on the 20th January.

Sir, I so disagree with The Times Leader about Universal Credit today. (19th January) Obviously temporary uplifts cannot continue indefinitely but we are still in the grips of a pandemic. Once we are through this crisis Universal Credit should, by all means, be reviewed. But to accuse the opposition of "playing politics" as Mr. Johnson has done is absolutely inane. They had asked for a serious debate in the Commons which is actually what Parliament is for.

****

JANUARY

The Chancellor Rishi Sunak is understood to be baulking at the £6.4 billion cost of extending the £25 Universal Credit for another 12 months, and has reportedly been considering **one-off payments of £1,000 or £500** for claimants instead. Many people think that that would be a stupid decision on several counts. If you need to go on to benefits after this payment is made due to changed circumstances, you wouldn't get this payment. And it is much easier to maintain discipline over money if it is a regular amount, rather than a large one-off.

The temporary uplift, introduced last March and worth more than £1,000 a year to those aged over 25, is currently due to end at the end of next month, and the Government is under pressure from campaigners and some of its own MPs to extend it. Citizens Advice said last month that 75 per cent of claimants would be unable to afford the basics if the £20-a-week boost was scrapped, up from 43 per cent currently.

****

A photo of 200 homeless people queueing in freezing temperatures in the snow for a soup kitchen in Glasgow has prompted an outpouring of anger.

****

MARCH 22ND

In *The Observer* yesterday there was an article about our uncaring and damaging welfare system. Sir Michael Marmot, who chaired a review on health inequality in 2010, has now said to *The Observer* that fiddling round the edges was not acceptable and that the whole welfare system needs dramatic reform. Benefits must be raised, he says, to curb the UK crisis in mental health. He says that "I have seen evidence that for some people in receipt of universal credit, there are mental health consequences. It is a brutalising system. Everyone should have at least the minimum income necessary for a healthy life. That means, ideally, all people of working age should be in work. That's the desirable state. And in work, they should be paid a living wage. If they can't work, for whatever reason, then the welfare system should be sufficiently generous for their health not to be damaged by that experience. We know what needs to be done. Let's do it."

Charlotte Pickles, a member of the government's Social Security Advisory Committee and an architect of universal credit, said the current system simply was not generous enough. "This £20 uplift, I think, is going to have to be extended further. Not just because the political fallout of it will be massive, but also because the benefits are too low at the moment."

Sir Michael Marmot also said that studies had shown that more generous labour market support could even have an impact on suicide rates during economic downturns, suggesting that a rethink "could prevent a great deal of suffering. The evidence has shown that the generosity of active labour market programmes, both unemployment insurance and efforts to get people back into work, breaks the link between the rise in unemployment and the rise in suicide".

And in the interest of fairness I give the **government's reply**:

"We are committed to supporting the lowest-paid families through the pandemic and beyond to **ensure that nobody is left behind**. That's why we've targeted our support to those most in need by raising the living wage, spending hundreds of billions to safeguard jobs, boosting welfare support and local authority funding by billions and introducing the £229m Covid Winter Grant Scheme to help children and families stay warm and well fed. We have also provided £32m for food distribution charities and £750m to tackle homelessness and rough sleeping next year."

I just find it strange that they don't even acknowledge that there might be some truth in what the people closely involved say. The reply to any criticism or worry is that they are giving out loads of money and there is no problem. All is well. **Nothing to discuss.**

****

Nine in ten councils have seen **a rise in people using food banks** and an increase in family disputes requiring mediation across most of England. Senior figures across local authorities are worried that a **further crisis in rough sleeping** and homelessness will emerge when the eviction ban ends at the end of May. Also in Bradford, for example, three times as much food was delivered from 21 sites during the peak of demand compared with pre-Covid levels and more than a third of teachers delivered food parcels to pupils' homes.

****

APRIL 6TH

A report has come out by the Evidence and Impact team at the **Joseph Rowntree Foundation** (JRF) about **poverty in the UK today**. This report was written in January, but I have only just seen it. I quote the reasons for the report and the main recommendations as I do feel it is a slur on our society that the poverty rates in this country are so high, and you just might have missed it.

"This report is being published in the midst of the coronavirus storm – a turbulent time when all of us have felt insecurity and instability. But our analysis shows too many of us entered the pandemic already at risk of being cast adrift into poverty, while often lacking secure housing, a reliable income or adequate support. It also shows that those of us already struggling to keep our heads above water have often been hit the hardest. Our response to the pandemic should be measured by how just and compassionate it is to people in poverty, whether they were already experiencing hardship or have been swept into it.

- We need as many people as possible to be in good jobs. Unemployment is expected to rise in the coming months, and we need to see further bold action to **retrain workers and create good quality new jobs.**

- We need to improve earnings for low-income working families and ensure more people are in secure, good quality work. Government must support people in the lowest-paid jobs, or people working part-time, to move into higher pay and access sufficient and secure working hours, including **bringing forward the Employment Bill.**

- We need to strengthen the benefits system. At a minimum, we need the temporary **£20 per week increase to Universal Credit** and Working Tax Credit to be **made permanent**, extending this same lifeline to people on legacy benefits such as Jobseeker's Allowance and Employment and Support Allowance.

- We need to **increase the amount of low-cost housing** available for families on low incomes and increase support for households who have high housing costs."

This is their annual 2021 report and goes into detail about how this can all be achieved. I really hope that members of the government are reading it.

****

APRIL 14TH

Apparently, HM Revenue and Customs mistakenly overpaid tax credits, as much as 17 years ago, to about 500,000 people on benefits. These people had no way of knowing they were being overpaid. The flaw is linked to an error on HMRC's part. In many cases it did not follow the correct procedure with assessments and failed to update systems with changes to personal circumstances. So now, in the middle of a pandemic, at the beginning of January this year, these claimants have had their payments drastically cut in an aggressive tax raid on the country's poorest families. As a result, as many as half a million struggling families are having to survive with significant cuts to their income, effectively wiping out any benefits brought in from the £20 a week uplift.

One single mother who lost her job during the pandemic said that her payments fell significantly in January, just days after her son was diagnosed with a brain haemorrhage.

Sir Iain Duncan Smith, the former Conservative leader, who was the architect of universal credit, said using the benefits system to claw back tax in this way was "a major mistake" that was "causing profound difficulties". Apparently, companies in England cannot take court action to recover most debts from more than six years ago, when they are considered "statute barred", but this does not, for some inexplicable reason, apply to the Revenue. *The Times* carried out this investigation under the Freedom of Information Act.

****

I keep saying to myself **'words fail me'** but then I get so angry about yet another piece of information that I have to find some more.

****

Tackle poverty to reduce crime. The Chief Constable of Merseyside Police, Andy Cooke, who is retiring after five years in the role, said if he was given a £5 billion budget to cut crime, most of it would be spent on trying to tackle poverty. Mr Cooke said the solution to crime in inner cities is building community cohesion. He told *The Guardian*: "The best crime prevention is increased opportunity and reduced poverty. That's the best way to reduce crime. So there needs to be substantial funding into the infrastructure of our inner cities and our more deprived areas. The solution is building the opportunities for young people, and levelling up the playing field. It's such an unequal playing field we have at the moment with job prospects, and with opportunities for the future. There's got to be some levelling up."

****

Well, as I said on April 6th, if the government reads the Rowntree report on poverty things could improve. The trouble is, of course, we know that Boris Johnson is a liar. A video has been shown this morning by Peter Stefanovic calling out a few of **his lies to parliament**. He showed Johnson lying about figures for our cut in emissions, our growth in GDP, nurses' pay, test and trace, and **poverty**. If he doesn't even acknowledge there is a problem with any of this, then nothing is going to improve.

****

APRIL 23RD

Food banks
A record 2.5 million emergency food parcels were handed out by Britain's biggest food bank charity during the first year of the pandemic. The Trussell Trust said that its outlets had experienced a 33 per cent increase in the number of parcels they distributed between April 2020 and March 2021. Almost one million (980,082) of these parcels went to children – more than one parcel every minute on average, according to the charity. It is the first time the total number of parcels have topped two million as they warned that low-income

families are experiencing 'historic' levels of need. The Trussell Trust said **poverty** was the main driver of food bank use, mainly caused by the low level of benefits, increasing numbers of families hit by the benefit cap policy, and gaps in the social security system.

It warned its figures present a partial picture, as unprecedented numbers of people are being helped by independent food aid providers and community groups, some of which sprang into action as a result of the pandemic.

Sabine Goodwin, coordinator of *The Independent* Food Aid Network, said: "Now, more than ever, our social security system needs to be reset, local authority support schemes involving crisis grants prioritised and adequate wages and secure work ensured.

"It's the Government's responsibility to stop hunger from happening in the first place so that everyone is able to afford to buy food and other essentials."

Of course it is a difficult time during this pandemic, but we do not want this government saying that **no child goes hungry** until it has read these reports.

****

An article in *The Observer* today highlights the effect the pandemic has had on the **poorest and most marginalized** people in society. James Bullion, who steps down next week from the Association of Directors of the Adult Social Services, says he is frustrated that minsters had still not laid out how they intended to **reform social care**. But he is also angry and concerned about the lack of sufficient support for rough sleepers, disabled people, older and frail people. He says that "if we had had **a quarter of the £37 billion** that's been used on test and trace that would have put us in a position where we would have transformed lives, we'd have had less risk, we'd have had fewer deaths". But there was a **silver lining** because in his area, Norfolk, they were able to access the list of the vulnerable people who had been told to shield. "For the first time," he says, "councils and the NHS had a shared list of people to work with. **And suddenly we had a model of intervention with food boxes and volunteers going to check people were OK."**

****

APRIL 28TH

There was a photo in *The Mirror* today **of a bed in a seven year old's bedroom** put there by Zarach, which is charity in Leeds that delivers basics to children in poverty. There was just a bed and nothing else, not even a floor covering of any sort. As they say, it just shows the "nothingness" some children are forced to live in through no fault of their own. There is a Just Giving campaign asking people to help make their houses into more of a home. So far, they have raised £8,000. The actions of so called 'ordinary' men and women are so far above those of this government. These are the people who the vulnerable in our society depend on. And they do not let them down.

****

And on the same day as we see this heart-breaking photo, Sarah Vine, wife of Michael Gove and journalist for the *Daily Mail*, in defending the Downing Street flat refurbishment, says that **Boris "can't be expected to live in a skip".**

****

MAY 24TH

There was a debate in parliament today on **child food poverty**. This was because 554,276 people signed up to an e-petition relating to child food poverty, which was started by Marcus Rashford. In order to understand accurately what 'child food poverty' and 'food insecurity' means, I will quote from Hansard on this debate.

"People are asked three questions: Have you had to skip meals because of a lack of money or not being able to access the food that you need?

Have you gone hungry and not eaten for those same reasons? Have you gone for a day without eating for those same reasons? The executive director of the Food Foundation said that 14% of households with children fell into the moderate or the severe category following their response to these questions.

The petition has three key asks of the Government: provide meals and activities during all school holidays, expand free school meals to all under 16 when a parent or guardian is in receipt of universal credit and increase the value of healthy start vouchers to at least £4.25 a week. Well this has apparently already happened, but it needs to be expanded."

Ian Lavery MP for Wansbeck said, "Child poverty is a political choice. It could be eradicated within weeks if there was the political will. There is lack of quality housing, and mass evictions are just round the corner. Fire and rehire is running wild and the benefits system is not fit for purpose. Soon the £20 uplift in universal credit will be cut. What an absolute mess."

Grahame Morris MP for Easington said, "Closing Sure Start centres and depriving local authorities of the means with which to support children are deliberate policies of this government and this is the consequence."

Nelson Mandela is also quoted when he said that, "Overcoming poverty is not a task for charity, it is an act of justice. Like slavery and apartheid, poverty is not natural, it is man-made and it can be overcome and eradicated by the actions of human beings."

Beth Winter says, "We should all be filled with anger about the fact that we in the UK, one of the richest nations in the world have allowed this situation to arise. We should be ashamed that food banks have been normalised in this country; it is a political choice and a shocking indictment of us."

This debate was one and a half hours long and I bring just a few points to your attention here. But, as always, what really matters is whether there is any action by the government.

****

JUNE 5TH

I think at this point we need to look at the gender make-up of the Cabinet. At the time of writing the Cabinet is made up of 22 men and five women. I think it is always important to remember this, but never more so than when you read the next chapter.

****

WOMEN

2021

Many women have shouldered the burden of this pandemic disproportionally, with children and elderly relatives to look after, and low paid jobs to try and manage. And if you became pregnant during this time, you were completely forgotten.

JANUARY
Self-employed women on Maternity leave have had no extra financial support from the government. They were told that Maternity leave should be treated like a holiday or sick leave! This is a blatant example of sexual discrimination. The charity **Pregnant then Screwed,** with support from Doughty Street Chambers and law firm Leigh Day, will be taking the Chancellor to the high court on Thursday 21st January for discriminating against women in the Self-Employment Income Support Scheme. SEISS was introduced by the Chancellor of the Exchequer in April 2020, to support self-employed workers whose trade has been adversely affected by Covid-19. The eligibility conditions and calculation method chosen by the Chancellor have a discriminatory effect on women as they do not exempt periods of maternity leave. The number of women affected is significant: currently calculated at 69,200. Pregnant Then Screwed are asking the Chancellor to take immediate steps to change the SEISS so that time taken for maternity leave is discounted when average earnings are calculated. Joeli Brearley, CEO and founder of Pregnant Then Screwed, explains, "The

government has had nine months to amend this scheme so that it doesn't discriminate against women; but they have chosen not to."

Pregnant Then Screwed is an independent charity which was launched on International Women's Day in 2015, as a space for mothers to share their stories of discrimination. The project quickly grew and today they are a charity dedicated to ending the systemic, cultural and institutional discrimination faced by thousands of pregnant women and mothers every year. They say that "we believe in a world where stay-at-home parents are valued for their contribution to society. We believe in a world where both parents are encouraged to spend time with their children. We believe in a world where childcare is free and is the best it can possibly be for all children and all those who care for our children. We believe in a world where both parents contribute equally to the running of a household whilst achieving their own ambitions. We believe that mothers deserve better and we believe that if we work together we can, and we will, create change.

"With the outbreak of the pandemic we've had heart breaking messages from so many women. For some this drop in income has left them and their young family in desperate poverty; while their male colleagues are in receipt of the full benefit. But this isn't just about the 69,000 vulnerable new mothers who have received a payment that is well below what they should have received. It is about the critical importance of maternity leave and ensuring that as a society we value it. Giving birth and caring for the next generation, particularly in a baby's first year of life, is work; it is mentally and physically exhausting work. Not only that but ensuring the next generation survives and thrives is surely the most important job there is. For maternity leave to be dismissed as the same as being sick or taking a sabbatical is not only insulting, but it sends out a very dangerous message about how this government views mothers and the integral role we play in a well-functioning society. This court case is about defending women's rights and showing the government that they cannot ride roughshod over the Equality Act".

****

Seven out of 10 of eligible mothers who have asked for furlough in this lockdown have been turned down. Mother Pukka, alias Anna Whitehouse, is asking 100,000 women to comment on one post with their experiences and to tag the prime minister.

****

JANUARY 28TH

Covid stay-at-home advert withdrawn!! This advert was deemed sexist, as whilst encouraging people to stay at home, it had four pictures depicting a woman at home cleaning, a woman ironing, a woman home-schooling and a man lounging on a sofa! Two opinions on this. One says, "who thought up this patriarchal patronising advert?"; the other says, "yep, that looks about right!"

****

FEBRUARY 18TH

The **charity Pregnant then Screwed** lost its court case today against the Treasury and the Government.

****

FEBRUARY 23RD

So, an interesting article in *The Observer* yesterday. It is all about **locking up more and more women**. And of course, if you lock up the mother you damage the child. So, this article is about women in prison, which is a cause close to my heart.

In 2006 Baroness Corston produced a review that argued that the majority of women should be diverted to probationary support in the community rather than be given a custodial sentence. This has been seen cross-party as accepted wisdom. Well, there are still twice as many women in prison as 30 years ago, but at least the intention was there. Not anymore. The government has just announced that it is spending £150 million to create 500 new prison places for women. They say that extra places are needed because an extra 20,000 police offices will lead to more female arrests! And when pointed out about how this will affect children their answer is...**are you ready for this**????? to bring more children in to sleep the night with their mother in prison, thus normalising prison for children. As a member of the Howard League for Penal Reform for over 30 years, I despair.

This is a letter we were all asked to send to our MPs by the Howard League.

Dear Oliver,

I am writing to express my concern that the government has announced it will increase the number of prison cells for women by 500 places. This is despite the number of women in prison falling and the government's stated policy to reduce the number of women entering into the criminal justice system.

Ongoing plans to recruit 20,000 additional police officers are cited in justifying this decision to expand the size of the women's prison estate. There is no sensible reason why more police must mean more women are arrested. Women who currently enter the criminal justice system are often victims of crime themselves. Very few women commit serious violent crimes. Police forces are already committed to reduce arrests of women and to divert women to services that meet their needs and reduce crime.

The government should be backing its own policy to reduce the numbers of women in the criminal justice system and not be spending money on an admission of failure.

These 500 new prison places will cost millions, not only to build but in running them year after year. The Howard League for Penal Reform has highlighted that the sums being spent will dwarf the money being given to women's centres and organisations working in the community to prevent crime and support women – work that the Ministry of Justice's own research shows reduces crime and turns women's lives round. At a time when self-injury by women in prison is on the rise, it is unacceptable for the government to be contemplating an expansion of women's prisons.

I would be grateful to hear your views on whether money should be spent on failing women's prisons or on women's centres and support on housing, families, and mental health in the community.

Will you raise these concerns on my behalf with government ministers at the Ministry of Justice? It is not too late to stop these plans and persuade the government to have the courage to back its own stated policy to keep women out of the criminal justice system wherever possible.

With best wishes, Sue Wood

And as yet, of course, no answer.

Many women's prisons are filled with women who should not be there. Two thirds of women in prison are survivors of domestic abuse, over half have experienced physical, emotional or sexual abuse during their childhood, and half of women in prison have committed an offence in order to support someone else's drug habit. Many are there for failing to pay their TV licence. There are those with serious mental health and addiction issues who have never been able to get the help they need and have found their way into the prison system via repeated minor offences. More than three in five are serving sentences of less than six months. This is not long enough to get any proper help but just long enough to lose your home, your job and your children.

I have had six letters published in *The Times* about prisons and the legal system over the years and one in *The Guardian,* and obviously it makes no difference whatsoever. So, women of the UK, don't expect any help or support from this government if you fall on hard times. **They are passionate about locking women up.**

****

MARCH 9TH

Today there was a debate in the Commons about **support for women leaving prison**. Over half of all women walk out of prison with **£46 and a plastic bag** and the threat of recall if they miss their probation appointment. Many will have been in a prison far from their home and so will have no contacts locally. Some might only have been in for a six-month sentence, which is too short to be enrolled for any rehabilitation or education courses but long enough to have your children taken into care and your home to be repossessed. For those who are victims of abuse, returning to their home is a huge personal risk. Once again, vulnerable women are at the bottom of the pile.

****

MARCH 14TH

Yesterday there was a gathering of women on Clapham Common to remember Sarah Everard, a 33 year old young woman who was kidnapped and murdered on the streets of London by a rogue police officer. These women wanted a **vigil on Clapham Common in her memory.** This was refused by the courts because of the pandemic. The organisers had asked the police to work with them to make it safe. They wanted stewards and other safety measures put in place, but the police refused to co-operate. So, the women came anyway. They all wore face masks and stood in peaceful silence. The Duchess of Cambridge had been earlier to leave some daffodils she had picked from her garden. It was not an official visit, but she remembered how it had felt when walking the streets of London in the dark on her own. Later in the evening, the women started to speak about their experiences from the band-stand and at that point the police moved in. They trampled over the flowers and candles, and arrested some women by man-handling them and pushing them to the ground. So, at a peaceful protest/vigil by women over the issue of violence by men to women we saw more violence by men to women. There is to be an inquiry, but this moment will be etched on the mind of every woman in the UK for a long time to come.

****

MARCH 15TH

And at an emergency summit meeting today about violence against women the **Women's Minister Liz Truss** was not invited to attend.

"There will be no minister from the Government Equalities Office at the meeting," says Downing Street.

****

Also today, there is a bill having its second reading in parliament which is called **The police, crime, sentencing and court bill** and it will be voted on tomorrow. This controversial bill will mean that police chiefs will be able to put more conditions on static protests.

They will be able to impose a start and finish time, set noise limits, and apply these rules to a demonstration by **just one person**. They are also going to ban any protests outside parliament. This is designed to stop people occupying public spaces, hanging off bridges, gluing themselves to windows, or employing other protest tactics to make themselves both seen and heard. The protest by Extinction Rebellion last year brought a lot of the city of London to a standstill, which is I think why this bill is being brought to parliament. However, the Labour Party opposes the protest measures. Shadow justice secretary David Lammy says the legislation is "a mess". He says the government is trying to rush through Parliament "poorly thought-out measures to impose disproportionate controls on free expression and the right to protest". Rights of Women, a campaign group, says the bill's focus is all wrong, and it fails to introduce long-called-for measures that could reduce violence against women and girls. Amnesty International UK predicts that if the measures become law, there will be more scenes like those at the Clapham Common vigil for Sarah Everard. The proposed law includes an offence of "intentionally or recklessly causing public nuisance".

One final measure clarifies that damage to memorials could lead to up to 10 years in prison. In other words, it is being said that this will mean it will be possible to have tougher sentences for **toppling statues than for assaulting women**.

At any time this would not be a good look, but now?

****

But so **much unrest in the UK** at the moment. Many, many protests taking place in major cities against this new **Police, Crime, Sentencing and Courts Bill**. At the moment this bill is at the committee stage in the House of Lords. There have been protests over the last three weekends with them being held this last weekend in London, Newcastle, Liverpool and Portsmouth. Obviously, there is a real concern over new powers being given to the police to stop peaceful protests. However, more and more violence is being used by a certain number of people. But also, there is a petition against the Bill which has just been launched and will be sent to the National Police Chiefs Council. Entitled **"Protect Your Freedom to Protest"**, it has already been signed more than 206,000 times. It reads: "The government is planning to make important changes to the law that will restrict the right to protest when lockdown restrictions ease. We oppose this new planned legislation and instead demand that the National Police Chiefs Council adopts a new, eleven-point Charter for Freedom of Assembly Rights – or explain why they refuse to do so."

****

In an article by Alice Thomson in *The Times* today, she records some interesting **rape statistics**. Approximately 85,000 women are raped each year. An estimated 90% know the man who raped them, meaning that approximately 8,500 women each year are raped by a man they didn't know. But only 1.4% of rape cases in England and Wales recorded by the police resulted in a suspect being charged. This is the lowest figure on record. Because of the dire situation with our criminal justice system, which has been starved of funds by this government, some cases now take over three years to come to court The number of women's refuges have dwindled due to lack of funding, so domestic abuse victims have nowhere to go. Sadly, the situation is that police, prosecutors and courts don't take women seriously and treat women victims more like criminals. Harriet Johnson, a barrister, says, "I see rape victims blamed, belittled, ridiculed and ignored by officers who are supposed to be supporting them." Women have **lost faith in the system**. Sammy Woodhouse, who was in a care home in Rotherham, said that the worst thing about being groomed, raped and beaten from the age of 12 by an older man was the fact that police and social services thought she deserved it. "Sometimes I was like a dead body on a slab," she said, "but everyone thought I was a slut."

As I continue to write this book I feel a lot of anger, but then I feel more and more despair.

****

MARCH 17TH
The Police Crime and Sentencing Court Bill was passed yesterday by 359 votes to 263.

****

MARCH 18TH
And so, yesterday in parliament in a debate on domestic violence, when Oliver Dowden's opposite number, Jo Stevens, questioned him about sentences for vandalising statues, he responded by saying that **"I really wish that Members in this House would take a more temperate approach towards this"**. Ms Stevens tweeted: "Apparently I wasn't "temperate" enough when asking Oliver Dowden why sentencing for attacking a statue is higher than that for raping a woman. Judge for yourselves."

So, Oliver goes on to say that rapists can get life sentences. Yes, Oliver, we know that, but the proportion of rapists being prosecuted in England and Wales has plummeted to just 1.7%. And new Home Office statistics suggest the alleged perpetrators of more than 98% of rapes reported to the police are allowed to go free. And of the 57,000 rapes reported to the police in 2018, they are only a fraction of the real figure because many victims do not report assaults. **And male MPs continue to denigrate, insult and belittle women MPs in the hallowed sanctuary of our House of Commons.**

****

MARCH 24TH

A nurse, Karen Reissmann, 61, who has worked as a frontline nurse throughout the pandemic, was handed a **fine of £10,000** in March for protesting over the government's proposed 1% pay-rise for NHS workers. As the organiser, she offered a risk assessment of her protest to Greater Manchester Police (GMP) and ensured it was Covid-safe. On 1st April, London law firm Bindmans, acting on Reissmann's behalf, wrote to GMP saying that the way the force had interpreted the law was wrong, that the protest should have been allowed to proceed, and that it should also withdraw the fine.

Reissmann, a nurse for 39 years, said: "Somebody calculated that if I used my 1% pay rise, it would take me 56 years to pay the fine off."

The force's determination to prosecute comes against the backdrop of the government's **police, crime, sentencing and courts bill**, which will leave police to use their own discretion, and potentially criminalise protests. The GMP applied a blanket policy that all protest was unlawful under the regulations. However, the letter states that "this approach was wrong in law and contrary to authority". And today in central London we see photographs of thousands of anti-lockdown and anti-masks protestors thronging the streets with no social distancing and of course hardly any masks. Will everyone be fined £10,000? I really do not understand what is happening here and it would appear that the police do not understand this new bill either.

****

APRIL 5TH

And two dreadful stories in *The Observer* yesterday. This really follows from the 'kill the bill' protests in Bristol. **The police have been accused of an abuse of power by using anti-terror style tactics against protesters after two young women claimed they endured terrifying ordeals at the hands of male officers pretending to be postal workers.** The women were caught up in a series of undercover raids by Avon and Somerset Police shortly after the protests. Katie McGoran, 21, who left the first "kill the bill" demonstration on 21st March before any trouble broke out, claimed she was mistakenly arrested after a male officer dressed as a postal worker tricked his way into her shared student house in north Bristol a few days later. She says the disguised officer and at least three other male plain-clothed officers followed her flatmate up the stairs before revealing they were police with a warrant. They then burst into McGoran's bedroom **and handcuffed her while she was only partially dressed.**

"It was frightening having all these policemen in my room after what happened to Sarah Everard and seeing footage of the vigil in Clapham," she said. "I was only wearing a T-shirt, underwear and a short dressing gown. I felt really vulnerable. I started having a panic attack. I was so scared. I was shrieking and asking to call my mum but they said 'no' and told my flatmate to go to her room." The officers, she claimed, kept her in handcuffs even after they realised she didn't match the picture of the person they were looking for. They watched, she added, as she struggled to put some joggers on: "I couldn't put them on because of the cuffs. I was crying. It was really humiliating." McGoran said they eventually uncuffed her but didn't apologise for the 20-minute ordeal. **"They were making jokes when they had caused me to have a panic attack," she said.**

The same day the police are said to have used similar tactics to raid another all-female shared student house in the city. The family of Grace Hart, who is 16, claimed she answered the door twice to a male officer who pretended to be a postal worker and who said that he had a package for her flatmate. Her father, Paul Hart, said she became suspicious so she started to close the door. "The officer," he claimed, "then barged in along with a group of at least three other plain-clothed male officers shouting 'police' and pointing Tasers at her."

"They pushed her up against the wall. They had Tasers out. She had red dots on her body," he said. "Three of those could have killed her because of the voltage. It's an excessive use of force. It's absolutely horrendous."

The officers, claimed Hart, searched the entire house, including his daughter's room, even though the person they were looking for wasn't there and **Grace didn't attend any of the protests**. Grace said she felt "violated" by the raid and added, "I'm now really nervous to open the door when I don't know who is behind it."

I write this book because I get angry. And I get angry on two levels. Once when I find out about all of these appalling stories and then again when I realise that not enough people really know nor care. There is disquiet in the community as these protests show, but sadly protests very rarely change anything. The only way to change is to have people of intelligence, wisdom, vision, compassion and integrity at the heart of our politics.

****

And we hear in *The Times* yesterday that Priti Patel is introducing **league tables** ranking police forces on their success in cutting serious crime. Chief constables are not happy about this, saying that it was a **return to targets**. Apparently, targets have historically resulted in a disproportionate focus on some cases at the expense of others. Kit Malthouse, who was Boris Johnson's deputy mayor for policing in London, oversaw the introduction of targets for seven categories including burglary, violence and theft from vehicles. The police watchdog later concluded that the Met had concentrated on those areas **at the expense of protecting abused children.** As one senior source said, "It is yet another land-grab by the Home Secretary. These targets will drive perverse behaviour in policing." Some police chiefs have already complained that she went too far when she demanded forces increase enforcement of protests and coronavirus restrictions and are not happy with the new national crime and policing bill.

****

APRIL 15TH

The Domestic Abuse Bill. This is another bill that will **disproportionately affect women.** As this bill faces its final vote in the House of Commons, the safety of migrant women hangs in the balance. If the Government **votes against existing amendments** to the Bill, some of the most marginalised women in society will continue to face an impossible choice: stay with an abusive partner and endure further emotional and physical harm, or call the police and face the threat of detainment, deportation or destitution, excluded from refuges, housing and welfare.

At the start of the year, three amendments that would give migrant women greater protection when reporting or fleeing abuse were voted for in the House of Lords. But as the Bill heads back to the Commons, charities expect the Government to vote against them. Originally introduced by Theresa May in 2019, the Bill was created to offer victims greater protection and see more perpetrators of abuse held to account. The legislation has been touted as landmark, and indeed it is very much needed for women in abusive households, but campaigners say the Bill will not be fit for purpose if it does not offer safety to all victims. In the UK, when a person is subject to immigration control, they have **no recourse to public funds** and cannot access mainstream welfare benefits. NRPF applies across the board to people subject to a time-limited immigration status. For those who are also victims of abuse, NRPF can also make accessing women's shelters extremely difficult as places are often funded by housing benefits.

If the three amendments are voted down, then migrant women in the UK will have no access to help of any kind. The reason many charities expect the amendments to be voted down is because of the Government's Support for Migrant Victims scheme, which is a 12-month pilot fund to cover the cost of support for migrant women with NRPF in refuge accommodation and to meet their basic needs. The Government has allocated £1.5 million to the scheme, but Southall Black Sisters say this is "wholly inadequate to meet the needs of all vulnerable migrant women who need crisis support". The scheme is also pitched by the Government as an evidence-gathering exercise of what long-term funding is needed, but charities insist there is plenty of evidence available. For Janaya Walker of SBS, the scheme is a way of avoiding meaningful action and an excuse not to vote for the amendments. "This is a tactic; an attempt to kick the issue into the long grass. We still have no detail as to who has been awarded the grant for the SMV contract or what kind of support will be offered."

So far, the Government has declined to comment. But we just continue to take note of the **lack of compassion** that we have come to expect of this government in every single aspect. And we watch closely to see how they vote. We must acknowledge that maybe they will not vote them down.

****

APRIL 19TH

But they do. The amendments to the **domestic abuse bill** have been **voted down** by the government. So, we were right to be worried. Amendment 43 would have specifically required the Secretary of State to take steps to ensure that **all** victims of domestic abuse, irrespective of their status, receive protection and support. MPs voted down the amendment by 352 to 226 votes. "Perpetrators know, at the moment, that they can use immigration status against vulnerable and frightened victims," Jess Phillips argued in the Commons last week. "If you tell the police, you'll get deported and you'll never see the kids again. If you go to the police, they'll lock you up in a detention centre. I have seen this thousands of times."

I watched the votes come in with disbelief. Nearly all men of course.

****

MAY 14TH

And so a survey which has just come out from that wonderful charity **Pregnant Then Screwed** found that one-fifth of the 936 women they interviewed in December were **made to wear face coverings as they gave birth** to prevent the risk of Covid-19 infection. The research shows women were left struggling to breathe or experienced panic attacks while wearing the masks, which goes against the UK guidance published in July 2020 by the Royal College of Midwives and the Royal College of Obstetricians and Gynaecologists. "Research that we did in December showed that just 53% of women are feeling listened to in labour," said Joeli Brearley, CEO and founder of Pregnant Then Screwed. "When you overlay that with the fact that 50 per cent of women who are having C-sections are being told to wear a mask, and 10 per cent of those in natural labour, you're adding a literal communication barrier when birthing restrictions mean that some women are birthing alone. Women that we've spoken to have had asthma, they've felt dizzy, one woman even threw up in her mask during labour. This is completely avoidable. The guidance needs to be made clear and communicated to all pregnant women that they do not need to wear masks in labour."

Maria Booker, from the charity Birthrights, has insisted that being made **to wear a face covering during childbirth is "completely inhumane"** and has called for all maternity services to make the guidelines clear to staff.

A spokesperson for the NHS said: "Guidance to hospitals has been **absolutely clear that women who are giving birth are exempt from wearing a face mask**, and every hospital in England should be following this."

But if that is the case, why did it happen? Who is looking after these women? Who is listening to their concerns? It was bad enough that women were not allowed to have a partner or other person with them during hospital appointments when pregnant. **Please, please listen to women, all women, and show that you care.**

****

MAY 19TH

The Institute for Employment Studies and the charity Gingerbread have reported that single parents have really struggled during the pandemic as they have been more likely to have been working in industries where there have been lots of job losses with more to come as furlough ends. At the same time, the cost of childcare has gone up.

****

MAY 25TH

There is still some concern about the fact that **pregnant women** are not in a priority group for vaccinations. Sylvia Richardson, president of the Royal Statistical Society, writes in *The Times* today that a study by the National Maternity and Perinatal Audit showed the harm Covid-19 could cause during pregnancy. It took until April to decide that pregnant women could be vaccinated but no faster than other members of their age group. Meanwhile, other countries such as Ireland began prioritising pregnant women. "These decisions", she says, "raises important questions about how these critical choices are made. Too often decisions affecting women's health are neglected or delayed. **This cannot be helped by the gender imbalance of the groups making these decisions.**"

Indeed. As I keep saying we are governed by a huge majority of men.

****

And we are all very concerned too, about one special woman.

****

NAZANIN ZAGHARI-RATCLIFFE

You may remember that when Boris Johnson was Foreign Secretary in November 2017, he told a Commons committee that Nazanin Zaghari-Ratcliffe had been "teaching people journalism" in Iran when she was arrested on charges of espionage. The claim was used by the nation as evidence to double her prison sentence, furthering allegations she had been spreading "propaganda against the regime". Her five-year sentence is now nearing an end.

Britain owes Iran around £400m for a cancelled arms deal in the 1970s. The deal was made with the country's then Shah, and would have seen 1,750 tanks and other vehicles sold by Britain to Iran. However, the Shah was toppled in the Islamic Revolution of 1979 and although paid for, almost none of the vehicles were delivered. Successive international courts have found that we are in fact legally obliged to pay this debt.

So **I wrote to Dominic Raab** at the end of December 2020.

Dear Mr Raab,

I am horrified to read in today's Times that the Foreign Office no longer takes any responsibility for British Citizens imprisoned abroad through no fault of their own. They say that they have no obligation to give any assistance or protection whatsoever. Of course we can see this with the case of Nazanin Zaghari-Ratcliffe. The lack of any help for her is a disgrace. An international court ruled in 2008 that we were legally obliged to pay our debt of £400 million. If this debt was paid then Nazanin would be freed. And she has had no access to British officials at all.

What exactly are you doing about her situation? Is this debt going to be paid as we are legally obliged to do?

And is it true that British citizens, falsely arrested overseas, have no legal right to consular assistance?

****

2021

JANUARY

I had a reply from the Foreign and Commonwealth Office on the 26th January. At the end of a reasonably long email, it finished with this paragraph.

You also raise the issue of a debt owed to Iran. We continue to explore options to resolve this 40-year old case and will not comment further while these discussions are ongoing.

I happened to find a similar paragraph in some correspondence some four years ago. I can only presume that discussions have been ongoing for nearly 40 years and so further comments will never emerge. But her due release date is the 7th March this year. At the moment, she is tagged and living with her parents due to the pandemic in the jail.

Foreign Secretary Dominic Raab said that he would leave "no stone unturned" in his quest to have Zaghari-Ratcliffe released on time. I repeat... **the date is 7th March.**

****

MARCH 6TH 1.30PM

And so, about now what should be happening? Well, **Nazanin Zaghari-Ratcliffe** should be being given her passport, being relieved of her electric tag, be packing her bags, be saying a fond farewell to her parents and be making her way to the airport in order to fly back to England tomorrow.

****

MARCH 7TH

Well, she was freed from house arrest today but has been ordered back to court next week so has not been allowed to leave the country.

****

MARCH 13TH

She has now faced a second set of charges.

****

March 20th

Nazanin Zaghari-Ratcliffe gets the verdict about her trumped-up charge tomorrow.

****

MARCH 26TH

Well, nothing yet. She could still be waiting for a verdict in her second court case on Easter Sunday, her family believes. After a court hearing on March 13th, Nazanin was told she would hear whether she'd be convicted of a second set of anti-regime charges in around seven working days. But this period has coincided with New Year celebrations in Iran – and Nazanin's husband Richard thinks it might not be resolved until after Easter, which this year is the 4th April.

****

APRIL 5TH

Nazanin Zaghary-Ratcliffe is still in Iran. April 3rd marked the first day back at work after the Iranian New Year. The UK debt remains unpaid. Apparently, the legal proceedings concerning the debt return to court in two weeks' time. Caught between the interests of two States, Nazanin will now be calling on the United Nations to call out Iran's practices of arbitrary detention and hostage taking.

****

APRIL 26TH

Fifty days after **Nazanin Zaghari-Ratcliffe** was due to be released from Iran I could find no news about her anywhere, until midday today.

Four minutes ago, suddenly on the news, we hear that she has been sentenced to a year in prison after being found guilty of propaganda activities against the regime in Iran.

She was also given a further **one-year ban on leaving the country**.

Her lawyer said she had been accused of taking part in a demonstration in London 12 years ago and of giving an interview to the BBC Persian Service.

She has not been taken to prison yet, apparently, and her lawyer plans to appeal.

Confirming the sentence, her husband Richard Ratcliffe told the BBC the court's decision was a bad sign and "clearly a negotiating tactic" by the Iranian authorities – who are in the middle of discussions to revive the country's nuclear deal. She is obviously being used as a bargaining chip and I firmly believe that she will not be released until the British Government pays its debt to Iran. The money is in a frozen bank account and has been there since 2002. However, it has remained there ever since, whilst arguments over interest and the legality of handing it over continue whilst Iran was under international sanctions.

So it goes on, and we wonder exactly what the Foreign Office is doing apart from saying oh dear how dreadful. Her six year old daughter had made a calendar and was crossing off the days until her Mummy came home.

****

APRIL 29TH

There was an urgent question in the House of Commons yesterday about the recent developments in her case. The PM and Dominic Raab have already condemned the Iranian government for the new unlawful sentence and said it is totally inhumane. So why was our Foreign Secretary not there in the House of Commons yesterday when discussing the case? Why did he send a junior minister instead?

Nazanin Zaghari-Ratcliffe watched the proceedings from Iran and said that she feels there "wasn't anything said that gave me grounds for hope". Again, empty words from the Foreign Office.

****

MAY 2ND

Oh my goodness, just a few minutes ago my heart started thumping and I held my breath. News came out that Iran was due to release Nazanin as the UK had paid its debt. However, sometime later this was denied and all the Foreign Secretary would say was that they were having legal conversations and they were not linked to the £400 million debt. But in the strongest language used so far, he does call her treatment a **"form of torture"**.

Her husband Richard maintains, however, that **she is** being used as a bargaining chip in the dispute over the unpaid debt, as well as leverage in talks over the nuclear deal between Iran and world powers which are being held in Vienna shortly. But he adds that he thinks that maybe we are in the middle of negotiations which could possibly be a hopeful sign. So we all hold our breath and hope.

****

MAY 4TH

This makes my blood boil. Boris Johnson insisted to reporters yesterday that the debt legally owed by the UK to Iran has nothing to do with the fact that they are imprisoning Nazanin Zaghari-Ratcliffe. They are not linked, he said, in spite of the fact that Iranian officials told state media on Sunday that **she would be freed once Britain has paid up**. The British Government has never made it clear why it has delayed paying this £400 million debt. So, what happens now? Will this woman ever be free whilst we have such uncaring men in this government?

****

MAY 7TH

On the Today programme this morning, Antony Blinken, the USA Secretary of State who is over here on a visit, was asked if America would 'stand in the way' if Britain decided to 'hand money to Iran'. He replied, "It's a sovereign decision for the United Kingdom and I am not going to get into details of any negotiation." There are fears by this government that paying the money would breach international sanctions against Iran. A British court has ordered that the money be repaid, but apparently issues remain over any interest due and sanctions blocking payments to Iran. The UK Government has repeatedly insisted that the debt and Ms Zaghari-Ratcliffe's incarceration are "separate issues". Well maybe they have been in the past, but it is obvious to anyone with half a brain that they are not anymore.

****

MAY 28TH

Absolutely no news about Nazanin Zaghari-Ratcliffe. I have just written to the Foreign Office again and await a reply.

****

And I get a reply this very afternoon which is amazing. Very prompt. It says all the correct soundbites such as:

It is indefensible and unacceptable that Iran has chosen to continue with this second, wholly arbitrary court case against Mrs Zaghari-Ratcliffe. We have repeatedly called on Iran not to return her to prison.

This Government remains committed to doing all we can to secure Mrs Zaghari-Ratcliffe's return home. Iran has deliberately put her through a cruel and inhumane ordeal.

The Prime Minister met Mrs Zaghari-Ratcliffe's husband in January last year to reinforce the UK's support for bringing his wife home. The Foreign Secretary remains in close contact with both Mrs Zaghari-Ratcliffe and her family – meeting with the family last on 3rd March.

(But it is now nearly three months since that meeting.)

And it finishes **We continue to explore options to resolve this 40-year old case and will not comment further as discussions are ongoing.**

You might find it interesting to look back at the reply to my previous letter on page 116. It is not good enough for me. So I write again.

****

MAY 31ST

Well, I get a reply once more but this time it is an automated reply. This is because they have been inundated with requests from people wanting to go on foreign holidays and needing advice. Well, I can totally understand that we are all desperate for a holiday after the long, dark dreary lockdown winter we have just had, but this is a woman who just needs to get home.

****

THE HOMELESS

2021

MARCH 17TH

A report by the Public Accounts Committee praised the initiative **'Everyone In'** for "quickly and decisively" housing rough sleepers, at the beginning of the pandemic, and so saving lives amongst this vulnerable group. But the programme also revealed that the numbers of people sleeping on the streets – 37,430 – turned out to be around nine times higher than official estimates. MPs slammed the Ministry of Housing, Communities and Local Government for still not having a plan to deliver on the Tory election pledge to end rough sleeping by May 2024. It was also unclear whether the Government would hit its target of providing 3,300 homes for these people by the end of March 2020. Despite £161m funding, the majority are expected to be placed in leased buildings rather than new housing stock, while the accommodation is only expected to be temporary, with average stays of two years. Meg Hillier, Chair of the Public Accounts Committee, said, "Rough sleeping was a massive public health issue long before the pandemic, and much larger than Government has previously publicly acknowledged. MHCLG now has a huge opportunity to capitalise on this success in the pandemic response and begin to reverse its long record of failed and abandoned housing targets and policies. People without recourse to public funds are still left exposed and risk losing support. Support for these people is urgent."

****

MARCH 27TH

The Home Office has quietly revived a controversial programme that employs councils and charities to gather personal data that can lead to **deportation of rough sleepers**. It comes after the Home Office introduced rules that make rough sleeping grounds for revoking someone's right to stay in Britain. Claudia Webbe, Labour MP for Leicester East, reports that 70 specialist organisations working with homelessness have expressed concern that this draconian and **inhumane policy** will make the work of outreach teams trying to support people sleeping rough much harder, as people fear that engaging with services could put them at risk of being detained and deported. Yet the Home Secretary did not even consult with these representatives before introducing these changes. Indeed, this is the second time in recent years that the Tories have tried to deport people for the 'crime' of being homeless. The UK government designated rough sleeping as an abuse of EU free movement rights, and some European nationals were removed under a previous incarnation of these rules. The practice was **declared unlawful by the High Court in December 2017**, yet this government clearly has little respect for legal precedent. This is the latest example of the government's mistreatment and demonisation of foreign nationals. It has sadly been a tried and tested technique of reactionary governments to gild their destructive administrations with a toxic veneer of appearing 'strong' on immigration. Yet, this divide and rule tactic has only ever brought misery to all working people, regardless of their country of birth. It is especially callous for the government to introduce these changes during a global pandemic. Did you spot the word **inhumane** there? We are of course talking again about the department run by **Priti Patel**.

****

Also this month, it is very concerning that the support for the homeless in the 'Everyone In' scheme has already been **scaled back**. Is this a surprise? Indeed, despite the UK's worst spike of Covid-19 cases arriving in January 2021, the scheme had already been criticised by charities and local authorities as running out of funds. Figures from April to June 2020 found that that almost two-thirds of the 4,227 people recorded as sleeping rough in the English capital were doing so for the first time – a 77% rise over the amount of people introduced to the streets in the same period last year. And most worrying of all is the fact that there were **449 children** and young people living on the streets in this period, an 81% increase from the previous year. This indicates that the economic fallout from the pandemic had pushed vulnerable people onto the streets that the 'Everyone In' scheme had vacated. **But the Prime Minister has pledged that he wants to end rough sleeping by 2024.** Well, that is a really worthwhile aim. However, in order to achieve this, his government must invest much more than the £750 million earmarked for the next year. The government needs to urgently revise how it measures rough sleeping and it must finally end the criminalisation of rough sleepers – no matter their nationality. Would it surprise you to know that t**he Vagrancy Act**, which was **introduced after the Napoleonic Wars in 1824, continues to this day to punish vulnerable people who are begging or sleeping on the street?** No, I thought not.

****

MAY 9TH

All evictions have been banned until the end of May because of the pandemic. But a recent report by the **House of Commons Housing Communities and Local Government Committee** said today that the issue has been a looming cliff edge for the duration of the pandemic. The MPs said: "We are very concerned that the government is waiting until there is a clear crisis before intervening, rather than ...taking proactive action to protect people." Well yes, that sounds about right and what we have come to expect. Polly Neate, chief executive of Shelter, said, "If the government doesn't act, the system will collapse under the weight of a growing evictions crisis. **The government's ambition to end homelessness will be totally undermined if more people lose their homes."**

****

MAY 30TH

And so tomorrow we could see thousands more people being made homeless as this ban on rental evictions comes to an end in England. I hope the government has plans to help the homeless. As the shadow housing secretary, Lucy Powell, says, "The housing secretary (Robert Jenrick) promised that no-one would lose their home as a result of the crisis, and he must make good on that pledge." **Absolutely he must.**

****

HOUSING

2020

AUGUST

Housing Minister Robert Jenrick has been involved in a few housing scandals which doesn't give us a lot of confidence. The longest running controversy concerned a planning decision made by Jenrick, against the advice of planning officers, for a £2 billion 500 apartment housing scheme in London led by billionaire and former "adult entertainer" and newspaper owner Richard Desmond. The decision was ultimately declared illegal. But Desmond had already made a donation to the Tory party. Mr Jenrick was also facing questions over a second planning row, involving the Jockey Club. He has called in an application for it to build 318 homes and a hotel at Sandown Park in Esher, Surrey. The intervention has raised concerns about conflicts of interest because of the Jockey Club's links to senior Conservative figures and donors. Its board includes Tory peer Baroness Harding, who oversees the Government's coronavirus test and trace programme, Rose Paterson, wife of Tory MP Owen Paterson, and Peter Stanley, who last year donated £5,000 to Health Secretary Matt Hancock's constituency office in Newmarket, where the Jockey Club is based. Racehorse owner Tim Syder gave the Conservative Party £12,500 in November, shortly before he joined the Jockey Club board in December 2020.

****

Then there is another U-turn by the government after Jenrick had announced new planning laws which said that house building could take place pretty much anywhere on greenfield sites etc without proper planning permission. But many MPs, particularly southern MPs, realised that their constituents wouldn't like their beautiful countryside being turned into housing estates. Estate agents cautiously welcomed the U-turn in house building planning rules as the government decided to shift the building focus to urban areas rather than rural ones.

****

OCTOBER

And the Government makes yet another U-turn. Robert Jenrick announced that all new homes produced through a controversial planning policy known as Permitted Development Rights will have to "meet minimum space standards". You might reasonably think this ought to be a given, but for too long, it has not. Permitted Development Rights (PDR) allow changes to be made to an existing building – such as an empty office block – **without planning permission**. The flats resulting from such conversions did not have to meet minimum space standards of 37m² for a one-bedroom, one-person flat, or 61m² for a two-bedroom flat. According to a new report from the Town and Country Planning Association and the London School of Economics, more than 100,000 homes have been produced in England in this way. However, quantity does not equal quality and PDR has caused more problems than it has solved. "Slums of the future", "human warehouses" and "rabbit hutch homes" are just a few of the ways in which office-to-residential conversions created through the controversial planning policy have been described. PDR has allowed developers to avoid minimum standards for access to light which has meant some conversions, such as Astra House in Harlow, have tiny windows which do not open fully, leading to poor ventilation, while others, like Green Dragon House in Croydon, had boilers that did not work for months because they were never intended to service a residential property.

****

2021

JANUARY 22ND

And Robert Jenrick is allowing Britain's **first new deep coalmine** in decades. Alok Sharma, who quit as business secretary this month to concentrate on climate etc, is said to be furious that **he wasn't even consulted**. Whilst claiming to be a climate leader ahead of the COP26 climate talks in Glasgow this November, our government is planning to allow a new coal mine to be built in Whitehaven, Cumbria. This new mine would allow the extraction of 2.78 million tonnes of coking coal every year until 2050, the year by which the UK will supposedly have reached net-zero carbon emissions. Jenrick said it was a local decision and nothing to do with him.

****

Grenfell Fire. Last year (2020), Dame Judith Hackitt, chairwoman of *The Independent* Review of Building Regulations and Fire Safety said that immediate industry reforms were needed. "We need a culture change in this industry," she told a conference. "You need to care about the buildings that you are in a supply chain for. **You need to care that the people who live in them and work in them and sleep in them feel safe and are safe. Until you care, this system will not change and will not work.**" A year later, questions prompted by Grenfell are still being asked and we are still waiting for the answers.

And so on February 10th we hear that the 2017 Grenfell Tower blaze, which killed 72 people, laid bare years of building standards failings in tower blocks. But it is not covered by the Government's widely criticised £5bn Building Safety Fund (BSF) announced today which only offers aid to developments **over 18 metres** that have unsafe cladding.

Housing Minister Robert Jenrick announced a further £3.5bn to strip unsafe cladding off buildings earlier this month, but he was accused of 'betrayal' for failing to axe the 18m threshold, saying anyone in buildings under this height will have the option of a 'long-term low interest scheme' with £50 a month minimum payments. But leaseholders could now receive bills of up to £75,000 to repair the problems, and even be forced into temporary accommodation. External Wall System 1 check certificates are now needed for mortgage firms to sign off sales. Independent fire risk expert Stephen Mackenzie said the Government is risking 'Russian Roulette' with lives by excluding buildings under 18m and non-cladding issues from the Building Safety Fund. He said the Government needs to stop 'penny pinching' and adopt a fix now pay later approach to speed up the remediation process, warning: 'Grenfell two is out there'. He said defective cavity barriers pose a huge risk when on buildings made with flammable materials such as wood, timber, and combustible cladding and insulation. He said a national risk register should be set up urgently to decide what buildings should be prioritised, which should take into account internal defects and the vulnerability of occupants as well as height.

Mr Mackenzie also said: "The whole thing is a mess, we need to go back and audit all the buildings, determine what's on them and triage them into very high, high, medium, low and very low risk. Then we need to tailor the state aid relief package and determine what is needed to fix these buildings. I don't think we are going far enough with the measures."

Cladding fire checks have been branded a costly "shambles", with leaseholders left in limbo over safety and facing huge bills. Post-Grenfell inspections to reassure residents their homes are fireproof have delivered radically different results at the same blocks in London. A fire safety expert last night said the Government-backed inspections were not fit for purpose. One 750-home complex in Royal Docks, East London, had THREE separate checks with different results in just 10 months. It means people who bought flats after being told they were safe are now unable to sell up and face costly repair bills because their cladding failed the latest External Wall System (EWS1) check. On Wednesday night, an **amendment to the Fire Safety Bill** that would have protected leaseholders from paying for repairs was **not accepted**, meaning **MPs did not get the opportunity to vote on it.** More than 30 Conservative MPs had signed the modification, put forward by Tory Stephen McPartland, who warned the current terms of the bill could allow freeholders to simply pass on the costs of any remedial work the fire service order them to do. **The rejection has come as another blow to the estimated 11 million leaseholders caught up in the scandal.**

Some residents of blocks below 18m are understood to have already received requests for upfront payment for full remediation, with freeholders instructing solicitors to carry out debt recovery. This could result in a **tide of bankruptcies and evictions** if replicated more widely before a government support scheme is operational. The cost of repaying these loans will then be passed on to leaseholders via their service charges, in a mechanism dubbed a 'cladding tax' by campaigners. The government has promised that repayments will not exceed £50 per month. But the details are understood to remain in development, with questions such as the impact of financial regulation rules and ultimate responsibility for the loan still unresolved. The government had originally said that further details would be released at the Budget in March, **but nothing was announced**.

Are we surprised? **Apparently, the government guidance sets no restriction on the use of combustible materials below the 18 metre threshold, meaning many have been built with dangerous systems.** Well I certainly did not know that.

****

FEBRUARY
Giles Grover, of the End Our Cladding Scandal campaign, said: "It is nearly four years after Grenfell and Ministers have utterly failed to address the serious failings the tragedy exposed. Our lives are

still being ruined, with no end to our suffering in sight. **Robert Jenrick's** attempt at what he believes is a fair and proper solution — forced loans on leaseholders — is deeply inadequate and will fail to address fairly the wide range of safety issues we face. **The first duty of the Government is to protect and safeguard the lives of its citizens; today it has failed in that duty and, in doing so, has failed leaseholders. Tonight, millions of people will go to sleep feeling trapped and abandoned. We won't forget this — and we will certainly not stop fighting in our campaign for fairness.'**

****

MARCH 12TH

U-turn?

The proposed **coal mine in Cumbria,** which had initially been viewed by Robert Jenrick as a local issue, is now being put on hold by Jenrick and being taken away from the local authority for putting to public inquiry. Greenpeace has hailed it as "fantastic news and definitely better late than never". Friends of the Earth added it was a "startling, but very welcome, U-turn" and urged the government to refuse permission for the project. It could have something to do with the fact that the UK is hosting Cop26, the UN climate summit, in November. A few weeks ago, one of the country's most eminent environmental scientists, Sir Robert Watson, said it was "absolutely ridiculous" the government was refusing to act.

****

MARCH 14TH

"Unlevelling down"!

This is what people are calling the £4.8 billion levelling up fund which has been given to places like Richmond and Newark. These just happen to be wealthy constituencies of Rishi Sunak and Robert Jenrick. But interestingly, the funds have not been given to Barnsley or Salford which are amongst the most socially deprived areas of the country but which unfortunately did not choose a Tory MP.

And now I hear that there are legal challenges for this government to answer about these claims that it funnelled cash to Tory areas with its "**levelling up" fund.** Now legal campaigners from the The Good Law Project will take the government to court, contending that the design of the £4.8bn 'Levelling Up' Fund is unlawful. They cite an investigation by the National Audit Office, which found that the government's list of targets for the cash had been published without supporting information to explain why they had been chosen. The House of Commons' cross-party Public Accounts Committee had also said **the lack of transparency** had led to concerns **of "political bias" in the allocation of funds. Forty out of the first 45 schemes to be approved in March had at least one Conservative MP.** The campaigners cite Chris Hanretty, Professor of Politics at Royal Holloway, University of London, who looked at the funding formula and evidence presented by the National Audit Office and government. **"On the basis of the data collated by the ministry and published by the NAO, there is robust evidence that ministers chose towns so as to benefit the Conservatives in marginal Westminster seats,"** he wrote.

****

APRIL 23RD

There are more and more large executive housing developments being built on greenfield sites. Ben Webster, Environment editor of *The Times,* reports yesterday that parts of England protected for their beauty are being blighted by a doubling in the amount of greenfield land opened up to sprawling "executive home" developments. Permission has been granted for development on an average of 294 acres of greenfield land per year within England's 34 Areas of Outstanding Natural Beauty (AONBs) since 2017, up from an average of 128 acres a year in the previous five years, according to research commissioned by CPRE, the countryside charity.

The High Weald AONB, which covers parts of Sussex, Kent and Surrey, is facing the largest amount of development, with 932 houses approved since 2017. Another 771 homes have been approved in the Dorset area, 592 in the Chilterns and 684 in the Cotswolds. The research found that twice as much land as the national average was used per new home in developments in AONBs, with builders focusing on large "executive" properties. Only 16 per cent of the homes met the government's definition of affordable, which includes those sold or rented at lower than market value. The government's planning guidelines state that "great weight should be given to conserving landscape and scenic beauty" in AONBs. *Well obviously I should hope so but it doesn't seem to be happening.*

Apparently guidelines state that large developments can be permitted in these areas in "exceptional circumstances" and where it would be in the public interest. These terms are not clearly defined, **creating loopholes for developers to use**. Crispin Truman, the chief executive of the charity, said: "The fact that some of our most highly prized areas of countryside are being lost to build more executive homes says a great deal about **our planning system**. Continuing with this 'build and be damned' approach just serves to line the pockets of greedy developers whilst undermining climate action, stalling nature's recovery and gobbling up our most precious green space that's vital for our health and wellbeing, all the while doing next to nothing to tackle the affordable housing crisis. Rural communities are crying out for well-designed, quality and genuinely affordable homes in the right places. We know this kind of development is possible."

Well indeed we all know that. So exactly what is being done about it? Robert Jenrick, does this have anything to do with you?

****

MAY 16TH
Survivors and bereaved relatives from the Grenfell Tower disaster have told the government '**enough is enough**' after a fire broke out at a block of flats with the same type of cladding. More than 40 people

needed treatment after the blaze ripped through the 19-storey New Providence Wharf development, near Canary Wharf in East London, on Friday 14th. Around a fifth of the building's facade features aluminium composite material polyethylene cladding panels, which were found to be a key factor in the fire which killed 72 at Grenfell in 2017. Survivors and relatives said they were 'horrified' by news of the latest blaze, adding in a statement issued by the Grenfell United group: "When will the Government take this scandal seriously? Enough is enough. The Government promised to remove dangerous cladding by June 2020 – it has completely failed its own target and every day that goes by lives are at risk."

Dither and delay again and again, with very dangerous consequences.

****

And so as we approach **June 2021** there is more and more controversy over the government's planning targets. A new analysis today **(May 25th)** says that over the next five years nearly 400,000 new homes will be built on greenfield sites in the south of England. That doesn't sound a very popular idea to me. Of course we need more houses, but they need to be affordable houses in areas where there are already facilities for an increase in the population.

****

JUNE 6TH

It is reported in *The Sunday Times* today that residents caught up in the safety scandal of Grenfell Tower are sharing posters and videos on Chinese social media platforms about bills they are facing of up to £100,000 to remove flammable materials. "**Do not buy in Britain**" they are saying.

****

JUNE 7TH

And yet we hear today that there is a proposal by Gladman Developments to build **143 new homes on the edge of the New Forest** just north of Ringwood. Chris Packham has criticised the plans as "selfish and shortsighted" because it is near a nature reserve and the ecosystem there has been designated a site of special scientific interest due to the vast range of wildlife it supports. Blashford Lakes is a 159-hectare nature reserve surrounded by lake, pond, river, woodland and grassland habitats. Up to 5,000 birds can be seen there during the winter, and lapwings and oyster catchers are often seen feeding on the lakes. Gladman says that 50% of the homes will be affordable and it will help tackle the area's housing shortage. Planning officers at New Forest district council have recommended that the application be approved.

Well no one is denying that we need more affordable homes, but there are questions to be asked here I think. First, why is an area of such scientific interest being targeted and why only 50% of affordable housing? We do actually need 90,000 social houses **built every year**, a target that has never been met by successive governments, but for goodness sake we need to build them in appropriate places near schools, surgeries, shops and public transport.

****

JUNE 13TH

And in *The Sunday Times* today, there is a report of a millionaire with investments in property and motorcycles who has given £150,000 to the Conservative party 48 hours after a government minister approved a controversial housing scheme for him. Where do these people get all this money from, I would like to know?! To me this is eye-watering stuff. His name is John Bloor and apparently he is one of the largest donors to the Conservative Party, having given more than £3million, including almost £1million in the run up to the 2019 general election.

Chris Pincher, a housing minister, gave the green light to a Bloor proposal to build hundreds of homes on **rural land in Herefordshire** and just three weeks after officials took control of a scheme in Berkshire.

Asked repeatedly whether he or his representatives had lobbied Robert Jenrick or anyone else, government officials said it would be **"too costly" to find out under the Freedom of Information laws.** Oh yes, we've heard that one before. So corruption and deceit continues at pace in the Housing department. There **is** a plan to build more affordable housing (I think) but this sort of planning is unacceptable.

****

And of course everyone who makes their way to our shores needs safe accommodation. As I keep trying to say, **we need cool heads, wise informed decisions and complete transparency.**

****

ASYLUM SEEKERS

2021

So how are we treating asylum seekers who land on our shores looking for help and refuge? Well, some of the following was reported before the present government took office, but the present Home Office does not appear to be showing much compassion.

JANUARY
Traumatised asylum seekers are being housed in rat-infested accommodation, with no access to medical aid, MPs have said. In a scathing report, the Home Affairs Select Committee said the housing for those seeking sanctuary in the UK was a "disgrace". The MPs said families were living in "shameful" conditions, including houses infested with mice, rats and bedbugs.

The Home Office contracted out the task of providing accommodation for asylum seekers in 2012 to Serco, G4S and Clearsprings Ready Homes.

The report added: "It is clear that in too many cases Providers are placing people in accommodation that is substandard, poorly maintained and, at times, unsafe. Some of this accommodation is a disgrace and it is shameful that some very vulnerable people have been placed in such conditions. Urgent action must be taken by the Home Office and Providers to deal with this issue. Even when significant concerns have been raised, a lack of alternative accommodation has led to vulnerable people remaining in housing that is unfit or unsuitable for many months until they are moved."

Yvette Cooper MP, the chair of the committee, said: "The state of accommodation for some asylum seekers and refugees in this country is a disgrace. And the current contract system just isn't working. Major reforms are needed. We have come across too many examples of vulnerable people in unsafe accommodation, for example children living with infestations of mice, rats or bedbugs, lack of health care for pregnant women, or inadequate support for victims of rape and torture. No one should be living in conditions like that."

Refugee Council Chief Executive Maurice Wren adds: "This report sends a crystal clear message to the Government: it must stop cramming desperate people into unfit, unsafe, rat infested housing. The committee paints a grim picture of poor conditions across the board, but it's particularly shocking that mums-to-be are being prevented from obtaining the urgent medical care and the nutritious food they need during pregnancy. There's simply no excuse for putting the lives of women and their babies at risk."

As usual this is the standard reply from a **Home Office spokeswoman** who said: "The UK has a proud history of granting asylum to those who need our protection and we are committed to providing safe and secure accommodation while applications are considered. We work closely with our contractors to ensure they provide accommodation that is safe, habitable, fit for purpose and adequately equipped and we conduct regular inspections to check that this is the case. We have also made significant improvements to the operation of the contracts including increasing the number of dispersal areas by more than a third. We will consider the Committee's recommendations and respond in due course."

We will wait for that response.

****

JANUARY 31ST

Asylum seekers lodging in Napier Barracks in Folkestone are told that their claims would be at risk if they complain about their lodgings. There is a distinct lack of information on their asylum claims. Napier Barracks is unhygienic with broken toilets and sinks, with a lack of any possibility for social distancing. It is now under lockdown because of an outbreak of Covid. Some of the 400 people there have been moved out, but those who remain are frightened of getting Covid as there is no room to socially distance, no washing facilities and the toilets are broken. They have been told that if they try to leave they will be arrested. Some of the men have slept outside in freezing conditions they were so scared of getting Covid.

Two days ago, on the **29th January,** a fire broke out at Napier Barracks and windows were smashed. This all comes after a petition was signed by more than 18,000 people to shut down the barracks because of concerns about the conditions inside. Fire engines turned up and all were evacuated and eventually they were allowed back in. But since then, heating and electricity in all but one of the blocks has been off, leaving the men, many of whom have Covid-19, in freezing conditions. Some of them spoke to *The Guardian* and said that drinking water supplies had not been replenished, forcing them to drink non-potable water from the bathroom block taps. Charities have attempted to provide warm blankets and food to the men in the last 48 hours, but have been turned away by police officers who are on the site, which is being treated as a crime scene.

Priti Patel described the destruction as "deeply offensive to the taxpayers of this country". She said this "type of action" would "not be tolerated" and that the Home Office would support the police to "take robust action against those vandalising property, threatening staff and putting lives at risk". **Shadow immigration minister Holly Lynch** said the claims were "reprehensible" and an "affront to the values of the British people" to lock people into accommodation with no way to self-isolate, and called for residents to be moved into Covid-secure housing "as a matter of urgency".

****

Exclusive from *The Independent* on 31st January. "It has now emerged that the Home Office, in its equality impact assessment of the plans to use MoD sites to house asylum seekers, justified the move by stating that housing these individuals in more 'generous' accommodation would '**undermine public confidence in the asylum system'.** Critics say the document shows ministers 'pandering to prejudice' and jeopardising health for 'political ends'." **Naomi Phillips**, director of policy and advocacy at British Red Cross, said the sites were "completely inappropriate and inhumane" as housing for refugees and called for them to be closed "urgently".

So, ignoring all of that, Mr Philip from the Home Office states that "these sites have accommodated soldiers and army personnel in the past – it is wrong to say that it is not good enough for asylum claimants".

In fact, they have not been used by the military for more than seven years and never of course during a pandemic.

****

FEBRUARY 21ST
The Ministry of Defence has reiterated the fact that **Napier Barracks** has not been used by the Ministry for well over seven years as it was not fit for purpose. Many asylum seekers have contracted Covid-19 due to the unsanitary conditions there and have been moved to hotels. These hotels are run by **Stay Belvedere Hotels LTD,** which is sub-contracted by Clearspring Ready Homes which stands to earn up to **£1bn** for its Home Office contracts despite the controversy over Napier Barracks. Inside these hotels some asylum seekers have complained of unwelcome sexual behaviour and there are claims that women were being abused. Staff have master keys and enter women's rooms and call them unpleasant names and they feel unsafe and scared. They have all also been told that they are not allowed to leave the hotels for any reason and that the police will be called if

they do. Questions also remain about how privately contracted staff are treated. Many of them are being paid little over £5.50 an hour according to a joint survey by *The Observer* and *ITV News*. Many of them are foreign nationals who say they accept the low wages because they are breaking the terms of their visas by working for more than 20 hours a week. The Home Office is looking into these allegations and states that asylum seekers are free to come and go in line with Covid restrictions and that they have access to a 24/7 migrant helpline.

****

FEBRUARY 22ND

And another interesting article in *The Observer* yesterday. Once more it is about **locking up more and more women.**

More immigration units for women refugees are being planned by the Home Office in spite of Priti Patel previously saying that women seeking asylum should be spared detention. **Is this another U-turn?** Apparently some pilot schemes offering alternatives to detention are being scrapped. There is now a new detention centre being built in Durham which will hold up to 85 women and there is no guarantee that children will not be housed there. So many of these women have suffered sexual abuse and physical trauma that to continue to lock them up is inhumane and detrimental to their mental health.

An immigration minister, Chris Philip, has confirmed plans were being finalised for a detention centre in County Durham. He said, "The public rightly expects us to maintain a robust immigration system and detention plays a crucial part in this. We are committed to making sure people with no entitlement to be in the UK are removed."

When I was a speaker for the charity **Save The Children** we were always proud to be able to say that the UK had one of the finest records and a long history of offering refuge to those who need it. For those of you who have read my book called "My Voice" you will find, on page 31, my 15-minute talk on what it is like to be a refugee child. I will just give here three quotes by children from page 35.

"We are not here because we are seeking a better life. We are here because we are seeking a safer environment."

"We don't want to be refugees. We want to be building up our own countries and making them good places in which to live."

"We are not refugees by choice. We are refugees by situation and circumstance."

It is of course up to you to decide which is the more humane approach.

****

MARCH 20TH

Remember the idea Priti Patel had about sending asylum seekers to Gibraltar or the Isle of Man? Well, they are furious because it has never even been discussed with them. This is the first they have heard about it! **"Is this a joke?" asks the Isle of Man.**

****

MARCH 24TH

Priti Patel has unveiled new plans in the House of Commons today to tackle the number of **asylum seekers** coming to the UK. She said her plans will tackle criminals who smuggle people into the UK illegally, as well as crack down on those who make asylum claims to which they are not entitled. She says that people coming in having paid gangs to smuggle them here would be sent back to 'third countries' and only people entering the country through legal channels will be allowed to stay. People smuggled in by small boats will no longer have the same entitlements as those who arrive legally under the Home Office plans. Charities, including the British Red Cross, have criticised the changes for **judging claimants on how they arrived and not just on merit.** British Red Cross chief executive Mike Adamson said, "The proposals effectively create an unfair two-tiered system, whereby someone's case and the support they receive is judged on how they entered the country and not on their need for protection. **This is inhumane**."

An open letter signed by 454 immigration scholars in the UK has stated that **"One cannot travel illegally if one is seeking asylum"**. They say that the plan circumvents international law and is based purely on assertions.

****

Asylum seekers are now being moved out of hotels in a **Home Office dispersal scheme** whereby different areas of the country take in and plan to house, hopefully permanently, a certain appropriate number. However, I suppose it will come as no surprise to hear that this scheme is not working and appears to be **absolutely shambolic**. Leyla Williams, deputy director of community centre West London Welcome, which supports migrants in London, said that every week she was seeing asylum seekers, including many pregnant women and children, "shunted from one place to another" with as little as two hours' notice and "no idea where they're being moved to. Identified potential victims of trafficking and modern slavery are expected to get into cars in which the driver refuses to tell them where they are being taken. Children are removed from their communities and schools without warning, and their teachers and friends are left wondering what has happened to them. People **aren't tested for Covid** before they are moved to shared housing, and pandemic travel restrictions appear not to have applied to the Home Office. On arrival, people find housing in shocking states of disrepair". Many of these areas are already over-crowded and are often very right wing communities who can pose a real threat to asylum seekers. Local councillors say their regions, in which many wards already exceed the dispersal ratio of one asylum seeker per 200 local residents, are being "oversaturated" with new people being moved in under Operation Oak, and that this is placing an "untenable" strain on local services. Some now often have a ratio closer to one asylum seeker to 80 local residents.

A Home Office spokesperson said the department was undertaking work to ensure that the distribution of asylum seekers was "spread evenly" across the UK.

****

But seven council leaders in the West Midlands wrote a letter to the Home Secretary, informing her they had decided to **suspend participation in the asylum dispersal scheme** because the Home Office contractor Serco was seeking to place more asylum seekers in areas that already exceed the one-to-200 ratio. The letter, seen by *The Independent* states: "Whilst we understand and fully support moving asylum seekers out of hotels, we were alarmed to see that 65 per cent of the wider Midlands allocation under Operation Oak are intended to be placed in our authorities by April of this year." They say that the current position is untenable and they cannot continue to be part of the dispersal scheme unless the situation is addressed. Many of the houses that asylum seekers are expected to live in are squalid beyond belief and have severe damp problems. They are left without money and forced to wait weeks to start receiving their weekly government allowance.

The home secretary, Priti Patel (yes I have to mention her again), said the department was "working closely" with councils in dispersal areas – of which there are about 180 – and "taking account" of their views.

But councillors in Yorkshire and the West Midlands have told *The Independent* that the Home Office contractors responsible for finding and managing asylum accommodation in their areas are failing to engage with them and "ignoring" concerns they raise about the viability of certain areas. I do not see this reported anywhere except in *The Independent*.

****

And another article in *The Independent* says that asylum seekers are being left without adequate shoes, clothing or suitable food in Home

Office hotel accommodation, in what has been condemned as **"dehumanising" treatment.**

A report by the Refugee Council reveals that people seeking refuge have been confined to their rooms for days because they have inappropriate footwear – for example only a pair of flip-flops – or are having to wait for their one set of clothes to be cleaned.

In other cases, people who are physically unwell have had no option but to eat food that is harmful to their health, and have been unable to access even basic healthcare, with some prevented from getting the Covid vaccine despite being eligible.

Thousands of asylum-seeking men, women and children have been placed in emergency hotel accommodation over the past year, often for months on end, as the pandemic has led to mounting delays in the asylum system. More than 8,000 people are currently said to be living in hotels. The Home Office started an operation in February to "accelerate" the movement of asylum seekers from hotels into longer-term accommodation, but this is proving to be a slow process as the contracted housing providers are struggling to procure housing.

The new findings, based on the Refugee Council's work with more than 400 asylum seekers across Leeds, London, Hull and Rotherham, expose "extremely concerning" gaps in support at the hotels. The charity has had to step in to provide basics such as shoes and coats and to make sure people receive the food they need. In some cases, they have also had to arrange for vulnerable people to be transferred out of hotels.

Shadow immigration minister Holly Lynch accused the Home Office of operating with a **"lack of compassion and competence" which has resulted in emergency asylum accommodation becoming the norm.**

The report describes the quality of food in hotels as a "major cause of concern", stating that "repeated poor-quality meals" are contributing to the declining physical health of people placed there.

****

MARCH 16TH

The Home Office has just announced that it will not reduce the number of **asylum seekers in Napier Barracks** as, in spite of an outbreak of coronavirus there, they are planning to move yet more people back in. Bridget Chapman, of the Kent Refugee Action Network, said it was "horrific" that vulnerable asylum seekers would be again "packed into entirely inappropriate communal living situations against the advice of PHE". She added: "The use of the phrase 'socially distanced' here is derisory. You cannot socially distance when you are being housed in a room with 27 other people and you're all sharing the same air." These barracks were described as unhygienic and completely unsuitable for human habitation months ago as I have previously reported.

****

APRIL 15TH

And talking about **breaking the law** and talking about **Priti Patel,** we read in *The Times* this morning that a judicial review has found that she **broke the law** after the **death of a detainee** in an immigration detention centre. A Nigerian man died in a centre at Harmondsworth, west London and one of his friends, a man called Ahmed Lawal, was scheduled to give evidence at the inquest. However, Patel proceeded with efforts to deport him by a charter flight before the inquest could take place and before any evidence could be obtained. According to the lawyers who brought the judicial review on behalf of Lawal, this is again **without precedent. Never before has a Home Secretary been found to have breached a detainee's human rights by refusing to allow them to give evidence at an inquest**. The Home Office said that the government would not appeal against the findings.

****

And it doesn't stop there because I have just found out that lawyers acting on behalf of former Napier Barracks residents say that previously unseen documents show that the Home Office placed hundreds **of asylum seekers** in military barracks where they were at "significant risk" of a fire breaking out. A report by the **fire safety inspectorate into Napier Barracks** in Kent found that the measures in place to reduce the risk of fire at the site did not ensure residents were "appropriately protected from serious risk". As I reported earlier there *was* actually a fire at Napier Barracks and it was a miracle that no-one was injured. The damning report was sent to Home Office contractors **on 30th November, 2020** along with a letter from the fire safety inspectorate ordering them to rectify the issues highlighted **within 28 days**. Lawyers acting on behalf of former Napier Barracks residents say, however, that the Home Office failed to comply and did not take action to rectify the fire safety issues until **March 2021**, when Home Office contractor Clearsprings carried out a fire risk assessment. The fire inspectorate's warnings were revealed during a court hearing surrounding the legality of the Home Office's use of Napier Barracks as accommodation for asylum seekers, with lawyers acting on behalf of **six former residents** arguing that the conditions amount to **being unlawful**. During the two-day hearing at the High Court this week, the judge is to consider whether the Home Office's decision to house asylum seekers in the military site b**reaches human rights law**. However, the Home Office has decided to continue using the site. Around 70 asylum seekers were moved there last Friday and more are due to be transferred in due course, according to the department.

****

Mental health doctors warn that the Home Office is putting vulnerable **asylum seekers** at heightened risk of suicide by placing them in immigration detention centres. The Royal College of Psychiatrists (RCP) is calling on the government to allow potential detainees with a mental illness to remain in the community so they can access the treatment they need from the NHS, or **risk a "significant deterioration" in their mental health.** It warns that the "perilous" conditions of removal centres are putting a vulnerable group of people – including torture and trafficking survivors – at a "much-increased risk" of worsening mental health and suicide.

Currently, the Home Office operates a policy called **Adults at Risk** whereby mentally unwell detainees found to meet a certain threshold for vulnerability will be released from detention – but the RCP says this assessment is not sufficient. "People with significant mental illness may have particular difficulty in being effective self-advocates. Their very vulnerability may prevent them from providing adequate evidence for that vulnerability," the report states.

It comes as **Priti Patel** plans to make it more difficult for trafficking survivors to be released from detention as part of her new immigration plans – a move she says will prevent serious criminals from taking advantage of modern slavery safeguards. However, the department's plans – **set to come into force from 25th May** – will mean that to be considered for release, suspected victims will be required to go through the Adults at Risk process and provide medical evidence that their ongoing detention would place them at "future harm".

Professor Cornelius Katona, lead author of the Royal College of Psychiatrists' report, said: "The perilous conditions of immigration detention centres are putting a vulnerable group of people at a much-increased risk of worsening mental health and suicide." He added: "Many have been subjected to horrifying events which are only compounded by immigration detention centres. **The government must end the practice of detaining mentally ill asylum seekers.**"

****

MAY 13TH
People Power! This is a fantastic story and it happened in Glasgow. On the first day of Eid when Muslims were wishing others peace and happiness, a border enforcement van drove into a large Muslim community in the suburbs of Glasgow to arrest two Indian men with a view to their being **taken to a detention centre and then deported**. Word got round and within a very short space of time more than 200 neighbours had surrounded the van, one person got underneath it and eventually the deportation order was stopped and the two men

were released! Scottish police turned up to protect everyone but said they were not involved with the deportation order. The two men were overwhelmed with the support of the local people. Nicola Sturgeon accused the Home Office of creating a dangerous and unacceptable situation and Glasgow central MP Alison Thewliss said it is "absolutely awful" but heartened to see local residents in Pollockshield "standing up for their neighbours and refusing to accept the brutality of the Home Office". The photographs of the crowd were amazing and some estimates were of well over 300.

There was initially no response from the Home Office in London and apparently the office of the responsible Secretary of State Kevin Foster cancelled all agreed interviews for the day. I wonder why?

****

MAY 14TH

A Labour union boss said that "**Priti Patel should be deported, not refugees**". He has just been suspended for this remark by the Labour Party and is apologising right, left and centre. Well true, we really don't want to deport anyone if we can help it, but I have said it before and will say it again, she is the worst possible person for the job of Home Secretary in my opinion and should be shuffled off as soon as possible.

****

MAY 16TH

A migrant charity has threatened **legal action against the Home Office** after this attempt to deport these two men in Glasgow. Mr Singh and Mr Sehdev, both aged in their 30s and reportedly a mechanic and chef respectively, have lived in the UK for several years and are 'part of a community', said refugee and migrant charity Positive Action in Housing. The charity's director Robina Qureshi said: "The Home Office have referred to these men as illegal. Well they are wrong, and we are now investigating legal action against the Home Office for casting such aspersions. The term illegal in this context is part of the hostile environment. It's not appropriate to use it for people who have lived in the UK for several years and are part of a community. The men now have legal representation and are in the process of trying to regularise their status. The fact that they had no active legal representation before means they were left vulnerable." Jelina Berlow Rahman, a lawyer instructed to represent Mr Singh, said he has been in the country since 2008 and "has a right to a private life, a family life". She added: "It was evident from the number of people who came together, that this was his community, that these were his neighbours, and that many were his friends – the majority of people knew him."

****

Fresh testimony from immigration detainees, shows that The Home Office has pursued a policy of psychological brutality by locking up scores of torture survivors in solitary confinement for indefinite periods. Interviews dictated from prison reveal some torture and trafficking victims have had to spend more than **23 hours a day in solitary confinement for periods of up to a year**. Their accounts portray mental health breakdown, self-harm and suicide attempts after the Home Office opted to place detainees inside the prison network as part of its Covid measures. The charity Bail for Immigration Detainees has written to senior immigration officials warning the prolonged solitary confinement of an estimated 500 detainees appeared to breach the UN's minimum standards for the treatment of prisoners.

One detainee, a European national arrested for an offence but **never charged**, describes being held in solitary confinement for three months from January for more than 23 hours a day. A torture survivor, he self-harmed and tried to hang himself. Many testimonies like this one raise questions over the government's continued hostile environment approach and also follow a change in rules that means that from the end of May more victims of trafficking are likely to be detained and forcibly removed from the UK.

****

MAY 20TH

On May 13th I wrote about the **two immigrants in Glasgow** who were prevented by more than 300 neighbours from being forcibly removed with a view to deportation. One man was a mechanic and the other a chef and had been in the UK for 10 years. Apparently, they have over-stayed their visa for several years. So, the Home Office is not letting it rest and are **pressing ahead with efforts to deport them**. The group of Sikhs in Scotland have accused the Home Office of pursuing a heavy handed and targeted approach to deporting members of its community. The Home Office says that "they will still be detained and deported at a later date". However, the director of Positive Action in Housing, a migrant charity, says "it is wrong to call them illegal – the Home Office is casting aspersions on the Indian community. They have been working peacefully for years in the community and it's just a matter of not having the right paperwork. They are not criminals and they are not costing anybody anything".

****

MAY 22ND

Priti Patel has been **photographed at the scene of an arrest** by the police of some alleged people smugglers. Staffordshire Police Chief Constable Gareth Morgan told *The Times* that he was concerned that Home Secretary Priti Patel had interfered in operational matters which could create the impression that "**policing is seen as the extension of government**". He calls for her to "stand back from policing agenda and allow officers to assert their independence". "She should let us get on with the job," he says.

****

MAY 24TH

And now we are beginning to hear about the new, radical and apparently brilliant border plan to stop illegal immigrants from ever landing in our country again. And of course this overhaul of our borders is the work of our **Home Secretary**. It will "slam the door on dangerous criminals" and "will meet the demands of the British people" she says. She will say in a speech today that she will pledge to create **"the world's most effective border system"** by implementing a **"fully digital border" by 2025.**

Well, I am sure that that is good, of course. We await 2025 with interest.

****

MAY 29TH

Today I hear that a **10 year old Italian girl,** Sara Bajraktari, has been told by the Home Office that she is not eligible for post-Brexit immigration status under the EU settlement scheme, despite the fact that her parents have been living in the UK since last year and have status. She and her brother, Erik, 16, moved to the UK to join their parents earlier this month after staying with relatives in Italy to finish their school year – but while Erik was granted settlement, Sara was refused. Sara's father, Mark Bajraktari, told *The Independent* he was left "speechless" after discovering that his daughter had been refused and expressed concern about his family's future in the UK. He and his wife, Leonora, moved to Britain in December – a move that had been postponed due to the pandemic. They both applied under the settlement scheme and were granted pre-settled status. In order to meet the threshold for pre-settled status, the two children had visited the UK for five days in December. However, whilst her brother who is 16 had a bank card which showed that he had bought items in Britain, Sara had only a flight boarding pass as evidence – which the Home Office did not accept as evidence that she was in the country. "What you have provided is not sufficient," the refusal letter states, "because online boarding passes provide no evidence of residency." And so they refuse her residency. Can you believe it?

Christopher Desira, director of law firm Sepharus, is assisting the family and said the Home Office was informally reviewing the decision. He said the case indicated "either poor decision-making or a poorly understood application", adding: "The child should have been granted pre-settled status based on the evidence submitted (airline ticket) to demonstrate the child was resident in the UK before 31

December 2020." He thinks it will get overturned once it has been looked at properly, but of course it is an extremely stressful and worrying situation, especially for a 10 year old child.

Does Priti Patel know about this case? I honestly do not see that it is a difficult decision to make.

****

JUNE 3RD

Six asylum seekers formerly housed in Napier Barracks have **won a legal challenge against the Government** after a High Court judge found their accommodation failed to meet a "minimum standard". The judge's judgement does not force the barracks to close, unfortunately, and the Home Office is now considering its next steps.

Well, we have a reply. A Home Office spokesman said:

"During the height of the pandemic, to ensure asylum seekers were not left destitute, additional accommodation was required at extremely short notice.

"Such accommodation provided asylum seekers a safe and secure place to stay. Throughout this period our accommodation providers and sub-contractors have made improvements to the site and continue to do so.

"It is disappointing that this judgment was reached on the basis of the site prior to the significant improvement works which have taken place in difficult circumstances. Napier will continue to operate and provide safe and secure accommodation."

Indeed, we hear that many more asylum seekers are still being moved into Napier Barracks.

****

Now you may think that the replies we get from the Home Office are reasonable and no-one is saying that the housing of asylum seekers is an easy task for anyone. But I believe that we need to treat people with dignity and compassion.

****

JUNE 6TH

Today it is reported in *The Sunday Times* that Kent, a conservative-led council, is considering bringing a judicial review against Priti Patel (what, another one?). So many unaccompanied child refugees are arriving at Folkstone now that they are at "breaking point". They are asking the government to make it mandatory for the children to be moved to other counties throughout the country. Apparently, the Home Office began a consultancy exercise nine months ago for doing this, but nothing was implemented. The children arriving also seem to be getting younger. Some 12 year olds and 13 year olds have arrived without family in recent months. There are also an unprecedented number of young girls on their own, prompting fears that they could be forced into prostitution by criminal gangs.

****

JUNE 9TH

Indeed, a leader in *The Times* today agrees with me about the difficulties of the safe housing of asylum seekers. There are no easy answers to the challenge of illegal migration, they say. But it is interesting to note that as Britain is no longer a signatory to the Dublin convention, having left the EU, we cannot require asylum seekers to make their claim in the first EU country they entered. They are able to seek refuge anywhere in the world.

****

JUNE 10TH

And to be fair to Priti Patel she has said today that she is introducing a new scheme similar to a rota that will allow migrant children to be moved to other counties to ease the pressure on Kent.

****

JUNE 10TH

But the good news does not last long, because also today, disturbing news is revealed in letters published by PHE yesterday. Apparently Priti Patel was advised by PHE back in September last year not to house asylum seekers in dormitories because of Covid. But at a hearing of the Home Affairs Select Committee in February this year, Priti Patel told MPs that the **Home Office had followed PHE advice throughout.** And of course it has been well documented here and elsewhere that the conditions in Napier Barracks were dreadfully overcrowded and indeed there was an outbreak of Covid with more than 200 men being affected. During a debate after an urgent question in the Commons yesterday, opposition MPs called for her resignation. Well yes, actually she misled parliament. But in my language I believe it to be a lie.

****

I think that the treatment by this government, and by the present Home Secretary, of many of those seeking asylum, is inhumane, neglectful and cruel. I feel ashamed to live in a country which treats any vulnerable people in this way.

****

And so now we go on to see how we treat vulnerable people who do not live in our country and yet who depend on us for so much.

****

CUTS IN FOREIGN AID

2021

MARCH 1ST

There is concern that this government is going to **slash the legally mandated budget of 0.7%** of national income on **foreign aid projects,** but there is particular concern today about a decision to **slash the aid to Yemen by 50%** and how that would be very serious indeed. It would continue the "slow, agonising and obscene process of starving to death" for millions of people, the former International Development Secretary Andrew Mitchell said this morning on the Today programme. A Yemeni aid worker said, "It is hard to describe how heart breaking the situation is in Yemen right now. We have already had aid cuts since the beginning of 2020 which have helped put 16 million people into hunger. Children are dying here every day. It is not a moral decision to abandon Yemen."

****

MARCH 2ND

And in the paper today confirmation that this aid has been **cut from 0.7% of GDP to 0.5%.** This move has outraged Save The Children as they say it puts millions of people at risk of starvation. Tobias Ellwood, chairman of the Commons Defence Select Committee, said that Britain had failed the first test of what post-Brexit Global Britain means in practice. Last night on the news there were films of young children in Yemen trying to keep their school open. They were running through the rubble to school where a **young boy of nine** was trying to teach them. He had been **blind from birth.** As he was being interviewed there were noises in the distance. "Oh that is gunfire," he said nonchalantly. This is just one story of course. But we really should not be allowing this government to cut this aid. I write again to my MP. I will say later if I get a reply!

****

MARCH 6TH

In the headlines today is the leaking of a Foreign Office document which says that Britain's humanitarian support to global conflict zones is to be **cut by two thirds.**

****

MARCH 7TH

And do you remember David Miliband? He now lives in New York and is the CEO of the International Rescue Committee, the global refugee charity. He should have become leader of the Labour Party after Gordon Brown, but was squeezed out by the affiliate votes of Len McCluskey's Unite union intent on revenge against the Blairites, and so his brother Ed Miliband became leader instead. Labour then lost at the next election. I think it is probably safe to say that if **David Miliband** had become leader of the Labour Party, they could have won the election, he would have become Prime Minister and there would have been no referendum and no Brexit. And definitely no cuts in foreign aid.

In *The Observer* yesterday he responds to the decision by the **British Government to halve the aid to Yemen in anger and disbelief.** He says that:

"At a time when acute malnutrition among children under five in Yemen is at record levels, and when the UK has made leading global efforts to avert famine the hallmark of its aid policy... it is hard to

imagine a more self-defeating decision for the UK, or disastrous decision for Yemenis. Without funding, UN and humanitarian agencies will have no choice but to scale back life-saving programming and more Yemenis will die. What we have seen today are not the actions of a "global Britain". That phrase rings hollow... Make no mistake, as the UK abandons its commitment to 0.7%, it is simultaneously undermining its global reputation."

Sir Mark Lowcock, head of United Nations' Office for the co-ordination of humanitarian affairs, warned that this decision would result in tens of thousands of deaths. And **Kevin Watkins,** CEO of Save The Children, says of the cut in funding to Syria, *"A 67% cut in UK aid to Syria after 10 years of war could mean removing education support from 350,000 children or leaving over 115,000 mothers and children under the age of five without nutrition support. It could also mean 1.9 million fewer medical consultations. That means mothers with children suffering from malnutrition and potentially lethal diseases being unable to access care – and it means more preventable suffering and lost lives.*

"This is just a fraction of the wider impact that these cuts will have on some of the most vulnerable people on earth. The UK is currently a world leader in funding education in Syria. And such drastic cuts will only make an escalating crisis even worse."

Well, I have just this minute got a reply from my MP. He acknowledges that the situation in the Yemen is the worst humanitarian crisis in the world and goes on to say that the government is committed to helping as much as they can both financially and politically. I do appreciate his detailed reply but there was so much defence of the government's actions on foreign aid that I couldn't let this pass! I replied, quoting the people above, and asking him if he thinks they are wrong. I also said that apparently there needs to be a **vote in parliament** if they are to change their manifesto commitment from 0.7% of foreign aid. And I quoted Andrew Mitchell MP when he said that "the government cannot balance its books on the back of the poorest people in the world". I ended by saying that I was sick and tired of the weasel words that this government uses when trying to explain the disastrous decisions they make about those who are in great need.

****

MARCH 15TH

UK scientists attack 'reckless' Tory cuts to international research.

Hundreds of key research projects aimed at tackling some of the world's major problems – from antimicrobial resistance to the climate crisis – will have to be cancelled or cut back thanks to budget cuts imposed by the government. Bob Ward, policy director at the Grantham Research Institute on Climate Change and the Environment, told *The Observer* that the cuts immediately undermined the chancellor's budget pledge to make the **UK a scientific superpower**. Universities were told that the budget for international development projects had been cut from £245m to £125m. Professor Alan McNally, of the institute of microbiology and infection at the University of Birmingham, described the cuts as devastating. "This is the only avenue we have had for meaningful funding of antimicrobial resistance research in countries where the research needs to be done," he said. **"This reckless and short-sighted act could create a gaping hole in the UK's climate research, just as we prepare to host the crucial Cop26 UN summit later this year,"** he added.

****

MARCH 21ST

A cross-party group of MPs are writing to the government stating that the cuts of the **foreign aid budget** are unlawful. Andrew Mitchell, a former international development secretary, is urging the government to put the change to the aid target up for a **House of Commons vote**.

Britain's cuts to overseas aid have actually also affected many African science projects and put them all at risk. The funding cutbacks have shocked scientists across Africa and dismayed Royal Society officials. "The cuts we were forced to make have been brutal," said Richard Catlow, the Society's foreign secretary. "We have seriously damaged our reputation as trusted partners in future collaborations. The relationships that we have built up have been badly and, I fear, permanently weakened. The business department's abrupt action means that Flair fellows [Future Leaders – African Independent Research (Flair)], who were expecting three years of support – will have their funding halted with only two weeks' notice, obliging the Royal Society to use its own funds to pay for another three months to soften the blow." One scientist directly involved in this work is Chris Trisos, at the University of Cape Town, South Africa. Armed with a Flair grant, his team has developed ways to track how climate change will affect different species each year for the rest of this century. Results were published in the journal *Nature*.

"We were about to start a new project to forecast how **climate change will affect wild harvested food plants**," Trisos said. "In Africa, millions of people rely on picking wild fruits and berries, but we know very little about how climate change might affect this essential nutrition source. We were going to study that. Then our grant was axed. I felt it like a physical blow when I was told. My group's future now looks very uncertain."

And for two years, the Rwandan-born scientist Anita Etale has been leading efforts to develop cheap methods to **clean contaminated water** supplies, a widespread problem in Africa. "The cuts could have implications for the whole world", said Etale. "I am trying to find ways to provide clean drinking water for people because that is a basic requirement of life. And if people cannot get that, then don't be surprised when you see refugees and migrants arriving on your shores."

I thought research on **climate change** was one of the government's top priorities. The incompetence and uncaring attitude of this government is affecting the whole world. And they would deny every word.

****

MARCH 30TH

Dominic Raab is accused of **breaking the law** as these cuts take effect without being put to the vote in parliament. He had initially promised that they **would be able to vote**. But here is yet someone else who holds high office in our government, for whom promises and the law are absolutely meaningless.

****

APRIL 27TH

The Government has been accused by senior MPs, including former Conservative International Development Secretary Andrew Mitchell, of sneaking out details on the quiet, of cuts in foreign aid. Mr Mitchell criticised Mr Raab for having "slipped out" details of reduced spending rather than announcing it in front of MPs in the House of Commons. A leaked memo, meanwhile, has suggested that the UK will slash bilateral funding for **overseas water, sanitation and hygiene projects** by more than 80% in a move Water Aid described as "savage". Dreadful at any time, of course, but in the middle of a pandemic it is brutal. The memo said the UK's water, sanitation and hygiene (Wash) budget faces an overall cut of 64% in 2021/22 compared with 2019, with bilateral aid funding for clean water scaled down by 80%.

Separately, a report by industry-focused media outlet Devex said ministers are planning to **peg back funding for polio eradication by 95%.**

****

And then there is this one.

The United Nations Population Fund (UNFPA) said on Thursday that the Government's expected contribution to its flagship programme for family planning this year will fall from £154 million to £23 million.

The 85% cut to the UK's contribution has been described by UNFPA as "devastating" for women, girls and their families around the world, with the **cash originally earmarked to prevent tens of thousands of maternal and child deaths, millions of unintended pregnancies and millions of unsafe abortions.** All of this is disgusting, but this last one offends me the most.

Mr Raab denies sneaking out the cutbacks, arguing that his department acted in a "fully transparent way" over the recent announcement. So that's all right then.

****

MAY 3RD

Dominic Raab has just given further details on the cuts to foreign aid. As you would expect they make disturbing reading. UK aid to individual African countries is being cut by 66% this year and aid to the Indo-Pacific region by 68%.

The scale of the cuts was described by a former Conservative Foreign Office minister, Liz Sugg, as "difficult to comprehend". She said the impact on education was being likened by experts to "acts of violence against the world's poorest women and girls". The cuts risk the future of a billion children and young people, according to an open letter from a group of organisations who work to prevent and treat some of the devastating conditions which are also known as diseases of poverty. These diseases include trachoma, an excruciatingly painful condition that often leaves people blind; intestinal worms, which are a major cause of malnutrition in children; and elephantiasis, a debilitating condition causing swelling of the legs. They affect 1.7 billion people globally, including 1.1 billion in the Commonwealth. The cut of £150m, reducing funding this year from £167m to just £17m, follows similar swingeing cuts revealed earlier this week regarding water and polio. Organisations that signed the open letter, including the Bill & Melinda Gates Foundation, Médecins-Sans-Frontières, Uniting to Combat Neglected Tropical Diseases and several leading British universities, warned that the cut could also lead to the needless waste of many life-altering treatments which have already been donated by pharmaceutical companies to tackle the diseases.

Much of the funding is used to get the treatments "the last mile", to the people in hard-to-reach rural communities who are often most affected by these kinds of diseases. Without this money, there is a real risk the donated drugs will be stuck in warehouses, unused, while people desperate for them suffer needlessly nearby. "These aid cuts risk children's lives," the letter reads. "What happened to the idea of 'Global Britain'? The UK has pledged to provide 236 million treatments, leveraging over one billion pounds' worth of donated medicines. This life-changing partnership is now at risk with the UK pulling out its funding." The organisations estimate that every £1 donated brings £26 of donated drugs, and point out that the entire budget for tackling NTDs represents less than one per cent of the total UK aid budget. "Why risk the future of one billion people for so little?" the letter asks. **The organisations have called for the UK to at least maintain 50 per cent of this year's budget and restore funding to its previous levels in the following years. And today, UNICEF has warned of "serious consequences" for vulnerable infants around the world after learning that the UK plans to shrink its core funding by around 60% to £16 million.** "Any cuts to these funds will have serious consequences for children," it said.

****

MAY 23RD

A report in *The Sunday Times* today says that hundreds of millions of doses of medicines are sitting in warehouses in the world's poorest countries and will go to waste after we pulled 90 per cent of our aid money for treating neglected tropical diseases. Charities say patients across Africa are to be told life-saving treatment will not go ahead or is being suspended as there is no money to deliver the drugs to towns and villages.

****

JUNE 6TH

Well, a group of backbench MPs, including former Prime Ministers such as Theresa May and John Major, are going to **try to force a vote** on the foreign aid cuts tomorrow in Parliament. As we have seen, the PM never allowed a vote to take place. These cuts broke a pledge that was in their manifesto and was supposed to be unbreakable. But of course we have seen that this is not necessarily a barrier to them changing their minds.

The rebels think they might have enough MPs to defeat the government. However, Rishi Sunak has spent the weekend apparently phoning round everyone to encourage them to vote against any change. The rebels are trying to introduce a clause into the advanced research and invention agency bill, but we still have to wait to see if the Speaker will allow it.

****

The timing of this revolt is potentially embarrassing for the government as it comes just before the UK hosts the G7 summit. It is interesting to note that all the other G7 countries are sustaining or increasing their aid budgets. And as pointed out by Andrew Rawnsley in *The Observer* today, the cash value of the aid cuts this year amount to about £4billion. He goes on to say that "the impact is devastating on some of the world's most vulnerable people, but the sum saved is not much more than a rounding error to the UK Treasury. No-one can seriously argue that the restoration of the aid is going to bankrupt Britain".

****

JUNE 7TH

1pm and still waiting to hear from the Speaker! But listening to some Tory MPs today, I am afraid that they just don't get it. Some keep harping on about how important it is to deliver the vaccination to all and sundry and that is what they will be trying to support at the G7 summit. But as their interviewers try to point out in vain, that is not much good if people are already dying of disease and lack of clean water. And listening to Lucy Frazer, the Solicitor General, on 'This Morning Britain' was very, very depressing.

And it is looking increasingly unlikely that the Speaker will agree to this vote.

3.37pm The Speaker has just announced that, having taken legal advice, he is not able to grant this amendment. BUT he said that in view of the importance of this subject, he will allow an emergency debate tomorrow if it is sent to him by 5pm today. This is an unusual step, but the Speaker is obviously very keen on getting a debate and, at some point, a vote. He said that he was prepared to look at other ways to force a vote on the issue if the government failed to allow one. He said: "I share the House's frustration. It is quite right that this House should not continue to be taken for granted but we must do it in the right way. I believe the government need to respect and need to come forward, not only for this house. The country needs this debated and aired and an effective decision taken."

****

But let us see what the government **is** happy to spend its **money on**. Yes, I know it has been brilliant at buying the vaccine, at providing the furlough scheme and for many other necessary schemes, but just maybe it could have made some savings elsewhere.

****

MONEY, MONEY, MONEY.

2021

MARCH 5TH

The redecoration of number 10 is said to be going to **cost £200,000.**

****

MARCH 6TH

We get reports today that **Boris Johnson is spending £12,500 on gourmet hampers and ready meals**. About 30 giant hampers of organic food have been delivered to the back entrance of Downing St every Tuesday along with about 100 specially prepared meals. These come from Daylesford. Daylesford was set up by Carole Bamford, wife of the chairman of JCB. Lord Bamford, his family and company, have donated £10million to the Conservatives and he supported the Brexit campaign. Just saying!

OK, I presume that Boris Johnson is paying for all this himself, but it is strange that he needs gourmet meals when it is OK for children to be given a load of rubbish, or actually no meals at all during the school holidays.

****

MARCH 17TH

This is one I really do not understand. Yesterday in the Defence Review it seems that we can apparently afford to increase the number of **nuclear warheads**. The review is expected to recommend lifting the cap on warheads from180 to 260. Just nine countries in the world still have nuclear weapons, so this puts the UK out of step with most of its European neighbours. It is not clear who the government thinks it might use the weapons against, or who it thinks might consider launching an attack on the UK. I have absolutely no idea how much this will cost, but at the moment we are spending 2.2% of GDP on defence.

Now if you have the time and/or the inclination, you might be interested to read the **Integrated Defence Review.** I will just quote the opening paragraph:

The Integrated Review is a comprehensive articulation of the UK's national security and international policy. It outlines three fundamental national interests that bind together the citizens of the UK – sovereignty, security and prosperity – alongside our values of democracy and a commitment to universal human rights, the rule of law, freedom of speech and faith, and equality.

Fine words and I think we need to keep them at the forefront of our minds.

****

MARCH 23RD

Well today is the anniversary of the first lockdown. And not a lot to report. But just something that I missed last June. Apparently in 2022 the **Queen's official fleet of aeroplanes** is set to be sold off as part of the defence cuts. The sale will leave her without dedicated aircraft for the first time in her reign and she will be forced to use the Prime Minister's private plane. Well, his RAF Voyager was refurbished last June to the tune of **£900,000,** which included a red, white and blue design on its tail fin and a white paint job changing it from the previous military-style grey. I mention it today because I have just discovered that a second Voyager has been revamped, which has also cost the taxpayer another **£900,000,** for the use of the PM, ministers and Royals.

I couldn't understand at first why there needed to be two, but I think the answer must be that the Royals would prefer to travel separately from the PM. And who could blame them? But maybe it is for safety and security reasons.

****

MARCH 29TH

Jennifer Arcuri has just told her story of her four-year affair with the PM between 2012 and 2016 when he was Mayor of London. The messy private life of Boris Johnson is well documented but this one matters because questions have been raised about her presence on three high-level trade trips and receipts of **£126,000 of taxpayers' money** in event sponsorship and grants. The Greater London Authority is currently investigating whether Johnson breached the Nolan Principles of Public Life, the code of conduct by which the city mayor is expected to abide, by not confessing his affair with Ms Arcuri. But Ms Arcuri is spilling the beans and saying he is not the same man that she knew anymore. How does this man think he can hide his misdemeanours? Or does he just not care?

But we now look forward to a press briefing by the PM at 5pm in the new (**£2.6 million of taxpayers' money**) press briefing room. So, will that strident blue background change magically to red when we have a Labour Prime Minister?

****

APRIL 21ST

The reason for the **new press briefing room** in No 9 Downing Street was because the PM wanted regular press briefings like the ones they have in the White House. So that is why it was **renovated at huge cost**

to the taxpayer and also why a press officer, Allegra Stratton, was appointed last October. Well, we haven't seen her at all in all that time. However, in an embarrassing **U-turn,** the facility, which was fitted out with microphones, control desks, cameras and computers, will instead be used by ministers. Ms Stratton, a former TV journalist and aide to Chancellor Rishi Sunak, will leave Downing Street to head up communications for the major climate change summit planned for Glasgow this November. Tory MPs are furious about this. Well, I think we all are. What an appalling waste of taxpayers' money. And another interesting point. It was fitted out by a Russian Agency, apparently. Probably loads of bugs about! Why couldn't a British firm do it, I would like to know? Labour have accused the prime minister of "running scared of scrutiny" in the wake of a rash of negative headlines over "Tory sleaze and dodgy lobbying".

****

APRIL 23RD
The Conservative chairman faces fresh questions about how the refurbishment of Boris Johnson's flat in Downing Street was funded after leaked emails suggested that a donation to the party was set aside for the project.

****

MAY 3RD
The Prime Minister says he cannot afford to live on the PM's salary of **approximately £150,000.** Well help is on hand. NHS staff are **posting £3.50** to Boris Johnson in protest against the government's proposed 1% increase in pay. More than 650 doctors and nurses have already sent the money equivalent to the weekly extra amount some staff will receive.

****

Apparently, the Prime Minister is to announce shortly that a new Royal Yacht is to be commissioned by the government and named after Prince Philip. It will cost about **£200 million of taxpayers' money**.

****

MAY 10TH

The Parliamentary Standards Commissioner has confirmed that the Prime Minister is being investigated over his holiday **in Mustique at Christmas 2019.** The ten-day trip, which the PM took with his fiancée Carrie Symonds, reportedly cost around **£15,000.** We were all told that they stayed in a villa owned by David Ross. Well, we know that name. He is the Tory donor who has suddenly resigned from Chair of the Royal Opera House. (see the chapter on the Arts). The PM says that Ross paid for their holiday, but Ross is now denying it and is saying that actually he did not own that villa! He says instead that he helped "facilitate" the trip. What does that even mean? So the commissioner has to find out who paid for it all. Goodness me, what a plot. Surely it can't be that difficult. And of course if you remember this is why he missed one of the Cobra meetings which took place just as signs of a pandemic were beginning to appear.

****

MAY17TH

And now the Parliament's Standards watchdog reportedly believes Boris Johnson's holiday to Mustique was worth more than double the **£15,000** he declared in the Commons register.

****

MAY 20TH

Oh No!! This is dreadful news. The gold wallpaper in the flat above 11 Downing Street is falling off the wall. It is too heavy, apparently, and so specialist decorators have been called in to rehang some of it. It cost **£840 per roll** so you would really think that for that sort of money it would at least have the decency to stay on the wall.

****

MAY 30TH

The new yacht that was spoken about at the beginning of this month has got the go-ahead. Boris Johnson wanted it to be called the Duke of Edinburgh but apparently the Royal Family have vetoed that idea. They say it is not appropriate for a modern royal family, they would not be having holidays on it or travelling on it and actually, surprise, surprise, they were not consulted.

It will be built in Britain and will be used to promote trade and British interests around the world. It will cost 200 million pounds. All very good. I just find it strange that this decision is taken so quickly and decisively when so many other decisions about money such as funding for schools and children's education are questioned and deferred over and over again. Yes, I know that we are talking about much larger funding here, but to my mind it should take priority.

****

JUNE 8TH

And so today I read in City A.M. an account written by Eliot Wilson who is co-founder of Pivot Point and a former House of Commons official. I think it has been in the news for a while, but I have only just discovered it. I find it shocking.

Apparently Ajax is the family name of military vehicles made by General Dynamcs UK who won a competition to supply the British Army with more than 10 different variants of tanks. There was an initial payment of £500 million. Just 14 have been delivered and they are completely unworkable. They have such major vibrations that the soldiers driving them get sick and have aching and swollen joints and suffer from tinnitus. These tanks cannot go faster than 20 mph, they cannot fire whilst moving, and reversing over objects higher than 20 cm is impossible. Now I am no expert in military warfare but even I can see that this is a complete disaster. In fact it reads like some sort of comedy script. The article goes on to mention that the amount of money wasted by the Ministry of Defence is an eye-watering £5.5billion and they have, actually, nothing to show for it. As Eliot Wilson says **"Not a single, combat-ready vehicle."** And he goes on to say "The head of DE&S must be the figure in charge of procurement and have clear accountability. Currently, no one takes the blame. The senior leadership of the MoD are spending billions of pounds, and their judgement must be sharpened by the fact that they will be held to account for failures."

Well of course they must be held to account. I do not understand why they are not.

****

Then, whilst looking again at the government's defence review, which was in the news on the 17th of March, I just happened to stumble on to this part of the report. It is titled: **Corporate report "Defence in a Competitive Age"**. It is hugely long and I read it with growing wonderment. I quote a miniscule fraction but I promise you, if you have the time and the inclination to look it up, you will be transported to **a parallel universe**. Here is one tiny part:

"The Prime Minister's vision for the UK in 2030 sees a stronger, more secure, prosperous and resilient Union, better equipped for a more competitive age, as a problem-solving and burden-sharing nation with a global perspective.

"The Prime Minister's commitment to spending £188-billion on defence over the coming four years – an increase of £24-billion or fourteen per cent – is an investment in that vision of security and prosperity in 2030.

"Our readiness to provide humanitarian relief overseas at speed; and our ability to provide specialist and rapid support in responding to global health risks, such as during the 2014 Ebola outbreak.

"Our people, from all four corners of the UK, the Commonwealth and beyond, are our most important resource. They give us our edge. We will need to attract a more diverse workforce with the skills and experience required to operate in the information age and invest in and exploit rapid technology development.

"From the renowned success of building field hospitals around the country, such as the Nightingale hospitals, to delivering vital Personal Protective Equipment (PPE) and supporting ambulance drivers, NHS hospital staff and care homes, Defence has been supporting on the front line and the complex planning effort behind it."

Goodness, yes, the army have been and always are wonderful in helping on the home front, and of course the defence of the realm is the top priority of all governments. Definitely no expense spared, and fair enough I suppose. But I just don't quite recognise this country that they are talking about and especially not the bit I have put in bold.

****

I leave this with you. But we will keep remembering the fact that our education system, our NHS and our foreign aid budgets are all inadequate to the point of negligence.

****

JUNE 9TH
Well, this is a bit tricky. Eight months ago, Liz Truss signed up to the WTO's government procurement agreement. This was in order that the UK could keep bidding for contracts around the world, which might help **offset trade lost from leaving the EU**. Well, that sounds really good. But it also requires British public contracts to be offered to global companies in a fair contest. Well yes, of course. But apparently, as *The Financial Times* first reported, the UK's schedule explicitly says "ships, boats and floating structures, except warships" must be

advertised internationally and awarded without discrimination. So, we are now thinking that actually this new yacht **probably won't be built in the UK if it is to comply with the WTO's trading rules**. Well, maybe someone else can build it more cheaply which would be good.

****

Because yes indeed, we have left the EU. Now why was that exactly?

****

BREXIT

Brexit has been almost as much of a shock to society as the pandemic. So how is it going?

2020

NOVEMBER

Large swathes of the Kent countryside, once known as the Garden of England, are being ploughed up and turned into **huge lorry parks for Brexit**. One of the Ashford parks will not be functional until the end of February 2021.

****

DECEMBER

The **Brexit transition period** finishes in little over a week, and the UK is still wracked by deep uncertainty about what next year will bring.

****

DECEMBER 20TH

Thousands of lorries were held in Kent as a result of France's decision to close its border to accompanied freight from the UK, following the spread of the new Covid-19 strain. There was inhumane treatment of 4000 lorry drivers parked for 20 miles on the M20 and on the Manston airport for five days without food or washing facilities, sufficient toilets or drinking water. Hauliers and businesses are still waiting for forms about imports and exports after Brexit. Amid concerns of similar HGV queues stretching for miles after the transition period, the government gave itself permission earlier this year to build 29 lorry parks across the UK to reduce these potential burdens. Of these projects, only seven inland border facilities will be operational by 1st January, according to a government website, the majority of which are in Kent, once known as the Garden of England.

****

DECEMBER 24TH

Because of Brexit we are pulling out of the much-praised **Erasmus scheme** for international students. Quizzed in the Commons last January, the prime minister promised MPs: **"There is no threat to the Erasmus scheme and we will continue to participate in it."** But the promise was dumped after the UK rejected the EU's requirement to join the programme for seven years, with the fee calculated based on national income. **"The decision not to participate in Erasmus is short-sighted and mean-spirited," Lord Ricketts said**. "The programme transformed the life chances of thousands of Brits, many from disadvantaged backgrounds. Those too young to vote in the referendum will be the ones to suffer." A replacement for the Erasmus study exchange scheme will begin next September, the government says. Downing Street is blaming the annual cost of Erasmus, put at "hundreds of millions of pounds", because more students come to the UK to study than travel in the opposite direction. Now, in a hastily-made announcement, ministers have pledged "over £100m" to a new "Turing scheme", named after the Second World War codebreaker Alan Turing. However, the financial commitment is far lower than the Erasmus scheme and it will certainly not be a full substitute. Once again, those who are not so well off will be the ones to suffer.

****

On New Year's Eve a letter from the government was sent to the residents of the White Cliffs Estate telling them that a new customs clearing lorry park was going to be built on the White Cliff site using a **Special Development Order,** which will bypass the usual planning permission process. The sense of fury over Brexit was palpable as local residents came to terms with this government letter telling them that from the summer, their rural idyll of farmland and ancient Roman ways would be transformed and dug up for this 12,000 lorry parking lot.

****

December 31st A hard Brexit!!!

****

2021

Seafood companies have only weeks to survive because of Brexit. Victoria Prentis, Minister of Environment, Food and Rural Affairs, did not read the Brexit papers thoroughly because of a Christmas nativity trail she was organising. Detailed paperwork about Brexit including fisheries only arrived seven days before the Brexit New Year date ("and one of those was Christmas Day"). And now, January 2021, there are so many different forms to fill in and permits to acquire that it is taking days for lorries to get anywhere. Fish are going rotten and food supplies in Northern Ireland are dwindling.

****

JANUARY 15TH
Jacob Rees-Moggs makes remarks about fish in the Commons. They are flippant, insulting and ignorant. "At least the fish are British fish and are happy fish", he says. **I write to the Speaker of the House** but he says in his reply that *"The language used by the Leader of the House*

that you describe was, in Parliamentary terms, "in order" and therefore this is more a matter of taste. All Members, including government ministers, take responsibility for their own remarks and actions and you may therefore wish to draw your concerns directly to the attention of the Leader of the House, via your local Member of Parliament."

Which of course I have done! No reply as yet.

****

JANUARY 19TH

Lorries from Seafood hauliers in Scotland protested outside Westminster. "Brexit Carnage" and "Incompetent Government Destroying Shellfish Industry" were the slogans written on their lorries. Last week SNP Commons leader Tommy Sheppard described reports of Scottish fish being left to rot due to bureaucracy as the "Brexit fishing disaster", demanding that the fishing industry is compensated for the loss in trade. He said: "Boats confined to harbour, lorry loads of seafood destroyed, the industry losing £1 million a day as firms go bust – all as a result of Brexit red tape imposed by this Government." Meat lorries were joining the protest today.

But a week ago an EU Commission official wrote to **the British shellfish industry** stating that a ban on British shellfish entering the EU would last indefinitely and not be uplifted in April as had been implied by the government.

****

JANUARY 20TH

There is a letter in today's *Times* from 150 musicians including Simon Rattle, Evelynn Glennie, and Elton John about the **UK's decision not to allow musicians to have free and easy access to the EU!!** This happened because the UK now has no freedom of movement within the EU. It was not the EU's decision, but the UK's.

****

JANUARY 23RD

British businesses that export to the continent are being encouraged by government advisers to set up separate companies inside the EU in order to get round charges, paperwork and taxes resulting from Brexit.

The leaders of the UK's five largest business groups have written to the government demanding action on the **substantial difficulties firms are facing over Brexit**. The government had admitted that more than 142,000 tonnes of food could be wasted over the next six months because of Brexit border disruption and red tape.

****

FEBRUARY 8TH

A fisherman **closes his 40 year old business due to Brexit red tape**. A decades-old shellfish trader based at a major British port has said that it has been forced to close due to new paperwork brought about by the UK's exit from the European Union.

Sam Baron, owner of Baron Shellfish Limited, announced in the Fishing News group on Facebook on Saturday that he was shutting down the family business after years of exporting lobsters and crabs to customers on the continent.

It was set up by Baron's father on the northeast coast four decades ago, according to *The Yorkshire Post*.

****

FEBRUARY 9TH

The Road Haulage Association have written a letter to Michael Gove saying that exports are down by 68% on this time last year. Their Chief Executive had repeatedly called for measures to lessen the difficulties but had been largely ignored. He said that Gove has never replied to his written requests for help.

****

Only about 10,000 customs agents have been recruited after a Cabinet Office Minister promised 50,000 to help with the blizzard of new red tape. And there are rogue customs agents with no experience offering to help out.

****

FEBRUARY 10TH

There has been a lot of reporting about the treatment of Uighars by China and the government have not yet granted a vote.

I write to *The Times*:

*Sir, Yesterday (9th Feb) MPs were expecting to vote on a plan to give British courts the right to decide if Britain's future trade partners are **committing genocide**. Instead the government used an old parliamentary procedure in order to block this vote and to give this role to select committees. The government has been accused of playing games in order to avoid defeat. This government has also been accused of stonewalling perfectly legal requests for information under the Freedom of Information Act and recently a journalist was arrested for taking a photograph of a peaceful protest on behalf of asylum seekers. At a time when we need strong and wise leadership we have instead a shameful moral vacuum.*

Not published but it explains the cowardice of this government.

****

FEBRUARY 10TH

In the Commons, the PM spoke about a **new battery factory for electric cars** to be built in Bridgend, Wales. It will be the best in the UK, in fact, in the world, he said. Trouble is, he got it wrong. It is being built in Northumberland. No.10 said sorry, but he **misspoke**. In other words, he doesn't have a clue.

****

FEBRUARY 18TH

Liz Truss, Secretary of State for international trade, refuses to answer questions about the cross-channel trade crisis sparked by Brexit. She has transferred all trade questions to other departments and refuses to answer questions about the shellfish and fishing exports and the inward trade to Northern Ireland.

****

Lord David Frost has been drafted into the cabinet to take charge of forging a new relationship with the EU. So, he is an unelected House of Lords bureaucrat and accountable to no-one. He is taking over from Michael Gove as co-chair of a Brexit committee.

****

Oliver Dowden has been berated by the **fashion industry** for telling them to use their 'star quality' in order to solve the Brexit visa problem. Dame Vivienne Westwood and Twiggy were among 450 leading fashion voices who signed a letter this month calling on the government to help the £35bn fashion and textile sectors. Oliver Dowden responded to the letter by saying that it was up to the European countries to ease visa requirements and red tape. They have accused him of being patronising and putting the livelihoods of 900,000 people at risk.

****

The UK's **seafood sector is reeling** after a double blow from the impact of Covid-19 on the hospitality sector, and also Brexit-related delays and red-tape issues which have severely hampered seafood exports to Europe.

Under the current EU rules, the export of mussels, oysters, clams, cockles, and scallops, cannot be landed in EU ports by non-EU states like us.

Before Christmas, fishermen were promised access to a market – tariff-free – but that hasn't been the case. These tariff-free barriers are quite an obstacle. They have to get past the first barrier, which is permission to send it first, and that's what they are all still waiting for. The government and news media have portrayed this as an overnight ban. **But it is important to be aware of the whole story**. Fishing waters are graded according to their water quality. Most of our fishing waters are grade B. This means that the shellfish have to be purified before they can be sold on. As members of the EU we were able to sell on un-purified shellfish quickly, which could then be purified at plants in the EU. Some fishing companies have purification plants, but many do not. At least two years ago, fishermen and women noticed that if we were no longer part of the EU then as a third country our food standards would no longer align, legally, and we wouldn't be able to export grade B, un-purified shellfish.

This was raised with government figures as a major concern. It was obviously ignored. We (the UK) helped establish these EU regulations to have a consistent approach for easy, free flowing trade of shellfish. A no deal or equivalent would result in this catastrophe if it wasn't looked at. George Eustice is lying when he says it was a surprise and when it is being peddled as an 'overnight ban'. When he was fisheries minister he was aware of these worries. If these fishing industries saw this coming then Johnson et al should have, as well.

The consequence of this is that many fishing companies, some of whom have been fishing for over 400 years, will go out of business. **It is not an overnight ban and the government should have been prepared.**

****

FEBRUARY 23RD

Boris Johnson faces a showdown with Tory rebels as peers inflict third defeat on the **genocide amendment**.

Holocaust survivors have written to Boris Johnson pleading for a meeting over the "in genocide amendment" to the trade bill ahead of the prospect of another Conservative rebellion over the fiercely contested issue. In an open letter to the prime minister, survivors Ruth Barnett and Dorit Oliver Wolff said they are "deeply concerned" the UK government is "not doing enough whilst the genocide against the Uighur Muslim minority in China's Xingiang province worsens". They continue, "Trade is not worth the price of a people. We simply cannot stand by when others remain silent. We cannot stand by whilst we carry on business as usual. Please meet with us ahead of the vote on the genocide amendment to discuss the changes we urgently need to see."

****

Almost 8,000 jobs have moved abroad because of Brexit, a report announces today. £1.3trillion assets have been transferred to Europe since the Brexit vote. Apparently, Dublin and Luxembourg are the most popular alternatives to Britain. Frankfurt, Paris, Madrid, Amsterdam, Brussels and Milan follow on in that order of popularity.

****

MARCH

Nearly two months after Great Britain left the EU single market and customs union, the volume of freight being shipped across the Irish Sea from the Republic of Ireland to GB is still down significantly, raising further questions about government claims that trading volumes are returning to normal. Companies trying to avoid red tape and potential delays associated with Brexit are sending freight on much longer sea routes directly to the continent, rather than using the traditional 'land bridge' route across Britain. There is a **49% fall** in freight volumes on Stena Line ferries from Ireland to GB and a **102% rise** in freight volumes going from Ireland to France.

The direct sea routes to France are slightly slower and more expensive than crossing the Irish Sea and then driving south through Wales and England to cross the Channel between Dover and Calais. But going direct avoids the new post-Brexit checks and paperwork associated with the Dover-Calais route, and the Stena Line figures are reflected across the industry. It means lorries never leave the single market, and they avoid new customs formalities. Stena has started a new route from Dublin to Cherbourg to go alongside its existing route from Rosslare to Cherbourg. It now has 14 weekly crossings between Ireland and the continent, compared to six last year.

****

MARCH 4TH

The EU is planning legal action to impose tariffs on cross-Channel trade, and to restrict access to the city of London, after the **UK moved unilaterally to delay implementing the Northern Ireland protocol for six months**. As part of its departure from the EU, the UK agreed to conduct checks on goods moving across the Irish Sea, going from Scotland, Wales and England to Northern Ireland. The latter has remained part of the EU's single market for goods to avoid a hard border with the Republic of Ireland in what's known as the Northern Ireland Protocol, in order to protect the Good Friday Agreement. The UK had until the end of this month to put forward these checks, but it has decided to extend the implementation period until October. This is a move that the European Commission, the executive arm of the EU, said breaches their agreement and therefore international law. The Irish foreign minister said that Britain's stance would poison relations and trigger legal action. "Unfortunately, what this means is that the EU ... see that they are **negotiating with a partner that they simply can't trust.**" And "this is not the first time this has happened".

****

MARCH 6TH

Matthew Parris in *The Times* today says "Frost's fight with the EU is political thuggery". Lord Frost has been made the new Brexit minister. He has taken over from Gove. This refers to my piece on the 4th March but Parris is concerned that people have missed it due to the budget. Frost actually declared the **new grace period extension unilaterally** without any consultation with the EU. Dublin says it could easily have been arranged by negotiation, but Frost didn't even give advance warning. And Frost and Johnson both agreed to all this in the first place. Johnson just wants to pretend he didn't sign it. And this, if you remember, is what Theresa May refused to agree to. How do they think that they can get away with behaviour such as this?

****

MARCH 14TH

The **collapse of Britain's trade with the EU** will continue into the summer after the failure to recruit up to 30,000 customs agents. This is despite government assurances that normal service has resumed, industry groups have warned. Businesses also reported that a lack of customs agents meant they were unable to respond to orders from customers based in the EU, or they found their goods were returned at huge cost. Small and medium businesses are likely to be hardest hit by the dearth of agents that play a crucial role in handling the mountain of new paperwork being imposed on firms that wish to continue trading in Europe. The scale of **Brexit chaos** at Britain's borders was starkly exposed today as official figures revealed that trade with Europe collapsed in January. Exports to the 27 countries of the European Union — collectively the UK's biggest trading partner — slumped by a record **40.7 per cent**, or £5.6 billion, while imports were down **28.8 per cent**, or £6.6 billion. The trade figures cover the month after the UK finally broke fully away from Brussels following the end of the Brexit transition period on New Year's Day. This is the biggest drop since records began. Separate data showed that the economy as a whole went into reverse in January at the fastest rate since last April with a 2.9 per cent fall in GDP.

****

MARCH 21ST

In a speech today Dominic Raab has announced that the UK should be ready to strike trade deals with **countries that ignore human rights**. China is a case that fits this description with accusations of genocide. But in a leaked video call, Dominic Raab told officials that Britain would not get many trade pacts in growth markets if it only dealt with nations that meet the standards set out in the European Convention on Human Rights.

But shadow international trade secretary Emily Thornberry said: "The mask has slipped, and the shameful truth of Tory trade policy is revealed. Now in private he says the Government is prepared to sign trade deals with any country, even those violating the laws drawn up by British officials after the horrors of the Second World War."

Amnesty International UK director Kate Allen said the leaked remarks "will send a chill down the spine of embattled human-rights activists right across the globe. This apparent willingness to sacrifice human rights at the altar of trade is shocking, but sadly unsurprising. It fits a depressing pattern on human rights from this Government." She added: "Trade is obviously important to all nations, but the Foreign Secretary shouldn't be throwing human rights defenders to the wolves like this. So-called 'growth markets' – countries like India, Indonesia or Brazil – are often precisely places where human-rights protections are fragile and under threat."

Is this what Global Britain is going to mean?

****

The EU threatens legal action against the UK over its alleged breach of the NI Protocol. It could lead to the UK having to defend its actions at the European Court of Justice. But absolutely nothing surprises me anymore. This has to be the most corrupt government we have ever had.

****

MARCH 28TH

Let's talk about **flowers.** They are so beautiful, especially at this time of year when spring is bursting out everywhere. But red tape and a labour shortage leave retailers in short supply. Are we really surprised by that? Plants from mainland Europe are now subject to health inspections in the EU. They are also subjected to inspections in the UK. So, it can now take up to 48 hours longer for plants to arrive from Belgium and the Netherlands. Delphiniums, lupins, and other hardy perennials, plus roses, fruit trees and house plants are all in short supply. David Green, the founder of Chapel Cottage Plants in Cambridgeshire, says that "Brexit is causing major problems because it is very difficult to get plants into the UK. The British grower is overwhelmed with demand". And what about our daffodils? Fields and fields of unpicked daffodils in this country have been shown on the news. Obvious, really. There are no Romanians to pick them. Some young Brits did turn up to help with the harvesting but it got a bit windy and wet, so they left, never to be seen again.

****

MARCH 30TH

27% of small firms have stopped selling to the EU either temporarily or permanently since Brexit. **The Federation of Small Businesses** has warned that what might have been dismissed as 'teething problems' in the first weeks of January were now looking more like permanent 'systemic problems'. Small importers have been hit hard by new paperwork, with 17 per cent temporarily suspending purchases from the EU. So there was also a rise in companies seeking expert help with the paperwork. More than half of those surveyed required assistance with customs declarations, rules-of-origin paperwork and new VAT obligations. The same proportion had set up, or were thinking about establishing, a presence in an EU country to make the process easier, the federation said. About nine per cent may secure, or are already using, warehouses in the bloc or in Northern Ireland for the same purpose. Mike Cherry, the Federation's national chairman, said: "These exporters tend to be among our most innovative and profitable small businesses, so it's troubling to see them bearing the brunt of changes."

****

APRIL 2ND

The Environment Secretary, George Eustice, is facing a threat of **legal action** from a solicitor **representing 20 shellfish firms** over claims that the government has misled the industry over its post-Brexit arrangements with the EU. He has accused the government of showing "negligence and maladministration" and that a group action was being considered for compensation.

Separately, **an exporter of mussels has sent a legal letter** to the Secretary of State saying the firm would sue for damages if the shellfish market with the EU was not opened up by September. Solicitors for Offshore Shellfish, a 30-year-old business employing 15 people in Brixham, Devon, wrote to the Secretary of State on 25th March stating that ministers and officials from the department had repeatedly given false hope to shellfish farmers, suggesting their businesses would be able to continue trading with the EU. "The assurances that were given by the department [Defra] gave rise to a legitimate expectation that export of LBMs [live bivalve molluscs] from class B waters from the UK to the EU would continue after 1 January 2021. In the event that our clients are unable to restart trade in September 2021, it will become necessary for them to dismantle and remove the offshore farm. This scenario (which we would hope to avoid) may result in a substantial damages claim," the letter said.

****

And **more unrest** in Belfast. There is rising discontent among unionist pro-British factions in Northern Ireland over arrangements linked to **Britain's exit from the European Union.** The arrangements are aimed at preserving a fragile peace in the territory by preventing a hard border with EU-member Ireland. The protocol removes the need for customs and regulations checks on the border with Ireland by shifting checkpoints for goods arriving from mainland Britain to Northern Irish ports. Unionists argue, however, that it strains ties with the rest of the UK by introducing trade barriers. Tension has also been stoked this week by a decision not to prosecute 24 Sinn Fein party members who attended the funeral in June of Irish Republican Army figure Bobby Storey in blatant violation of Covid-19 guidelines. And so, manhole covers, masonry and petrol bombs were thrown at police late Friday evening, and again on Saturday about 30 petrol bombs were thrown at police and police cars were torched. This problem is just not going to go away.

****

APRIL 4TH

In a brilliant article by William Keegan in *The Observer* today he says that the Brexit elite cannot hope to fool us for much longer. He cites the businesses who are in dire trouble and the students who won't be able to travel across Europe or take part in the Erasmus scheme, and goes on to say that actually regarding the vaccines it is not greed and capitalism that worked for us as Boris Johnson announced, but that everyone knows it **was the NHS and our scientists who came to the rescue.** He goes on to say that there was **"nothing that Britain did to develop the vaccine that could not have been done within the EU.** "Indeed", he says, "that knowing as I do how much British influence in Brussels was appreciated by other member states, I suspect that if we had remained inside the union we should have acted as a beneficent influence, preventing them from getting into such a tangle over vaccines." He goes on to add that, "if only Johnson could do a U turn on Brexit and put country before party". What? Has he not been following the stories here in my book?!

****

There are more and more **violent riots in Northern Ireland** due to the problems with trade after Brexit. Well, the Prime Minister was told that the Good Friday Agreement could be put in jeopardy with the border down the Irish Sea, and indeed as we have seen these forecasts are coming true.

****

MARCH 25TH

The UK's meat industry faces a permanent loss of up to half of all its exports because of ongoing problems with "mountains" of Brexit red tape, a leading trade body has warned. The British Meat Processors Association (BMPA) said "systemic weaknesses in current trade arrangements meant a potential loss of trade for UK exporters of between 20 and 50 per cent".

****

MARCH 26TH

A new report by the BMPA found meat producers also face up to **£120m a year in extra trading costs every year** because of the deal forged by Boris Johnson's government at the end of last year. Mr Hardwick said it was taking "twice as long and costs us twice as much to get products to the EU as it did before the end of the transition period". It comes as a new report by peers urged the government to consider an agreement with EU on common standards to reduce the "substantial barriers" for British traders. The peers' report cautioned that, without action, the physical checks currently in place on animal and plant products could become a "permanent barrier to trade" – with meat and live shellfish products particularly badly hit by the new inspection regime. Baroness Verma, the committee's chairwoman, said: "The Brexit trade deal struck with the EU may have prevented the nightmare of a no-deal exit for the UK, but **a lot of unfinished business remains between the two sides**." She added: "The government must take an ambitious approach to trade ties with the EU. Swift action and further funding is needed to minimise future disruption."

However, *The Independent* revealed last month that the prospect of **fresh talks with Brussels had been dashed** by the appointment of hardliner David Frost as the new Brexit minister.

****

APRIL 11TH

And the **Northern Ireland problems** also continue. Boris Johnson was constantly being warned about the possibility of trouble if the Brexit deal continued to insist on a Brexit sea border. He chose to ignore these warnings and the violence has escalated over this week. Jonathan Powell, who was the chief British negotiator in Northern Ireland from 1997 to 2007, says **Johnson lied** about the effects of his Brexit deal and says the current return to violence requires statesmanship rather than gamesmanship. "And it means no more using it (Ireland) as a battering ram in a new post-Brexit conflict with the EU." The Irish government is calling for a special crisis summit to address these rising tensions, but so far **Boris Johnson is refusing to set one up**. Peter Hain, who was Northern Ireland Secretary between 2005 and 2007, said that "compared with the attention Tony Blair, John Major and Gordon Brown gave to Northern Ireland it has been treated with casual indifference. Frankly I find it deeply upsetting". He also said that Johnson "should have been over there days ago and that the situation in Northern Ireland must be gripped by the highest level of the UK government". So once again, we see a complete disregard by the Prime Minister for the results of his Brexit deal.

****

APRIL 23RD

French block ports on fishing row.

There is a major Brexit row as French fishermen planned to blockade French ports last night in a protest at lost access to UK waters. Angry trawler-men are set to besiege the port of Boulogne-sur-Mer, near Calais, and have accused No 10 of treating them with "contempt" by shutting their boats out.

"This night of action is a warning shot," said Olivier Lepretre, head of the regional fishing committee.

Lepretre said UK authorities had only granted licences to 22 out of the 120 boats seeking permission to fish between six and 12 nautical miles from the British coast.

Local mayor Frederic Cuvillier offered his support to the fishermen, calling for the EU to "wake up" and protect the European fishing industry from Brexit's impact.

"The cruel truth is that there is no fishing deal," said Cuvillier, a former Socialist fishing minister, describing the situation as "desperate".

Fishing became a hugely fraught issue in negotiations late last year over an agreement to govern Britain and the EU's post-Brexit trade relationship. The UK had insisted it wanted to take back control of its waters, while EU coastal states sought guarantees that their fleets could keep fishing in British waters.

London and Brussels eventually reached a compromise that will see European boats gradually relinquish 25 percent of their current quotas during a five-and-a-half-year transition period.

British fishermen, many of whom sell their catches in Europe and rely on rapid transport, have also been deeply unhappy with the post-Brexit situation, saying that extra red tape is threatening their livelihoods.

****

APRIL 25TH
Cornish Fishermen

Tom Wall writes in *The Observer* today about the frustrations and anger of Cornish fishermen. **The UK-EU trade agreement**, which came into force in January, gives British boats a greater share of fish that can be caught in UK waters, but also allows European boats to fish in those waters until at least 2026, with many in the industry expecting that to continue for years to come. Border hold-ups and requirements to purify shellfish before export to the EU have hit earnings and led to some consignments being left to rot, as I explained earlier.

Bosustow, 48, a Brexit supporter, who lives in Newlyn, which is home to England's biggest fishing fleet, says that he will not be supporting the Tories on 6th May. "We are not going to forget when it comes to voting time," he says. "I don't feel like they [the Conservatives] deserve my vote at the moment."

Further down the quay, Brackan Pearce, 28, is restocking his trawler. He travelled up the Thames as part of a flotilla of fishing boasts demanding control of British waters during the referendum campaign in 2016. Now he feels betrayed. "**They lied to us**. They've used us to get Brexit. Without the boats going up the Thames, Brexit would never have happened," he says from the deck of his boat. The deal, he says, is the worst of all worlds. "It's a complete sell-out. It's a betrayal. The deal we have got is lose-lose. We have got friction at the borders and they [EU fishing boats] have still got access to our waters." Johnson has lost his support: "**I can't vote Conservative**." The port's harbour master, Rob Parsons, has seen the impact of border checks and delays up close. "Fishermen would say it has been 'a lash-up' – it means it's been really bad," he says. In January, next-day delivery became two to three days and that hugely impacted on the price."

The fishing industry continues to be hit with no help, or even any understanding or empathy, forthcoming from the government.

****

APRIL 28TH

Britain's **leading cultural organisations** have warned Boris Johnson that time is running out to solve the "crisis" for companies wishing to tour in Europe.

The heads of **Royal Opera, the Royal Shakespeare Company** and scores of other organisations have claimed that despite the Prime Minister's promise to fix the visa problem, over the last three months there has been little progress. Since Brexit, organisations and individuals wishing to tour in Europe have to spend hundreds of pounds and provide numerous documents for separate visa applications to each country they intend to visit. Touring has also been made harder with the imposition of limits on the number of stops hauliers — carrying orchestral equipment, for example — are allowed to make within the European Union. The government is being urged to negotiate a visa waiver for performers with the EU and provide an emergency fund to support extra costs now faced by artists when they work on the continent. Around 76% of artists have said that Brexit will stop them performing in Europe, according to research by Encore.

Deborah Annetts, Chief Executive of the Incorporated Society of Musicians, said: "It is extremely frustrating that despite the firm commitment made by the Prime Minister last month to fix the crisis facing the creative industry, we have not witnessed any real progress achieved by his officials to deliver on this pledge. Unravelling the huge bureaucratic obstacles preventing touring musicians and other creative workers from working in Europe is now an urgent priority as we look beyond coronavirus, otherwise work will be lost and businesses will go under. This letter should send a strong message to the Prime Minister that empty promises will not cut it, and to sort this mess out the government must negotiate a bespoke visa waiver agreement with the EU as well as bilateral deals on work permits with key EU member states."

Once again, we hear the phrase **empty promises**.

****

APRIL 30TH
"A very black day for Britain". The owners of Yorkshire's last distant-water fishery have been scuppered after government representatives

walked out of talks with Norway. The owners of a super trawler, called the Kirkella, have hit out at the collapse of these fishing talks, which has left hundreds of crewmen without work. Not only were there around 100 direct jobs, but hundreds more were employed in the supply chain. The Kerkella cost more than 40 million pounds to build and was christened by Princess Anne in May 2019, just two years ago. Mark McGorrin is the Chief Mate and he says that one of his proudest moments was sailing the Kirkella up the Thames and under Tower Bridge for the ceremony. He has been involved with fishing since he was 16. But now the trawler, which **normally catches more than 8% of all the fish sold in the UK's chip shops,** is tied up in the docks in Hull as they are no longer able to fish in the Arctic Norwegian waters and are now without any viable long-term opportunities.

UK Fisheries CEO Jane Sandell said they had been promised a "sea of opportunity, not the scuppering of an entire industry". She goes on to say that "George Eustice owes our crews and the Humberside region an explanation as to why the Department for Environment, Food and Rural Affairs (Defra) was unable even to maintain the rights we have had to fish in Norwegian waters for decades, never mind land the boasts of a 'Brexit Bonus', which has turned to disaster. In consequence, there will be no British-caught Arctic cod sold through chippies for our national dish – it will all be imported from the Norwegians, who will continue to sell their fish products to the UK tariff-free while we are excluded from these waters. **Quite simply, this is a disgrace and a national embarrassment."**

MP Karl Turner said it was an "incredibly sad" day, adding: "For years the industry have been warning that separate deals would need to be negotiated, but here we are in 2021 with the Kirkella tied up in Hull's King George dock in East Hull. **Brexit was supposed to be the fishing industry's salvatio**n, yet Hull is having hundreds of jobs and millions in investment left high and dry."

So once again we see a valuable and essential part of the fishing industry wantonly destroyed by this government, with money wasted, livelihoods gone and promises broken.

A spokesperson from Defra said: "We have always been clear that we will only strike agreements if they are balanced and in the interests of the UK fishing industry." And went on to say, "Norway is a key partner and we will continue to work with them over the course of the year."

So not much sense of urgency there then.

****

MAY 2ND

"Utter Confusion." In *The Times* yesterday these were the first words in the **travel section** by Ben Clatworthy. He was talking about **the international tourist industry.** And he goes on to say that the words **"total disarray"** would be appropriate as well. He writes about the appalling level of bureaucracy which as he says sucks the fun out of travelling. There are 10 forms to fill in, long queues to stand in, tests and more tests which can be expensive if done privately and having to take ages to try to find the results certificates, and the passenger location form with questions that need re-reading multiple times in order to be understood. For Britons, he says, **much of the stress is caused by our government** and it doesn't have to be this way. If the government maintains its requirements that UK border force officials check all arrivals' documents, then they need to have the resources to be able to do so. This needs to include the technology to reopen e-passenger gates to prevent huge queues.

I would not have thought that this was rocket science so let's hope the government is reading and learning.

****

The hospitality sector is experiencing a recruitment crisis, after many EU citizens left the UK. As 75 per cent of services are set to return from 17 May, an industry leader expressed anxiety over a lack of staff. Kate Nicholls, Chief Executive of industry body UK Hospitality, said "many EU citizens left the UK permanently as a result of Brexit". And she said: "some left for good when the pandemic started. There are foreign workers from the sector who made the decision to go back to Europe over the course of the last year."

Almost a quarter of hospitality workers in the UK are foreign nationals, according to Ms Nicholls. She said: "We have a large number of Eastern European, Polish, Spanish and Italian workers working in housekeeping, kitchens, restaurants and hotel management. In terms of future requirements, the system the UK government has put into place is going to prevent EU citizens from filling jobs post-pandemic. We have got domestic unemployment in the UK, shortages of people who are available for work and it's about making sure that hospitality is seen as an attractive employment sector in the future."

****

MAY 5TH

And to emphasise the opinion that I have of this government and its Prime Minister, **Michel Barnier** is publishing **his** diaries! They are called 'The Great Illusion'. These are a few excerpts as reported in *The Guardian* today by Jon Henley. 'In the image of its author,' he says, 'it is mostly courteous, measured and precise: a sober, matter-of-fact – and, to those who followed Brexit's twists and turns, broadly familiar – account. But that makes its asides and rare outbursts all the more forceful.'

"The UK's early problem," writes Barnier, "was that they began by 'talking to themselves'. And they underestimated the legal complexity of this divorce and many of its consequences. Britain's post-Brexit future was determined by 'the quarrels, low blows, multiple betrayals and thwarted ambitions of a certain number of Tory MPs'. Soon, however, the talking turned to Conservative party infighting, and by the end it had become 'political piracy' ... They will go to any length. The current team in Downing St is **not up to the challenges of Brexit** nor to the responsibility that is theirs for having wanted Brexit. **Simply, I no longer trust them," he writes.**

His sympathy does extend to May, "a courageous, tenacious woman surrounded by a **lot of men busy putting their personal interests before those of their country".** How often do we hear this? In the end, Barnier writes, the Prime Minister "exhausted herself, in a permanent battle with her own ministers and with her parliamentary majority".

He goes on to write: "I do wonder what, until now, has prevented the UK from becoming 'Global Britain', other than its own lack of competitiveness. **Germany has become 'Global Germany' while being firmly inside the EU and the eurozone."**

Well, I will wait for these diaries to be published in English and I will read them with enormous interest.

****

MAY 6TH

The PM has sent **two Royal Navy vessels to Jersey** because there is a post-Brexit dispute over fishing waters between Jersey and France. French fishermen have sent 60 fishing vessels to the south coast of Jersey and have threatened a **blockade.** So far, the protests have been peaceful and there have just been fireworks set off, but there was talk of the French stopping all electricity to the island as it receives 95% of its electricity from France through three undersea cables. Apparently, under the new rules, EU boats wanting to fish within 12 miles of the UK coast need to be licensed and prove they have a history of fishing in those waters in order to carry on operating. This includes submitting evidence of their past fishing activities. But there seems to be some **confusion about the new licences**.

Ian Gorst, the island's External Relations Minister said, of the 41 boats which sought licences under the new rules last Friday, all but 17 had provided the evidence required. "The trade deal is clear, but I think there has been **some confusion about how it needs to be implemented,** because we absolutely respect the historic rights of French fishermen to fish in Jersey waters as they have been doing for centuries," he said. "I do think a solution can be found. I am optimistic that we can provide extra time to allow this evidence to be provided."

But the French government has also expressed its anger at what it said were unilaterally-imposed conditions on the fishing licences, including the time French fishing vessels could spend in Jersey's waters.

So, this is an astonishing situation, **directly caused by Brexit**, whereby we are having to deploy the Navy in a stand-off with France. Obviously, it has to be sorted out diplomatically, but it is just another example of inadequate government.

But one hour after writing this I see that two French military ships are heading to Jersey. For goodness sake, these are just honest and brave fishermen trying to do their dangerous job to bring fish to our tables and they are now in the middle of this totally unnecessary debacle.

****

MAY 7TH

And of course today the papers are full of the actions over the fishermen in Jersey. And also of course the tabloids do not tell the accurate story because it is so much more fun and exciting to ramp it all up and to make it into a **gun-boat fight** on the high seas than about the **inadequate licences** issued to the French by the British. Here are a few headlines:

The Metro **Smash and crab**

The Mail **Le Grand Surrender**

The Sun **Take Sprat**

The Star **'Allo 'Allo French retreat after Brexit Battle. Good Moaning, we've sent them packing with their tails between their logs.**

How do we ever make any progress of any kind when certain aspects of our press display headlines like these? These headlines are puerile, inaccurate and are aimed at the lowest of the low. For goodness sake, grow up.

****

MAY 9TH

And as *The Observer* editorial states today: "It somehow seems nothing changes which must be how Little Englanders like it. The sad thing is they do not realise how very stupid – and deeply insular – they make Britain appear to the rest of the world." And "Let's be clear. Boris Johnson gives not a fig for fish or fishers. From Cornwall to Scotland, Britain's fisheries, which he vowed to protect, are being laid waste by his deceitful, damaging Brexit deal."

Great Britain? Global Britain? No. Little England.

****

Meanwhile, John Dixon, **second mate of the Kirkella, feels forgotten** by the government. He says that "the government ministers are agreeing to meet with the French fishermen to discuss their historic rights, they haven't even given a thought to our historic rights to fish in Norway. It's really frustrating they've just put us all on the backburner." He voted for Brexit for various reasons, not just for fishing, but feels the Government has failed to live up to what was promised. He said: **"I voted for Brexit because I believed in what they was telling me, and all of the fishing community voted for Brexit because we believed them and what the Government was saying.** We believed that we were going to have this independent coastal state and were going to be able to widen our horizons and do all these wonderful things and it just hasn't happened. They should be able to make it work, we're not asking for the world, we're not asking for something more, just asking them to keep in mind our heritage and fishing rights. **We just want it like it was before Brexit and so does Norway."**

Trevor Datson, spokesman for UK Fisheries Limited, who operate the Kirkella told 'i' the grounding of the ship was a "crippling blow". He said: "She's our flagship and **she's a flagship for British fishing**. The fact that **the government has betrayed us**, has let us down so badly, is something that we're all still trying to come to terms with." The crew of the Kirkella are "share fishermen" which means they are non-salaried but get a share of the value of the catch.

Mr Datson is not optimistic that the Department for Environment, Food and Rural Affairs will find a solution and thinks it likely they will lose their crew for good to other trades. He said: "The crew are all effectively laid off. We are desperately trying to find ways of looking after them, but it's made incredibly difficult by the Government. **Why would we trust Defra to do any better next time round?** It's in the hands of people who have so catastrophically failed and let our crews down when a deal was so easily achievable."

And to read more about this amazing fishing sea trawler and her crew go to page 94 in the book **"For the Love of the Sea" by Jenny Jefferies**. Here are the stories and favourite recipes of everyone to do with the fishing industry with a foreword by Marcus Coleman, the CEO of Seafish. This is such a topical and important book. We read about how so many families in the industry have been involved for centuries. The fishing industry today is being ignored by this government and many livelihoods have already been lost or destroyed because of Brexit.

****

MAY 10TH

Labour has accused trade secretary Liz Truss of a "catastrophic blunder" which could mean that UK companies that sign up to the government's flagship freeport programme will be shut out of export markets worth £35bn a year. "Rollover free trade deals signed with 23 countries including Canada, Switzerland, Norway and Singapore feature clauses specifically excluding manufacturers benefiting from freeport tax breaks," said Shadow Trade Secretary Emily Thornberry.

She said this meant companies taking advantage of new freeport zones at East Midlands Airport, Felixstowe & Harwich, Humber, Liverpool City Region, Plymouth & South Devon, Solent, Thames and Teesside will have to pay tariffs at potentially punitive rates on exports to these countries, which together make up almost 10 per cent of the UK's global export market.

Well, the government is denying that there has been any error so let's hope that they are right. Time will tell.

****

And also today, there is a huge row going on in the government about a **new trade deal between the UK and Australia**. The UK is hoping to clinch a deal very soon and are almost there. In fact, they would very much like it to be done before the G7 meeting in Cornwall on June 10th. Ministers hope a deal would help the economy to surge ahead as it recovers from the pandemic. However, there is a clause in the exporting of meat to the UK where guidelines allow public-sector bodies to use imported food that would be **illegal to produce in the UK** if they can justify doing so **on cost grounds**. MPs on the Commons food and rural affairs committee have called for the closure of the loophole for hospitals, schools, prisons and government departments, warning that ministers should "lead by example" on food standards. The headline in *The Independent* today reads: **Australia trade deal could mean children and patients eating meat reared in ways illegal in UK, warn experts.** This is hugely worrying because although Australia says their standards are as high as the EU's it is actually well documented that this is not so.

Welsh hill farmers are very worried that they will be put out of business and so are the Scottish crofters. Australia says: "don't worry we won't be exporting a lot to you, you are too far away and it will be expensive." Their main trade deals are with SE Asia. But of course, Boris Johnson wants to settle this before the G7 conference.

****

MAY 14TH

There is an interesting report in *The Times* today by James Dean, US Business editor of *The Times*. **He is questioning the government's insistence that any difficulties with trade since Brexit are due to "teething problems".** Lord Frost has said that he is very encouraged by the recent figures which show that British exports to the EU had risen by 8.6% in March compared with February. "Striking," he said, that "goods exported to the EU now exceed average levels from 2020." However, James Dean says that he was working from a **low base.** The 2020 average is essentially meaningless as a comparison as all exports the world over were severely hampered by the pandemic. Discounting that quarter, you need to go back to the third quarter in 2009 to find a lower level. However, he says that at least there was a Brexit deal for goods. There was nothing for services, which makes up the other 80% of the UK economy. Dean says that, "the Bank continues to forecast reduced investment and lower productivity growth as a result of 'lower trade between the UK and the EU' and 'higher barriers to trade'." He goes on to say: **"This is something that Frost and his friends in the cabinet need to overcome before they can begin to talk up the new regime."**

****

Now if you are about to tuck into a meal of Australian beef, lamb or chicken, you had better skip this bit! For today, May 19th, as reported in *The Independent*, animal-welfare organisations are horrified by the prospect of a deal because they are also saying that Australia has much lower legal standards on animal welfare than the UK, including: cutting off sheep rear ends, including skin and flesh, often without anaesthetic, barren battery cages for hens, chlorinated chicken, sow stalls which result in extreme confinement for pregnant pigs, and growth hormones treatment for beef. As I said it is all well documented.

RSPCA chief executive Chris Sherwood said: "Just days ago, the government vowed to be a global leader for animal welfare, with Defra publishing a wide-ranging and comprehensive strategy. Now the Department for International Trade is looking to sign a quick trade deal with a country still using worse systems which could undermine that pledge."

Minette Batters, President of the National Farmers Union, says she is "increasingly concerned" about the direction of trade talks with Australia, as well as negotiations with New Zealand and the US. She warned the government that there was a risk of "irreversible damage" for farmers across the country.

"It's clear that negotiators from Australia and New Zealand are sticking firm to their hard-line demands for the complete removal of tariffs on all their exports to the UK," writes Ms Batters. She says this would make it "all but impossible for British family farms to compete with vast volumes of imports from the southern hemisphere produced in a very different manner".

****

MAY 20TH

Simon Nixon in *The Times* today talks about the government's strategies for levelling up. He says that there can be no levelling up without a prosperous and successful London. Yet London's future has never looked less certain. It has been hit harder by the pandemic than any other region, it has experienced the highest number of deaths per capita, the biggest increase in unemployment and has had the highest number of employees on furlough. Then it has had the second shock **of Brexit**. The lack of a deal in services has created difficulties for many sectors including finance and an estimated 10% of bank assets have been transferred to Europe. He says that "The reality is that if the government is serious about levelling up it has no option but to be serious about London too". He goes on to say that "What is needed now is a new longer term deal to keep services running until the economy recovers. In the short term at least, levelling up means spending more money in London not less".

****

MAY 24TH

And now for those lorry parks that were initially set up to hold around 1,700 lorries in case of Brexit border disruption. Well, there is one that is still being constructed, would you believe, beside the M20 in Sevington, a suburb of Ashford in Kent.

It is causing massive disruption to local people as it is lit up all night and can be seen from villages several miles away. It has been called "as bright as Wembley Stadium" and "hideously ugly" by locals.

Mandy Rossi, who lives in nearby Willesborough, said that it is "hideously ugly" and has taken "a massive, massive chunk" out of the landscape. "It's just this massive lit-up area," she said.

Apparently, it is officially known as an "inland border facility".

****

JUNE 6TH

We are now back, once again, to Northern Ireland. Lord Frost has admitted that the **Government had underestimated the impact of the protocol in Northern Ireland**, which Boris Johnson signed up to in a bid to secure a trade deal with the EU. The UK has said it will delay new checks on goods arriving into Northern Ireland from Great Britain, agreed as part of the UK's withdrawal deal. He insisted the UK's unilateral move to extend grace periods on border checks was legal under the Brexit trade deal. But it is absolutely not.

He also said that the EU's previous threat to block vaccine exports had "significantly undermined" post-Brexit measures in Northern Ireland. The EU disputes this, and is preparing to **launch a legal challenge**. EU Commission Vice-President Maroš Šefčovič has called it a "violation" of the part of the deal relating to Northern Ireland and said legal action was imminent.

****

JUNE 8TH

Well tomorrow Maroš Šefčovič will meet Lord Frost in London for talks. He will be warning Lord Frost that "patience is wearing thin" in Brussels over the government's "confrontational" attitude. He will offer at least eight concessions aimed at easing some of the disruption to daily life in Northern Ireland. The move to go beyond EU law would be a big concession, especially as Frost has accused Brussels of "legal purism" that threatens the Protocol's implementation. If there is no breakthrough by next month and the government does not implement the protocol, the EU is ready to impose trade sanctions including retaliatory trade tariffs.

****

JUNE 9TH

Well, the talks have broken up with no agreement and Joe Biden has flown in ahead of the G7 summit. Ever proud of his Irish connections, he has accused the government of "inflaming" tensions in Ireland and Europe.

****

JUNE 12TH

So, the stand-off between the EU and the UK over the Northern Ireland Protocol continues. Interestingly, in *The Times* yesterday, James Forsyth, political editor of the Spectator, says that actually both sides could be more pragmatic and a deal could be worked out. This, of course, is in spite of the fact that it would mean the PM breaking a deal that he signed up to.

But then we read Matthew Parris today in *The Times* and we begin to understand why it is more likely that this is never going to happen. There are many quotes from Boris Johnson over the years in this article and it becomes absolutely obvious why it is that, as Mr. Parris says in his headline, **"Our closest allies no longer trust Johnson".**

Let us not forget that Johnson used to be Foreign Secretary. And they will remember his remarks. These are some of them.

'The Financial Times's columnist, Philip Stephens, reported that "At the Foreign Office (Johnson) was heard to muse as to whether **Angela Merkel** had served in East Germany's Stasi secret police." He even said "As Hitler did" when he said that the European Union was trying to create a European super state.

Then **President Macron** will remember many rude remarks by Boris Johnson.

And Tommy Victor, a former Obama spokesman who is close to Biden replied, "We (Democrats) will never forget your racist comments about Obama." Apparently Boris had said he regarded the "part Kenyan" **Barack Obama** as having an "ancestral" dislike of Britain.

Also when foreign secretary, he described St Patrick's Day celebration as "lefty crap." How can he be so appallingly rude?

Mr Parris finishes by saying "So does it matter that in Cornwall he's in the company of a handful of foreign leaders whose vote he doesn't need? Yes, because Britain needs their trust and, for now, Boris is Britain. He does not inspire that trust. Northern Ireland is perhaps the first example of why this matters. It won't be the last."

****

So will the EU bend their rules, will Boris Johnson extend the period of grace unilaterally (the present one expires at the end of this month), will the EU charge tariffs, or will Boris Johnson compromise in a sensible way? Anyone's guess.

****

And also today I see that **EU fishermen** have been granted the right to "plunder" UK waters of red mullet, scallops and lobster after

Britain failed to set limits on the amount that can be caught in a post-Brexit agreement. The move has infuriated green campaigners and UK fishermen with one accusing Whitehall of being "utterly negligent". No limits will be placed on how much non-quota stock, such as lobster, scallops and red mullet, 1,600 EU boats are allowed to collect.

****

And now the **steel industry** is furious as it is looking as though the government is going to drop EU import restrictions on about half of all UK's steel imports. Gareth Stace, the director general of the industry group UK Steel, said this decision was a "hammer blow" and "utter madness" that would leave UK producers vulnerable to import surges. **"On their first major test in a post-Brexit trading environment, the UK's new system has failed our domestic steel sector," he said.**

So never mind the Northern Ireland Protocol, that is our steel, farming and fishing industries that have been betrayed by a Prime Minister who doesn't do detail.

****

JUNE 15TH
The trade deal with Australia has been signed. British farmers have been sold down the river.

****

JUNE 18TH
UK exports of food and drink have fallen by more than 40% in the first quarter of this year.

****

And the last word on Brexit (in this book only!) goes to William Keegan of *The Observer*. "Brexit is proving to be the unmitigated disaster we 'Remoaners' feared. I am not surprised that Gordon Brown has called for the UK to rejoin the EU, although he does not believe that this will be possible in the short term. Brown's slogan for the referendum campaign would have been 'leading not leaving'."

Exactly. How much better to have stayed in the EU and worked to reform it? Of course it was not perfect, nothing is. But as with so many things, our Prime Minster ignores all difficulties and just denies them in order to **"get Brexit done"**. As Mr Keegan says, "In a sane and decent world... he ought to be suspended from public office for life."

****

Get Brexit Done?

No, Brexit has only just begun, and it will go on ...and on...and on...

****

THE ARTS

2021

MARCH 26TH

Music industry figures say they are yet to see any proof of negotiations with European Union countries on post-Brexit touring, or any details about those talks, despite government promises to the contrary. However, Boris Johnson told MPs that officials were working "flat out" and having "plenty of conversations" with European counterparts during a Liaison Committee yesterday. But several figures from music organisations which are in contact with the government told *PoliticsHome* they had not yet received any information from the Department for Digital, Culture, Media and Sport about those negotiations and the countries involved. "There is no evidence of any bilateral negotiations. We haven't had any evidence or reassurance up to now," Naomi Pohl, General Secretary of the Musicians' Union, told *PoliticsHome*. "What the Prime Minister said yesterday was really encouraging and I really hope the government has an appetite to address it. But we have had nothing solid from them so far on which countries they have actually spoken to and we haven't had a single progress report. The MU and UK Music will be following up with DCMS Secretary of State **Oliver Dowden** as a matter of urgency following the Prime Minister's comments."

****

MAY 1ST

The Musicians Union has just reported that the Government has announced that it plans to impose a **50% funding cut** to "high cost" subjects at Higher Education in England, **including music**. This is because music and the arts are not among its "strategic priorities". The 51-page consultation document is based on a statutory guidance letter written by the **Education Secretary, Gavin Williamson.**

The document reads: "The Government proposes that the courses... that are not among its strategic priorities – covering subjects in music, dance, drama and performing arts; art and design; media studies; and archaeology – are to be subject to a reduction of 50 percent." It adds that while the Government wants "provision in those subject areas to continue to be widely available, we believe they are nevertheless lower priority for OfS funding than other high-cost subjects".

The MU's response to the proposal is that halving funding would be **"catastrophic"** and would affect "our members' work, the financial viability of music courses, and training for the next generation of musicians and music professionals". They are responding to the consultation document and working with other bodies such as UK Music and Music HE, but as they say there is not nearly enough notice to enable HE institutions to plan before September.

I just find this news so disrespectful to the arts in this country and to education generally. What does Gavin Williamson think he is doing?

****

APRIL 26TH

"Welcome to Tory-run Soviet Britain."
This was the headline to a very disturbing article by Richard Morrison of *The Times* yesterday. He writes about **the arts** and he writes that "No organisation receives a penny from the government's Cultural Recovery Fund unless it signs what is effectively a **muzzling**

agreement requiring it to praise the government in a public statement."

He goes on to say that "And there's something else that makes the blood boil. It's the way that Boris Johnson and his culture secretary Oliver Dowden, can drop everything to meet football club chairmen for 'emergency meetings' yet do nothing to sort out the real crises affecting the cultural industries". He also goes on to highlight the under-funding of local authorities which will mean that many libraries, museums, sport centres, art venues and performing organisations already closed due to the pandemic will be forced to close altogether. "This is the issue the government should be addressing, not the machinations of self-interested billionaires." But he says that this is not sexy enough to make the headlines and there are not many votes in it. "By such cynical calculations do we now allow Britain to be run. The impact on our lives and local activities will be what we deserve."

He writes every week and his criticism of the Culture Secretary during this pandemic has been scathing.

****

MAY 2ND
Government in Culture War. Two resignations. What is going on?
I note today that the two billionaires who co-founded Carphone Warehouse, the mobile phone shop, have both just quit their roles as chairmen of prestigious arts venues. **Sir Charles Dunstone** resigned from the Royal Museums Greenwich Board in February, but this was only reported in *The Financial Times* this weekend. He left because Oliver Dowden (that name again) refused to renew the term of Aminul Hoque, a lecturer at Goldsmith University, as a trustee. Hoque is a Bangladeshi-born Briton and only the third person from an ethnic minority background to be a trustee. He led its response to the Black Lives matter movement last year. Apparently, the museum's trustees were prepared to quit en-masse over Dowden's refusal, but Dunstone prevented the move in an attempt to protect Paddy Rogers, who joined

as Director in 2019. The Greenwich museum is also responsible for the Cutty Sark, the National Maritime Museum and the Royal Observatory. Mr. Hoque told the *Financial Times* that he was "shocked, bewildered and baffled" by the government's decision. But actually it is said that with the backing of Downing Street, **Oliver Dowden is believed to have blocked many re-appointments** at top institutions in favour of candidates more in tune with the government's thinking.

****

And I do have to just add this because honestly you couldn't make it up. Well, you wouldn't want to make this up. Reported in *The Sunday Times* today they talk about the senior Conservative advisor called Dougie Smith. Heard of him? No, nor have I. He is married to Munira Mirza, who is the director of the No 10 policy unit and a longstanding aide to Johnson. **They say he is "best known in Westminster for previously running sex parties and is regarded as the 'most powerful man you've never heard of' in the government.** Seldom seen in No 10, he nonetheless is said to exert huge influence over public appointments and some secretaries of state including Oliver Dowden whose department approves those named to cultural bodies." Thank you, Liam Kelly and Tim Shipman (of *The Sunday Times*) for letting us know about that.

****

BUT that venue which is so close to my heart, the **Royal Opera House,** is also about to lose its chairman. David Ross is said to be quitting his chairmanship **after just eight months** into a four-year tenure. Apparently, there is a perceived conflict with his role as chairman of the National Portrait Gallery. It seems that Oliver Dowden has asked him to do another four years there, in which case he will have to step down from the Opera House. So, this is a different reason but nevertheless very strange. David Ross is very close to the Conservative Party, allegedly paying for the PM's holiday in Mustique, and a prominent Conservative donor. Also, Oliver Dowden's name is there, both of which just make me very suspicious.

But of course it is more than that. It is the whole attitude by this Government to the Arts in general. It has been described as **cultural cleansing.**

And **on May 7th** Richard Morrison, the Arts critic of *The Times,* **says "Butt out! Cronyism has no place in our cultural institutions".**

****

MAY 16TH
Simon Rattle, conductor of the LSO (for the moment), has appealed for government support to help them to survive the difficulties created by **Brexit and the pandemic.** The orchestra depended so much on international touring – much of it in Europe – for 40% of its income and now they have to find ways to survive.

With the new Brexit rules it will be impossible to continue as normal. Even the basic things which means that the truck of instruments has to return to England after two venues will mean that they cannot go from one country to another. So, concerts will have to be planned in a totally different way. "We're of course grateful for what public funding we get, but it's a drop in the ocean of what this great orchestra will need to survive," he told *The Guardian.*

****

MAY 21ST
Richard Morrison in *Times 2* today calls out the department of Oliver Dowden. Apparently **amateur choirs** cannot get back together yet with any more than six people. As Mr Morrison says, six people is not a choir. "It takes a degree of bungling bordering on genius to anger over 2 million people but that is what Oliver Dowden has achieved." The word 'apparently' is there because the instructions are so contradictory as to be baffling. Crowds of people can shout their heads off at sporting events and in pubs, but meticulously organised choir rehearsals are too dangerous. "It is lunacy," he says. "Dowden

should stop wasting his time and our money telling museums what to display and attend to the stupidity evident in his own department."

****

MAY 24TH

And on the Today programme this morning, Dr Declan Costello, an ENT surgeon specialising in voice disorders, is working on a report to show that **singing and the playing of musical instruments is safe.** He said that he finds it very strange that at pubs, restaurants and sports events crowds of people can shout and sing and yet amateur choirs are not allowed more than six people. The Department of Digital, Culture, Media and Sport have provided no evidence for this instruction and he is asking to see it.

****

JUNE 5TH

Oliver Dowden has been ridiculed by musicians, artists and crew members for boasting about a fantastic post-Brexit deal he has just made with Iceland, Norway and Liechtenstein. This deal will enable artists to travel to these countries visa-free for their music gigs. It is in fact the same deal that was offered to the UK by the EU during Brexit negotiations, which the UK refused.

Broadcaster Gavin Esler tweeted: "Liechtenstein. Population 38,000. Iceland 370,000. Norway 5 million. 'An ambitious approach'. Folks: the UK government thinks we are all idiots. At some point it might be good to prove them wrong."

Photographer Kevin Cummins also focused on population and market size, writing: "The Isle of Wight festival capacity is 50K. The population of Liechtenstein is just over 38K. Clearly a huge audience awaits the influx of British musicians and actors."

****

And so concert halls, theatres, opera houses, and other arts venues are cautiously beginning to open up. But we do not forget the cut in Arts courses or the problems with foreign touring due to Brexit regulations, or the many other difficulties faced by the creative arts today. They are never at the top of any government agenda, but the ignorance of their difficulties, by this present government, has been staggering.

****

So, what has the government been doing? It is important to look **beneath the bluster.**

****

CONTRACTS, TRANSPARENCY, CHUMOCRACY', AND THE MINISTERIAL CODE

2020

JANUARY 23RD

Peter Cruddas is to become a peer in spite of disapproval of a peer review body. Peter Cruddas, a former Conservative Party co-treasurer, donated £50,000 to the Prime Minister's campaign to become leader of the Tory Party in 2019. Overall, he has given more than **£3.5million** in **donations to the Tories**. The businessman quit his role with the party in 2012 after cash-for-access allegations. They relate to allegations he offered access to the then Prime Minister, David Cameron, in exchange for donations of more than £200,000. The watchdog commission advised the present Prime Minister that it could not support Peter Cruddas being made a Lord. In February the Prime Minister ignored the recommendations and appointed him anyway. Three days after being introduced to the Lords, Cruddas gave the Conservative party £500,000.

****

FEBRUARY

Priti Patel's senior civil servant Philip Rutnam resigns because of her bullying and shouting and swearing.

****

NOVEMBER

Priti Patel (again!) was accused of bullying. A report into her conduct found that she had broken the ministerial code of conduct, but the PM ignored the findings and kept her in her job. So again, her **senior civil servant Sir Alex Allen resigned** instead of her.

****

Boris Johnson's decision to stand-by Priti Patel after **bullying reports, triggers legal action**. A union representing senior civil servants has announced that it is launching a judicial review seeking to overturn the PM's ruling that she did not breach the ministerial code. They say that the PM needs to understand the damage he has done to confidence in the code.

2021

FEBRUARY 14TH

There is to be a judicial review into a **"handshake deal"** between the Conservatives and a company called Public First which has close links with the Conservative Party and in particular Michael Gove and Dominic Cummings. Last week the Government's own legal representatives admitted that it had breached procurement law by persistently failing to publish details of Covid-19 contracts. On March 3rd last year the government struck a deal with Public First and paid £23,000 for services between March and May 2020. The value of the deal was capped at £840,000 and the company billed the government for £550,000. There was initially no contract, just a handshake. There was no competition or tendering process. A judge will hear evidence tomorrow, the 15th.

****

FEBRUARY 20TH

A court has ruled that **Matt Hancock acted unlawfully** when his department did not reveal details of contracts it had signed during the pandemic. It was claimed that the government **breached its own transparency policy,** which requires the publication of details of public contracts worth more than £10,000.

****

MARCH 3RD (BUDGET DAY)

The UK government is censured for lack of transparency and accountability. The global coalition for **transparency and anti-corruption** has put the UK "under review", heightening concerns about the government's commitment to openness following a series of scandals. In a letter to the government, seen by Sky News, the **Open Government Partnership** said the **UK had failed to live up to its pledges** to improve transparency and accountability. The rare intervention means the UK will become the ninth of the international coalition's 78 members to be placed under review, joining a list that includes Bulgaria, Malawi, Malta and South Africa. The Open Government Partnership has no power to impose punishments, but the news has come as a shock, **as the UK played a key role in the group's foundation in 2011 and is currently its biggest funder, donating £6.8 million over three years.**

I am **constantly** amazed that this government doesn't seem to realise what is being done in its name a lot of the time.

One of the country's leading advocates of open government told Sky News he was stunned by the decision, saying: **"This is shameful."** Kevin Keith, chair of the UK Open Government Network, said: "It shows how far we have fallen in a decade and is symptomatic of wider problems including the unlawful failure to publish contracts awarded during the pandemic."

****

MARCH 5TH

Sir Philip Rutnam has been awarded **£340,000 payment**, in one of the highest compensation awards made to a departing Whitehall official, in order to avoid an employment tribunal hearing. But ministers are still facing a judicial review brought in by the FDA union that represents senior civil servants over Johnson's decision to clear Patel of bullying under the ministerial code. The shadow home secretary said that "taxpayers will be appalled at having to pick up this bill for the home secretary's unacceptable behaviour".

****

There are so many **chumocracy consultancy contracts** for exorbitant levels of money. In May *The Guardian* revealed that out of 177 contracts given to commercial firms as a result of Covid-19, 115 (worth over £1 billion) were **awarded without tender**. A company run by one person who had previously worked with Michael Gove, and another with Dominic Cummings, was given an £840,000 contract to test the effectiveness of the Government's coronavirus advice (most of us could have told them for free actually: the advice isn't working).

****

MARCH 5TH

Certainly, the publication of coronavirus contracts appear to show that Boris Johnson misled parliament. The Prime Minister had claimed that the contracts, which are subject to a legal challenge and cronyism allegations, were "there on the record for everybody to see". But a final order handed down by the High Court on Friday said the government had in fact only published "608 out of 708 relevant contracts". The revelation comes after a High Court judge also found Matt Hancock had acted unlawfully by handing out contracts without publishing details in a timely way after a case was brought against the government, again by the Good Law Project.

But there we are. There doesn't appear to be any comeback or criminal accountability and these people continue to lie their way through life.

****

MARCH 6TH

The Good Law Project has previously challenged the government in court over alleged cronyism in PPE contacts, clean air, and access to remote education during the pandemic. And I have just discovered what happened with some of those challenges. Campaigners from the Good Law Project say the latest document from the court confirms that the Prime Minister misled MPs even after it was ruled that the government had broken the law. "Government has not only misled parliament and placed inaccurate information before the court, it has misled the country. We have a government and a Prime Minister contemptuous of transparency and apparently allergic to accountability. The very least that the public deserves now is the truth."

This is an appalling indictment on our Prime Minister and his government and is extremely serious. Where is the judgment and the sentence?

****

MARCH 21ST

The PPE contract by the government last year is still being kept secret. In *The Independent* yesterday it was announced that Clipper Logistics, whose boss gave the Tory party £750,000, secured the order to supply the NHS **without facing any rival bids**. When the High Court ruled this to be unlawful, the Prime Minister insisted again that the contracts were "on the record for everybody to see". However, *The Independent* reveals that this deal has still not been published on the government's official website almost 12 months on.

****

MARCH 29TH

And it is not just the present Tory PM in trouble (again and again and again) but a previous Tory PM, **David Cameron**. Apparently, he told friends that he stood to **make $60 million from share options** in a company at the heart of a lobbying scandal. Lex Greensill, an Australian financier, was given privileged access to 11 Whitehall departments and agencies by Cameron, who was later hired by Greensill as an advisor at his financial services company with share options worth millions of pounds. Cameron subsequently sent a series of texts to Rishi Sunak, the chancellor, lobbying him to grant hundreds of millions of pounds in taxpayer-funded loans to the company. But the company has now collapsed, threatening 50,000 jobs, which means that Mr Cameron's share options have been left worthless. However, he has been cleared of breaking lobbying rules by a watchdog after reportedly asking Rishi Sunak to support Greensill Capital through the Government's Covid Corporate Financing Facility. It was said that as he was an employee of Greensill Capital, he was not required to declare himself on the register of consultant lobbyists.

But this doesn't look as though it is going away any time soon. Sir Alistair Graham has said, "There clearly should be a full inquiry because it sounds like a genuine scandal in which the public purse was put at risk without proper political authority." What is it with Tory MPs? Scandal after scandal about sex and money.

****

And so, **"Politicians seem incapable of being open and transparent"**. This is the headline of the editorial in *The Sunday Times* yesterday. They quote Kevin Keith, chairman of the UK Open Government Network, who says that "The UK government's reputation for openness and accountability is in freefall. That reputation needs to be clawed back. Behind closed doors is no longer an acceptable way of governing the country". My goodness, was that ever the correct way to run this country?

****

MARCH 29TH

Chumocracy again. Well, we know about Baroness Dido Harding as the head of the NHS Test and Trace task force, married to a Conservative MP, but there is also Mike Coupe, director of testing at NHS Test and Trace. He was a director of Sainsbury's and a colleague of Harding's at the supermarket chain. Campaigners have won a judicial review into their claims that Johnson and Hancock acted unlawfully by appointing their "chums" to these jobs in their fight against Covid. I would imagine that their defence is going to be that they had to act quickly in order to get everything up and running as soon as possible. But, surely they should have been doing all this in January and February as it was becoming obvious to very many people that we were about to be hit by a global pandemic? At the heart of the claimants' case is the charge that the posts were not advertised in the way they normally are in the public sector, so those with wide experience in the field were not able to put themselves forward. And they also point out that because all are unpaid positions, the government was guilty of indirectly discriminating against others outside the well-off, predominantly white group from which the three were chosen. While the claimants have stressed that at no stage have they sought to remove any of the three from their posts, they say they are acting to ensure that future governments are bound to act **fairly and lawfully in making public appointments.** Well, that will be the day.

****

APRIL 4TH

Two businessmen have decided to **summon Matt Hancock to the High Court** to justify why he is allowing non-essential shops to open before pubs and restaurants. They say that businesses such as theirs have spent a small fortune on doing everything asked of them by this government in order to make their premises Covid safe. They add that the risk of Covid-19 transmission is higher in shops than it is in pubs and restaurants.

I must say that when we visited pubs during the last lifting of the lockdown, we were very impressed with all the measures that had been taken, so I think they have a good point. But everyone will have their own views on this one. Shops etc will be able to open a week today on the 12th but the hospitality industry has to wait until the 17th May.

****

APRIL 11TH

The **lobbying scandal involving David Cameron** and financier Lex Greenshill continues apace as it appears to get more and more disgraceful. *The Sunday Times* has revealed today that Cameron not only tried to lobby Rishi Sunak but also Matt Hancock, and the Treasury ministers Jesse Norman and John Glenn. Greenshill also met Dido Harding and Sir Simon Stevens, Chief Executive of the NHS. The details of all of this are extremely complicated and I am not qualified to explain them. I just notice the reactions of certain people who are. Sir Alastair Graham, the former chairman of the Committee for Standards in Public Life, has described this as the **"biggest lobbying scandal in a generation"** and he said that Cameron had "tarnished British Politics". He went on to say that lobbying rules need to be reformed. But I say that you cannot reform anything in politics until you have senior politicians who have some sort of a moral compass. Last night Cameron's spokesman refused to respond to these allegations. Why does he need a spokesman exactly? Possibly because he is nowhere to be seen.

****

APRIL 12TH

Well, well, David Cameron must have heard my thoughts!! Well, mine and many others to be fair. Last night he came out of the woodwork and said that he had done nothing wrong. Yes, he thought the rules needed changing so that there was no scope for misinterpretation as he calls it. In other words "not me, guv". But people are saying that

that is not really the point. The whole thing has a 'smell' about it. A 'whiff' of distrust and opaqueness which really does not look good.

****

APRIL 13TH
Campaigners, including Transparency International, have said the saga "highlights deep flaws in the UK's approach" and that an inquiry should cover the **lack of transparency in lobbying, enforcing the ministerial code and the revolving door between government and the private sector.** We all agree with that, but we are still wondering when the inquiry of the government's handling of the pandemic will see the light of day.

****

APRIL 14TH
Labour will today pile pressure on Boris Johnson to agree to a **full-scale committee inquiry** into the **Greensill lobbying** affair in a Commons showdown this afternoon. MPs blasted Boris Johnson's plan for a "whitewash" No10 review of the scandal, saying the government can't be trusted to "mark its own homework". The opposition will force a vote to establish a committee-style probe with the power to ask witnesses – including Mr Cameron, the Chancellor and other ministers – to give evidence. However, Boris Johnson insisted his planned review of the scandal, to be led by top Lawyer Nigel Boardman, would have the "maximum possible access". But speaking in a Commons debate in response to an Urgent Question on the affair, Labour's Jon Trickett told MPs: **"It sounds like a whitewash to me."**

Boris Johnson also says that he wants this done as quickly as possible. Well, well, that will be in direct contrast then to the proposed inquiry into the **government's handling of the pandemic.** Lord Saville of Newdigate said today that he would **be amazed if an independent inquiry could be completed in less than seven years and it might take substantially longer.** Well, if they read this book and the others

I have mentioned, I think it could be speeded through. I say a couple of months at the most.

And the result of **the vote in parliament today about whether to have a fully independent inquiry into the Cameron lobby scandal** has just been announced. It has been **voted down** and so instead it will be a review conducted by a good friend of The Conservative party, Nigel Boardman. So, it is looking as though it will indeed be a whitewash.

However, around an hour after the vote, the **Commons Treasury committee** said it would hold **its own inquiry into Rishi Sunak** and his officials' role in responding to lobbying from David Cameron, who tried to secure Covid rescue funding for Greensill Capital, where he worked as an adviser. It came after Keir Starmer said the Greensill scandal marks the return of "Tory sleaze", amid questions over the former prime minister's lobbying for the financial firm. This is another story that is not going away any time soon.

There is also concern and outrage after it emerged that the former head of civil service procurement, Bill Crothers, became a part-time adviser to Greensill Capital while still working as a civil servant, in a move approved by the Cabinet Office. Apparently, this is absolutely not allowed.

****

APRIL 15TH

Well, not only not allowed, but absolutely **without precedent**. In fact, this is fast becoming the biggest scandal as it is affecting our **civil service,** which is the envy of the world for its expertise, impartiality and intellectual prowess. But do you remember that a civil servant resigned five months ago after the PM rejected his advice that Priti Patel, with her bullying, had broken the ministerial code and should resign? Well, his name was Sir Alex Allan, who just happened to be *The Independent* **adviser on the ministerial code** and the PM has not yet appointed his successor. So, no wonder, that with no one to hold them to account, ministers, including the PM, continue to break the code, tell lies and to break the law.

****

APRIL 16TH

Matt Hancock, our health secretary, has just been accused by Labour of **breaking the ministerial code** (again) after it emerged that he was given a 20% share in a company owned by his sister shortly before it won a lucrative NHS contract. Topwood LTD of Wrexham, a document-shredding firm, was **awarded a three-year contract** – reportedly worth £30,000 – by NHS Wales.

But we know that the ministerial code is completely ignored by our present politicians.

****

And today **May 28th** we discover that this **was** a break of the ministerial code, although Johnson calls it a minor breach, whatever that means. Well actually, I think it means he doesn't have to resign. (At least not yet!)

****

APRIL 19TH

Well, the Sunday papers yesterday were all over the **Cameron lobbying scandal** which gets bigger and bigger. It is all well documented and extremely complicated, so I will just quote the words of a few reporters which illustrates the seriousness of it all. Andrew Rawnsley in *The Observer* writes: "The ethics of government need a deep clean. That's not likely to happen when Boris Johnson is Prime Minister". He goes on to say "A former Prime Minister is at the heart of this scandal that points to **something rotten** about how we are governed and is now embroiling not just politicians, but also the civil service."

So many more ministers are facing questions about their involvement with Greensill, the most serious being **Matt Hancock,** our health secretary, and Greensill's financial ideas **for the NHS**. Gabriel Pogrund in *The Sunday Times* writes, "Why did a former prime-minister agree to lobby Hancock, a cabinet minister, on behalf of a dubious financier? How could Greensill have received such access to the NHS? And why was he allowed to use the nation's most beloved institution to promote his brand and his company?"

And Liz Truss, our international trade secretary, was dragged into the lobbying scandal yesterday when it was revealed that she has appointed a Greensill advisor to a top role. She gave Julie Bishop, ex-Australian foreign minister, an unpaid role on the G7's Gender Equality Advisory Council. Ms Bishop had taken a job with Greensill Capital in 2019. She made the announcement on the Government website, as the UK currently holds the G7 presidency.

And then there is the concern about the **steel tycoon Sanjeev Gupta**. On April 9th, *The Financial Times* reported that suspect invoices had been used to secure Greensill loans to Gupta that were later sold to investors in Credit Suisse funds, raising suspicions of fraud. John Collingridge reveals in *The Sunday Times* that Gupta planned to raise money from Greensill based on circular transactions with connected companies. This could have had the effect of artificially boosting his working capital. But as Oliver Shah writes, also in *The Sunday Times*, "There are reasonable grounds for authorities to investigate Gupta. So where is the **Serious Fraud Office (SFO)?**"

He goes on to say that "The SFO's record does not inspire confidence. More slobbering labrador than rottweiler... it is **underfunded and underpowered**".

This scandal will run and run for a long time yet. Boris Johnson is being pressed to have a full independent inquiry rather than the in-house Boden inquiry, but to quote Andrew Rawnsley once more, **"This Augean stable needs mucking out, but it is unlikely that Mr Johnson will be a vigorous shovel".**

****

APRIL 20TH

A senior **Amazon executive** is being lined up for the role of the government's special advisor, despite warnings from the Cabinet Office over serious **conflicts of interest.** And almost in the same breath the head of the government's ethics (what?) watchdog has called on Boris to give up the power to decide whether ministers should be investigated for breaching Whitehall's sleaze rules. Lord Evans of Weardale, who is the head of the committee on **Standards in Public Life,** said that the government's new advisor on ministerial interests should be free from political interference in order to decide which cases needed to be investigated. He said the PM should also give up his power to decide whether a minister had breached the ministerial code (what's that again?) and hand that responsibility to the new advisor. But where is this new advisor? As I have previously remarked, the post has been vacant since the resignation of civil servant Sir Alex Allan. Well, Downing Street has just said that his replacement was likely to be announced in the next couple of days. We wait with bated breath. But then they say that Johnson is unlikely to adopt any of the committee's recommendations!

****

APRIL 21ST

The Government is facing a lawsuit after a contract to supply face masks was awarded in July 2020 to Pharmaceuticals Direct Ltd (PDL) without any competition. The Good Law Project, which is investigating how coronavirus contracts were awarded, said details of the deal were only disclosed in March after it wrote to the Government.

The Department of Health and Social Care said due diligence was carried out on every contract and ministers had no involvement in awarding them. It said all contracts are published online, in line with transparency arrangements. But the BBC reported that even when the £102.6 million deal involving PPE equipment was finally published, the contact details for the supplier were **blacked out**. Then an admin error revealed that a former **Conservative parliamentary candidate** was the contact for a £100 million deal for personal protective equipment. And in what appears to have been a clerical error, a separate document published with the contract gives the name Samir Jassal as the "supplier's contact".

Mr Jassal twice stood as a Conservative candidate at general elections and has **met Boris Johnson and David Cameron**.

Jo Maugham, the Good Law Project's director, said: "The first lockdown ended in June. How can we still have needed PPE so urgently as to award a vast £100 million-plus PPE contract without any competition in July?"

****

And another story today involving **contracts by this government** has also just emerged. Now if there hadn't been any other dodgy contracts, I think this one would possibly have escaped notice. However, last March, 2020, at the beginning of the pandemic, James Dyson who is now based in Singapore wrote to the PM offering to make ventilators for the NHS. And replying to his question Boris Johnson assured Sir James Dyson his employees would not have to pay extra tax if they came to the UK to make ventilators during the pandemic. In fact, the actual texts are out there and he wrote, "I will fix it." And on another occasion: **"I am First Lord of the Treasury and you can take it that we are backing you to do what you need."**

The Prime Minister was heavily involved in efforts to get hold of ventilators and in touch with many businesses as the pandemic took hold.

Both Number 10 and Dyson stress the terrible urgency of the situation last year, rejecting the notion that the conversations were in any way inappropriate.

However, Labour said the revelations were "jaw-dropping" and declared: "Tory sleaze has reached the heart of Downing Street. The prime minister appears to have used the power of his office to personally hand public money to a billionaire friend in the form of tax breaks".

Labour leader Sir Keir Starmer suggested it was 'one rule for those that have got the Prime Minister's phone number, another for everybody else'.

In the end the ventilators were not required as medical understanding of the virus evolved. But under the **ministerial code**, ministers are supposed to have an official present when discussing government business and to report back to their department as quickly as possible if a conversation does take place where that is not possible.

So, whilst we can understand the urgency of this request (and who wouldn't pick up the phone to Mr Dyson if you think he can solve a problem for you?), nevertheless it does sound as though there was a more conventional and above-board way of doing it. And if it was any other prime minister? And in PMQs this morning he was shouting and blustering and accusing Keir Starmer left, right and centre of all sorts of ridiculous actions. Obviously, he was just trying to move the talk away from things that he would rather forget.

****

APRIL 22ND

Ex-veterans minister Johnny Mercer today said that Johnson's Government is **"the most distrustful, awful environment"** where **"almost nobody tells the truth"**. Mercer was reportedly sacked by text after being summoned to see the Chief Whip, Mark Spencer, last night after expressing frustration at a lack of progress on legislation to protect British veterans, who served during the Troubles, from prosecution. Spencer told Mercer he had to resign there and then so as not to create any more fuss, and he'd "get a nice letter" from the PM if he did. Mercer told the Chief Whip to "f*** off", and walked out. Ten minutes later, the Chief Whip texted Mercer to inform him that he had been relieved of his duties. The PM wrote him a nice letter anyway. Mr Mercer said on Wednesday that "nothing has been done" over the "gross betrayal of people who signed up to serve in the military", as he gave a damning account of Boris Johnson's Government.

****

The Conservative chairman faces fresh questions about how the refurbishment of Boris Johnson's flat in Downing Street was funded after leaked emails suggested that a donation to the party was set aside for the project.

****

More cronyism and corruption

Contracts worth billions of pounds awarded by the government for PPE supplies during the Covid crisis should have raised "red flags" for possible corruption, a report has claimed. A review of nearly 1,000 contracts worth £18 billion issued between February and November identified £3.7 billion, about a fifth of that total, as having the potential to involve fraud or cronyism. The campaign group Transparency International said that 24 PPE contracts worth £1.6 billion were awarded to those with known connections to the Conservative Party, while three contracts worth £536 million went to politically connected companies for testing related services. Details of these contracts were much more likely to be published late than those where no political connections were found. Chief executive Daniel Bruce said: "The Government's approach to procurement during this critical period has already dented public confidence at a time when the trust of its citizens is most needed.

We must now have full accountability for the eye-watering amounts of taxpayers' money spent on the response – with the award for each of the 73 contracts we highlight in our report subject to a thorough audit."

****

APRIL 23RD

Lord Udny-Lister, one of Boris Johnson's closest aides, has left his role as the prime minister's special **envoy to the Gulf**, Downing Street said yesterday. This is very sudden as he has only been in this role for two months. Could it have anything to do with the story about Saudi Arabia, I wonder? Apparently, the PM had asked Lord Udny-Lister, a Middle East expert, to check on a Saudi Arabia-backed takeover bid of Newcastle United Football Club. It came after the *Daily Mail* reported that the Prime Minister was contacted when the £300m deal ran into difficulties.

****

And Boris Johnson's phone? Yes, the phone has a story all of its own. Johnson has had the same phone number for more than a decade, and he refuses to change it. Cabinet Secretary Simon Case is said to have raised the issue with the PM last year, telling him he was being asked for help by MPs, lobbyists and others in the business world so often because his number was too widely known. He risks national security and his own safety by using an unsecured private phone. He should be using an encrypted device issued to him by security advisers. Instead, he has continued to use the personal phone he has used for 10 years, leaving him open to hacking by spies, malicious interlopers – and yet more humiliating leaks.

Security expert Philip Ingram said: "**This clearly poses a security risk**. If he's using a device which is not under Government control, then there could be apps which could compromise the data on the device. **He will 100% be targeted by hostile intelligence services like the Russians and the Chinese.**"

Well, we think the Russians are already in the new press briefing room which is now not being used for its original purpose. Difficult to know if this is good or bad.

****

APRIL 24TH

The chickens I think are at last coming home to roost! The media, this morning, is bursting with news about **the Dyson affair**. Why? Because 'you know who' has written an explosive blog about the PM. We are talking about **Dominic Cummings,** once chief advisor to the PM, chief advocate for Brexit and Vote Leave, breaker of lockdown rules and who then fell out with the PM over his handling of Covid and so left his post at No.10 in November 2020.

The PM, yesterday, accused Dominic Cummings of being the person who leaked his emails to James Dyson. He also accused him of being behind a number of other damaging leaks against him, including details of the second lockdown and the expenses of the refurbishment of his flat. Hmm, we don't think this was a wise or sensible move by the PM. Dominic Cummings knows everything about the PM's activities last year and has kept all the evidence. And he is to give evidence to MPs on the government's response to the Covid crisis on **the 26th May** when he said "I will answer questions about any of these issues for as long as the MPs want".

So, what exactly did he say on his blog?

Dyson text messages: "I have not found the ones that were leaked to Laura Kuenssberg (BBC political correspondent) on my phone nor am I aware of being sent them last year. **I am happy to meet with the Cabinet secretary and for him to search my phone for Dyson messages.**"

Lockdown leaks: "The Cabinet Secretary told the PM that the leak was neither me nor the then Director of Communications and that all the evidence definitely leads to Henry Newman and others in that office. The PM was very upset about this. He said to me afterwards, 'If Newman is confirmed as the leak then I will have to fire him and this will cause me very serious problems with Carrie as he is her best friend...(pause) perhaps we could get the Cabinet Secretary to stop the leak inquiry?' **I told him that this was 'mad' and totally unethical and that he had ordered the leak inquiry himself.**"

Flat expenses: "The PM stopped speaking to me about this matter in 2020 as I told him I thought his plans to have donors secretly pay for the renovation were **unethical, foolish, possibly illegal** and almost **certainly broke the rules** on proper disclosure of political donations if conducted in the way he intended. I refused to help him organise these payments. I would be happy to tell the Cabinet Secretary or Electoral Commission what I know concerning this matter."

Well, this story is going to run and run and we will all be looking out on the 26th May! But there again, of course, in the contents of this book alone we have known all along that this is what Boris is like. But what a mistake to make. To act out of revenge and not think it all through and, as one of Cummings allies told *The Times* today, "You've stuck a pair of size tens in a hornets' nest. You don't want to do that."

****

APRIL 24TH

There was a brilliant article in *The Independent* by Tom Peck yesterday. He writes about the leaks and corruption and the appalling state of this government and at the start of his article he writes that as we read it he wants us to keep saying in a small whispered voice, over and over again the phrase, "**These are the people running the country. These are the people running the country.**" It has a certain rhythm to it, he says. Then he adds that if you are able to follow on with the words "during a pandemic in which 150,000 people died", then feel free, but he acknowledges that it won't be easy.

****

APRIL 27TH
Lies and the Government and the Ministerial code

And the civil servants' union has won the right to challenge Boris Johnson in the High Court after he backed Priti Patel in the bullying row over Philip Rutnam. At a hearing in London two days ago, Mr Justice Linden granted the FDA (the First Division Association of civil servants) permission for a full hearing of the judicial review claim. **The FDA is challenging Mr Johnson's decision that Ms Patel's conduct did not breach the ministerial code**.

****

APRIL 27TH

A report in *The Times* today by Fiona Hamilton, crime and security editor, reveals that a **Chinese company** has been given more than £12 million in security contracts at the border, in prisons and at the Home office. Nuctech, which has close ties to the Chinese state, has provided its scanning equipment in key areas of UK infrastructure despite bans in the US and Canada and Lithuania. The Chinese Research Group questioned why it was being awarded contracts amid growing concern about Chinese encroachment and attempts to steal western intellectual property. The Home Office said, "Any company securing a contract with the Home office undergoes stringent due diligence checks." Why does that not fill me with confidence? What with the Russians in the new press briefing room and the Chinese in the Home Office, it is beginning to look as though this government, in addition to everything else, is completely incompetent and negligent with **our security.**

****

Transparency in government

Labour cabinet minister David, now Lord, Clark said that "Unnecessary secrecy in government leads to arrogant governance and defective decision-making". He said this in the proposals he brought before parliament in 1997 which led to the **Freedom of Information Act**. And as George Greenwood writes in *The Times*, "we can see that compliance with transparency laws is weakening and arrogant government threatens to return". Actually, I say it already has returned, but the more people who say this the better.

****

APRIL 28TH

The Electoral Commission

Well, the Electoral Commission has decided to investigate the refurbishment plans of No 11 Downing Street after it found that it had "reasonable grounds" to suspect an **"offence or offences" may have occurred**. It would appear that although the PM has paid for the refurbishment now, originally he was given a loan from the Tory party to the Cabinet Office. If this has not been declared, then it is in breach of the **ministerial code.** Of course, this is in all the media outlets and is being called 'cash for curtains' and it means that so many other inadequacies are being ignored. This will continue to be probed and discussed and it is actually not looking good for the PM. In PMQs on Wednesday, in trying to answer Sir Keir's questions he bluffed and raged and turned red and shouted and pointed his fingers and could not complete a single sentence.

People obviously have divided opinions about everything but what has united us all is their snub to John Lewis! Carrie said she wanted to get rid of the 'John Lewis nightmare'. Well actually **we all love John Lewis,** are devastated that they are closing some of their stores and we agree with John Betjeman when he said that nothing bad could ever happen at Peter Jones (which was owned by John Lewis). So, Carrie, really not a good thing to say. But John Lewis have the last word. **Their new advert** says "Time for an interiors refresh? We pride our Home Design Service on having something for *almost* everyone"!

****

APRIL 28TH

But at last, **a new Ministerial Advisor has been appointed** after the resignation of Sir Alex Allan five months ago. Lord Geidt is a Crossbench Member of the House of Lords, a Privy Councillor and a former Private Secretary to The Queen. However, **Boris Johnson will retain powers to quash any investigations and exonerate himself and ministers.** Boris Johnson overruled recommendations from Jonathan Evans, the chair of the committee on Standards in Public

Life, who said the adviser should be given powers to launch their own investigation. Lord Evans wrote to the prime minister on Wednesday, questioning why this power had not been included.

"We note that the adviser will still lack the authority to initiate investigations," he wrote. **"We will want to consider how far the new arrangements provide the degree of independence and transparency that the committee believes is necessary."**

Jonathan Jones, the government's former head of Legal Service who quit over concerns about the government's intention to break international law last year, said Johnson had endorsed a ministerial code that said his government should uphold "the very highest standards of propriety ... **there must be no bullying and no harassment, no leaking, no misuse of taxpayer money and no actual or perceived conflicts of interest".**

He said the public now needed confidence that the code would be respected, but the code has no legal status. **"The problem is we can have no confidence that these standards are being enforced or that any action will be taken when they are breached,"** he said. **"Its enforcement depends purely on prime ministerial whim."**

Jones said there was "a strong case for creating a new ministerial code with legal force. This could include tighter rules on conflicts of interests, declaration of donations, use of public assets, and leaking". Surely this has to be necessary when you have a government like this. In the past it hasn't usually been needed because most MPs have behaved with some degree of morality and resigned with dignity when found to be in breach of the ministerial code.

Remember the days? Edwina Currie over eggs and Cecil Parkinson over an affair?

****

APRIL 28TH

More lies as in PMQs today the PM accused Sir Keir Starmer of not voting for the EU trade agreement when it is on public record that he actually did. Johnson refuses to apologise for this false accusation.

****

MAY 2ND

And the former speaker of the House, **John Bercow,** gave an interview to LBC breakfast when he said that although he finds the PM perfectly amiable towards him he nevertheless **does not treat Parliament with respect**. He said that "the truth matters, parliament matters and telling the truth in and to Parliament matters". He also said that in his opinion Brexit **"is the most colossal foreign policy blunder of the post-war period"**. Speaking to Nick Ferrari at Breakfast, the ex-parliamentarian said he hoped to be wrong about Britain leaving the European Union but that he still needs convincing.

****

And we just skip ahead to **June 20th** when we hear that John Bercow has switched allegiance from the Tories to the Labour Party.

****

And connected to this are stories about the **Electoral Commission.** In a report by Nick Cohen of *The Observer* he reveals that the government have been targeting the Electoral Commission ever since it investigated Tory MPs and Vote Leave supporters. Amanda Milling, co-chair of the Tory Party, said the government wanted **to either abolish it** or undertake wholesale change. At the moment, this commission and the parliamentary commissioner for standards are the only bodies short of the police that can hold the PM to account and the Conservatives know it. Kathryn Stone, the parliamentary commissioner, may soon be investigating various items connected to the PM, but Nick Cohen in *The Observer* says that even if she recommends the Commons suspend Johnson they can use their majority to frustrate her. He goes on to say **"a party that once stood for traditional morality had baked in privilege and venality until it has reduced itself to ashes"**.

Just as I think it can't get any worse, I see a phrase like this. It sums it all up in one brilliant sentence.

****

MAY 2ND

Douglass Ross, leader of the Scottish Conservative party, was on the Andrew Marr show today. He was asked if Boris Johnson should resign if he was found to have broken the ministerial code over whatever was going on with his wallpaper. "Of course," he said. **"I think people expect the highest standards of the highest office in the land."**

Well that was a straight answer to a straight question. But wallpaper is hardly the most concerning problem that needs looking into at the moment.

****

Well, just to skip ahead once more for the moment: Today **May 28th** it has been ruled that Johnson did not break the ministerial code in the refurbishment of his flat which we now think cost around about £200,000. However, he was told by Lord Geidt that he acted unwisely and without rigour, suggesting he had little clue as to how it was being funded and was 'unwise' not to keep closer control.

****

Senior ministers wanting to know what is in **the Queen's Speech** next week have been told they must be **filmed reading it** in order to cut down on leaks. Can you believe that? If they want to see the information about some of the **25 bills** that will be outlined on May 11th, they have been ordered to examine it while being recorded remotely, to ensure they are not taking pictures or sending images.

This is now the level of trust in the present government, although admittedly not really surprising, because of all the leaks that have been going on.

MAY 5TH

Britain is at last preparing to grant full diplomatic status to the European Union's ambassador in London, concluding a dispute that has strained relations between the two sides for the past year. João Vale de Almeida took up his post as the EU's first ambassador to London last spring after Britain's exit from the bloc, but was denied formal recognition.

Reported in *The Times* today, Foreign Office sources said Downing Street's decision not to grant full credentials had had an "unhealthy, chilling effect" on talks between British diplomats and Brussels, even if Almeida was "not constrained in any way". News of the change in status came as **the EU formally signed off last year's Brexit trade deal.** João Vale de Almeida took up the role in February last year after Brexit was confirmed, but he was not given the same status as other ambassadors.

One source told the newspaper: "It is a silly dispute but has had a corrosive effect." Yes, I can certainly believe that.

****

More Lies

Caroline Lucas, leader of the Green Party, has sent an open letter to the Speaker of the House of Commons, together with the leaders of the other political parties.

This is part of her letter:

As you will know, one of the Nolan principles is that holders of public office should be truthful. It is also set out in the Ministerial code. We believe the Prime Minister consistently fails to meet this standard. This is not a question of occasional inaccuracies or a misleading use of figures:

it is a consistent failure to be honest with the facts, or to correct wrong information at the earliest opportunity when misleading information is given. This, we believe, amounts to a contempt of the House.

Jan 29th 2020. At PMQs, the Prime Minister said "The economy under this Conservative Government has grown by 73%". The truth is that under Conservative-led governments since 2010, the UK's GDP has grown by around 20%. The higher figure refers to economic growth since 1990, which includes 13 years of Labour governments.

Feb 5th 2020. At PMQs, the Prime Minister repeated this falsehood about economic growth and added another "We have cut CO_2 emissions in this country since 2010, on 1990 levels, by 42%. That is an astonishing achievement, and at the same time, the economy has grown by 73%". The reality is the decline of about 38% in CO_2 emissions has happened since 1990 not 2010.

March 4th 2020: At PMQs, the Prime Minister said "We have restored the nurses' bursary". This is at best highly misleading. Student nurses were awarded a £5,000 maintenance grant, but still have to pay tuition fees which they did not under the nurses' bursary.

June 17th 2020: At PMQs, the Prime Minister said "There are hundreds of thousands, I think 400,000, fewer families living in poverty now than there were in 2010". Again, this is not true as was made clear by the Children's Commission and the office for Statistics regulation. Yet there has been no retraction or apology to the House from the Prime Minister.

Feb 10th 2021: At PMQs, the Prime Minister said that Bridgend was "going to be the one of the great centres of battery manufacturing in this country if not the world". False claim with no retraction.

Feb 22nd 2021: In reply to a question about the details of Covid-related contracts, the Prime Minister said "As for the contracts that the hon. Lady just mentioned, all the details are on the record". Again, this was untrue and directly contradicted a High Court ruling which found that the Government was in breach of the law for not putting everything on the record. We would ask that this complaint be given precedence, allowing us to table a motion formally calling attention to the matter and asking that it be referred to the Committee on Standards and Privileges.

****

MAY 6TH

According to a report in *The Times* today, Ministers have awarded more than **£600 million worth of contracts** to tackle the Covid crisis, which is a third more than previously disclosed. The total spent on Covid-related contracts by the government exceeds £30billion.

****

MAY 16TH

Well, the **Cameron lobbying story** is very much in the news as he is called before a liaison committee to be questioned about his involvement with the Greensill affair. As Will Hutton in *The Observer* states, "It was excruciating. To watch a former British Prime minister before a committee of MPs last week trying to explain away his aggressive lobbying of ex-colleagues on behalf of Greensill which has since collapsed into insolvency was as humiliating as it was distressing." He goes on to say that "Cameron personifies a fundamental Tory frivolousness about both the consequences of power and how it is exercised". Absolutely. They have lost touch with ordinary life so much that the normal moral code seems completely off their radar.

****

So it was especially interesting to read **Andy Burnham today**. In the local elections for mayor of Manchester he won in every single one of the 215 wards. But as he says he lives in a completely different world from his previous life as an MP and government minster in the House of Commons. He says, "This isn't a situation where there's a security cordon that I walk through every morning and then I'm sort of taken away from that life that everyone else is living. I am commuting with everybody. ... I'm on public transport, I'm having a pint in the pubs outside. I kind of walk about and I make a point of this so people can come and talk to me." He feels that there is a lost connection between MPs and people's lives.

I think we would all agree with that.

****

MAY 16TH
Priti Patel has been accused of breaking the Ministerial code. (What, again?) She has been accused of a 'glaring and flagrant' breach of the Ministerial Code after she lobbied a fellow minister on behalf of a healthcare firm, Pharmaceuticals Direct Ltd, trying to seal a £20million deal for PPE last April. She denies any wrongdoing.

****

MAY 19TH
Yesterday was the first day of a **High Court hearing of a judicial review being brought against Matt Hancock by the Good Law Project and Every Doctor**. They are accusing the government of a "catastrophic waste of public funds", saying that a "substantial amount" of the PPE procured from the companies they chose had been unusable. Multibrands, a company in Bradford, wrote to the government in March last year advertising its capacity to supply 100 million masks from its warehouse in China. Apparently, they heard nothing from the government but they allege that the Department of Health unfairly prioritised Ayanda capital, Pestfix and Clandeboye and awarded them contracts worth about £700 million. The senior advisor for Ayanda Capital worked for the department for International Trade and was awarded a £252million deal for PPE. However, an undisclosed number of the masks did not meet standards and couldn't be used by the NHS. Pestfix had been prioritised because one of its former directors was an "old school friend" of the father-in-law of a senior civil servant

involved in procurement at the Department of |Health. It had no previous healthcare experience but was awarded a contract worth £108 million.

Well, the case continues and is due to end next Tuesday the 25th May.

****

MAY 20TH

The government seems to be facing a number of **threatening legal actions** at the moment. Here is another one. Apparently, government guidance for all **care homes** is that residents **over the age of 65** are not allowed to be taken outside their care home for any reason whatsoever, even now. The government says that there is too much risk that they could bring the Covid pandemic back into the care home. This is when all have had their second vaccine including the staff and including family members who want to take them out. But a pressure group called John's Campaign has started legal proceedings in a pre-action letter sent to the Department of Health and Social Care. They are saying that this ban on over 65s is unlawful. The letter requests the DHSC send a reply within 14 days, which will inform whether the campaign will apply for **a judicial review**. John's Campaign is named after Dr John Gerrard, who died in November 2014 after a hospital stay. It was founded in his honour by his daughter Nicci and fights for rights for relatives to be able to stay with people who suffer with dementia. There seems to be some confusion as to whether this is against the law or whether it is just guidance, but the campaigners are saying that each resident should be individually assessed rather than this blanket ban (or advice). It would appear that many heads of care homes would agree with this.

It really does seem to me to be draconian and lacking in any sort of common sense or compassion. But this is what we see over and over again with this government.

****

MAY 22ND

Daniel Morgan, a private investigator, was brutally murdered in the car park of a London pub in **March 1987**. Despite five police inquiries and an inquest, no-one has been brought to justice over his death, and the Metropolitan Police has admitted that corruption hampered the original murder investigation. *The Independent* panel, which was established by Theresa May in 2013, said its findings were originally to be published at last this Monday the 24th.. But last week **Priti Patel demanded that the findings of the report be handed over to her**, prior to publication. She says it is for "security issues".

But one source with close knowledge of the five Metropolitan police inquiries into the case and the documents involved, said: "There are no national security issues involved. There are **national embarrassment issues.**" So, this row has **delayed publication** of this long awaited report and the family are furious. They said that the report's delay was a "kick in the teeth" and served only to "betray and undermine the very purpose of the panel". In a statement, they added: "The Home Secretary's intervention is not only unnecessary and inconsistent with the panel's independence, it is an outrage which betrays her ignorance – and the ignorance of those advising her – with regard to her powers in law and the panel's terms of reference."

So it will be interesting to know when this report will see the light of day.

****

MAY 24TH

Is the Ministerial Code really that important? Priti Patel was on the Andrew Marr show yesterday morning and he asked her if she thought the ministerial code still matters, especially after she has been found to have broken it and the PM is under investigation over it. She replied, "I think at this stage **this isn't about breaking codes** and things of that nature, we're all just getting on in government doing very **difficult jobs** actually, coming out of this pandemic, and all ministers are currently focusing on doing that job."

Well, I do agree that it certainly is a difficult job being a minister during a pandemic, or any time actually, and it has been obvious to a lot of us for a long time that the current ministers are not of the calibre necessary for a time such as this. If you are afraid of being exposed as not being up to the job by being truthful, then you should resign. You need to read what Erskine May says about the ministerial code and lying to parliament, which you can easily find on page 41 of the brilliant book by Peter Oborne called **"The Assault on Truth"**.

****

MAY 25TH
On Friday evening (21st) new guidance was put up on a website to say that people living in **eight hotspots with increasing Indian variant** cases should stay in their towns and not travel in or out. Of course, no-one saw this and it transpires that none of the leaders, public health officials or local authorities of these towns had been consulted by the government. So, it came as a complete surprise to everyone when some journalists discovered this message about three days later. And then there was complete confusion. Were people allowed to travel to Portugal, which was on the green list, could they travel to work or to school, could they visit relatives or what? Actually, Tory MPs were furious with their constituents being virtually locked down with no warning and so it was made clear in the House eventually that this was guidance only and people should really use their common sense and decide what the risks to them were. "The guidance is just guidance," Zahawi, the vaccine minister said, desperate to appease them. So people were free to ignore it if they felt like it. Though obviously he would rather they didn't. Was that more or less clear? **Incompetence and confusion yet again.**

****

MAY 26TH

Dominic Cummings Day!

Dominic Cummings gave evidence to the Science and Technology Committee and the Health and Social Care Committee and spoke for more than seven hours. Well, this will have been well documented elsewhere so I am not going to comment on this marathon in detail. But there were a lot of serious accusations there, which someone needs to address. One comment that I found interesting was when he said that any parliament which offers people a choice for leadership of Johnson or Corbyn must be seriously flawed. And he also said that any government that had him and Boris Johnson at the top must be "crackers". He was also very critical of Matt Hancock and accused him of lying many times during the pandemic. Hancock was answering questions in the Commons this morning and there was a really interesting question to him, from the Shadow Health Secretary, Jon Ashworth. He asked Matt Hancock whether the accusations by Dominic Cummings were true, or if not, did the Prime Minister hire a fantasist and a liar to be his advisor? But of course this question was not answered.

****

JUNE 9TH

In PMQs today Sir Keir Starmer asked the PM four questions about the resignation of Sir Kevan Collins and the future of our children's education. After each question I sat on the edge of my chair waiting for the answer. But of course there was no answer to the questions asked. Once again it was all shouting and gesticulating and accusing the Opposition of absolutely anything he could think of. Indeed, he was pulled up by the Speaker once for not answering the question. And all the time he was shouting, he referred to our children as 'kids'. It jarred with me every time as, to me, it sounded disrespectful and slovenly.

****

Also today:

Transparency and openness? I don't think so. In *The Times* today George Greenwood reports that "a tribunal has criticised the Cabinet Office for a 'profound lack of transparency' as it overturned the department's attempt to withhold information about a secretive unit, called the **Clearing House**, that centrally screens freedom of information requests". I actually cannot believe that I am writing this. Almost all freedom of information requests should be 'applicant blind' and yet there were concerns that departments had been sending this 'Clearing House' details of journalists with FoI requests, leading them to be treated differently. The judge has ruled that the department must disclose all information related to the handling of complex requests. As the leader in *The Times* today says, "This ruling is a victory not only for OpenDemocracy ... but for all those who recognise the need for the government to be subjected to rigorous scrutiny." It goes on to say that this is not the way that an accountable government should operate and the judgement is particularly shaming for Michael Gove, the relevant minister, who had sought to brush off investigations into the workings of the clearing house as 'ridiculous and tendentious'. "Mr Gove must now ensure that the details about the Clearing House's methods are published."

****

JUNE 11TH

This goes back to the first item in this chapter. Today the Good Law Project sent a pre-action letter to the government. It said: "The nomination of Peter Cruddas for a peerage was unlawful because of apparent bias. A fair minded and informed observer presented with the facts of the matter, would conclude that there was a real possibility or danger of bias in the defendant's decision making." Well yes, we all thought it sounded very fishy at the time but then we are getting used to all these donations flying around the place mostly in the direction of the Tories. The Lib Dems are demanding a criminal investigation. So we will just keep an eye out and see whether justice is done or seen to be done.

****

JUNE 13TH

Well today it is reported in *The Sunday Times* that Lord Evans, who is chairman of the committee on Standards in Public Life, will make a Proposal in an emergency review being published tomorrow in the wake of the Greensill scandal. One of the proposals will suggest that all ministers should be **banned from lobbying for five years after leaving office.**

Well, we should be encouraged by this I suppose, but what an indictment on our government that it should even be needed.

****

JUNE 15TH

You may remember the case of **Daniel Morgan,** which I wrote about on May 22nd. We were concerned that the report was delayed yet again by Priti Patel demanding to see it.

Well, it has been published at last today. Most people are concerned with the fact that the Met have been accused of "institutionalised corruption" but that is beyond the remit of this book and I am concerned about the actions of the Home Secretary. I am going to quote the words of Baroness Nuala O'Loan in *The Independent* review, because once again it illustrates the intransigence and obstructiveness of Priti Patel. The Baroness says:

"Before I finish, I would like to touch on the regrettable **last minute delay** to the publication of our report. We had expected to publish on Monday **17th May** and the Home Office had been aware of this for several weeks. Senior Home Office officials had indicated to us that this was a convenient date, subject to the final decision of the Home Secretary. However, at the last moment we were told this would not be possible, due to a backlog of Parliamentary business arising as a result of the pre-local government election 'purdah' and the period of mourning for His Royal Highness, the Duke of Edinburgh. We were told that it was likely that the report would be published in Parliament on **24th May**. Again at the last minute, and very much to our surprise, the Home Secretary informed us she would not publish our report in Parliament until she and her officials had time to read it to ensure the report did not give rise to any issues under Article 2 of the European Convention on Human Rights, or on National Security grounds. We do not wish to rehearse the discussions which subsequently took place, other than to say how disappointed we were that the Home Secretary chose to adopt this stance when she did. **We are unaware of any such intervention previously. We do not believe the Home Secretary's approach was justified in this case**.

Nonetheless, our aim throughout the discussions was to ensure that Daniel Morgan's family had the opportunity to view our report as soon as possible. We have achieved our aim."

Why does Priti Patel behave in this way? What is she afraid of?

****

JUNE 15TH

The Speaker of the House, Sir Lindsay Hoyle, is furious with Boris Johnson. The PM sent out an embargoed press release to the media yesterday afternoon and then gave a press conference at 6pm about the easing of the lockdown **without first debating it in the House.**

The Speaker said it was "entirely unacceptable" that the Prime Minister held his televised news conference without informing the MPs in the Commons first and that he "must now lead from the top and follow the guidance" in the **ministerial code,** which states major announcements should be made first in parliament.

We await eagerly for that day.

****

JUNE 18TH

The Electoral Commission. Well, I have mentioned this a lot in this chapter and it is so important because it is able to investigate serious breaches of conduct by any government. But Ministers have announced today that a new Election Bill will remove its ability to prosecute criminal offences under election law, arguing it is a "waste of public money". Well, they have never been bothered about that before.

The Electoral Reform Society says that it is "a thinly–veiled government power grab".

What are they so afraid of? Our democracy is being drained away without a backwards glance.

****

JUNE 25TH

The Good Law Project has just reported that the High Court has ordered the Government to pay 75% of their costs in their successful legal challenge against **Michael Gove** for the unlawful award of a contract to associates of his and Dominic Cummings at Public First. They say that the "Government had planned to ask for permission to appeal the ruling but last night decided this wouldn't be wise and withdrew, belatedly accepting their conduct over the Public First contract had been unlawful."

The Judge today was crystal clear as to who won this case:

"In this case, it is clear to the court that the claimant (Good Law Project) was the overall successful party in the case...it sought a ruling that the decision to award the contract to Public First was unlawful, and the Court has made a ruling to that effect. Also, it was successful in defeating the Defendant's arguments about standing."

So once again the Ministerial Code has been broken, this time by Michael Gove.

****

So, I finish this chapter by quoting the final words of Ted Hastings, the superintendent from my favourite programme, 'Line of Duty'. He said:

"What's happened to us? When did we stop caring about honesty and integrity?" Thank you, Jed Mercurio. I think we all need to sit down in a quiet place and ponder the answer to that question.

****

PUBLIC INQUIRY

2021

MARCH 7TH
A group of family members of coronavirus victims have reportedly called for an **immediate public inquiry** into the pandemic crisis. The Covid-19 Bereaved Families for Justice UK group, which consists of 450 relatives of people who have died during the pandemic, has told the BBC an urgent review was necessary to limit the ongoing effects of the coronavirus crisis and prevent more deaths. They are threatening to **sue the government**. The group's lawyer, Elkan Abrahamson, told the broadcaster an early inquiry should be held prior to any complete formal proceeding, which is expected to take place once the pandemic is over.

Boris Johnson keeps putting this inquiry off for some reason, but these people have had enough.

****

APRIL 13TH
Well, the Prime Minister has lost very little time in ordering **an unprecedented formal inquiry** into the lobbying scandal of his old rival and mate, David Cameron. Government sources stressed that the decision on Monday was not a personal attack by Boris Johnson on his

old rival but said it was clear that the public deserved a transparent explanation of the scandal.

Campaigners including Transparency International have said the saga "highlights deep flaws in the UK's approach" and that an inquiry should cover the **lack of transparency in lobbying, enforcing the ministerial code and the revolving door between government and the private sector".** We all agree with that, but we are still wondering when the inquiry of the government's handling of the pandemic will see the light of day.

****

MARCH 15TH

Boris Johnson accepts he made a mistake in delaying the first lockdown.

Britain's first coronavirus lockdown came late because the Government's scientific advisers were using out-of-date data, close allies of Boris Johnson have claimed. As the first anniversary of the March 23rd shutdown approaches, senior sources have insisted Mr Johnson would act 'harder, earlier and faster' if he could go back in time, according to The Daily Telegraph. But they have claimed the PM was let down by his expert SAGE advisers who badly misjudged how quickly the virus was spreading. Mr Johnson was accused of costing lives and being too slow in his initial Covid response, which saw the country's borders remain wide open despite huge transmission in Europe and a voluntary lockdown which left it up to individuals and employers to decide what precautions to take. About 40,000 people died from the disease in the first wave. But yet again Boris Johnson blames other people for his mistakes and takes no responsibility for his actions whatsoever. WHEN IS THIS INQUIRY?

****

MARCH 18TH

When will the inquiry into the handling of the pandemic by this government begin? The campaign group Covid-19 Bereaved Families for Justice is calling for a judge-led, statutory inquiry to be convened urgently. Families bereaved by Covid-19 have warned Downing Street they will start legal action against the government after Easter unless Boris Johnson urgently launches a statutory public inquiry into the government's handling of the pandemic. Lawyers for 25 bereaved spouses and children on Wednesday gave Downing Street two weeks' notice that without a commitment they will go to court to claim ministers are breaking the law by not launching an inquiry now. Rachel Reeves, shadow minister, has been speaking to those who are bereaved and whose grief is still raw and recent and who are desperate for an inquiry. "Justice is being denied, and they can't have closure until they better understand what happened," she added. She urged the government to work with bereaved families to decide how the inquiry should be set up. "We can learn from the Chilcot and Hillsborough inquiries as to how this can be started in this parliament. With such a huge loss of life, justice delayed will be justice denied."

The government consistently refuses to be pinned down on when an inquiry should start, and who should lead it.

****

APRIL 7TH

And in another report today by Amnesty International it says that the UK is in a "headlong rush into abandoning human rights". They go on to say that "Their increasingly hostile attitude towards upholding and preserving human rights legislation raises serious concerns. On the right to protest, on the Human Rights Act, on accountability for coronavirus deaths, on asylum, on arms sales or on trade with despots, **we're speeding towards the cliff edge**." Amnesty International's UK director, Kate Allen, says, "For years, the UK has been moving in the wrong direction on human rights – but things are now getting worse at an accelerating rate." The report – which details 2020 global human rights trends, as well as those of 149 individual countries – condemns "the UK's high **Covid-19 death rate, one of the highest in Europe**, which saw at least 74,570 deaths over the course of the year, many of them in care homes, the failure to provide adequate PPE and regular testing, the direct discharge of infected patients from hospitals to care homes, and blanket imposition of do not resuscitate orders, all gave rise to further serious concern," the report says. "Having made mistake after lethal mistake during the pandemic, the government is now shamefully trying to strip away our right to lawfully challenge its decisions, no matter how poor they are. The refusal to conduct an urgent independent inquiry into its handling of the pandemic is a shocking demonstration that there is no appetite from this government to learn lessons and apply them in real time," said Allen. "There **needs to be an inquiry** that gets to the bottom of all of this."

The government's decision in July to resume military exports to Saudi Arabia resulting in about £1.4 billion sales, while slashing foreign aid to Yemen, was also heavily criticised in the report. Amnesty expressed serious concern about the government's reviews into the Human Rights Act and judicial review, both of which "are being **sped through during the pandemic** and could seriously diminish the public's capacity to challenge government decisions," said Allen.

This is a damning and much needed report by Amnesty International. There have been so many dreadful decisions by this government, most of which I too have written about in detail, but it is so good to see it all corroborated by Amnesty International. The actions of this government are shameful and every day there is something awful to report. As in the title to my preface, I find at least six impossible things to believe and write about before I have even got out of bed! When will people open their eyes and see?

****

APRIL 26TH
The Government has "no capacity" at present to launch a public inquiry into the handling of the coronavirus pandemic, it has

told bereaved families today. An inquiry "now is not appropriate" and people who would need to give evidence are "working round the clock" to keep society safe, families were told in a six-page letter from the Government Legal Department. So yet again Members of the Covid-19 Bereaved Families for Justice Group were told that the Government is "focused entirely" on responding to the pandemic, in particular on the vaccination rollout and preparations for a third wave. The PM has already made it clear that there will be an inquiry when the time is right but that time is not now. "There is simply no capacity for Government to pause these efforts and divert resources to an intensive independent inquiry. The very people who would need to give evidence to an inquiry are working round the clock to respond to the pandemic and keep us all safe. It is not anticipated that the Government's workload will ease in the coming months."

Co-founder Jo Goodman questioned how the Government can be "too busy to answer to a judge-led inquiry, and yet have time to conduct in-house parliamentary inquiries". She added: "How long will grieving families be left without answers, without assurance that the mistakes that led to our loved ones' deaths are not repeated? We are still living through the pandemic – procrastination is not only an insult to the bereaved, it also prevents the Government from protecting future lives to the best of their ability."

But we know that the government has no intention of holding an inquiry for months and months.

****

APRIL 30TH
Boris Johnson is still refusing to hold a public inquiry into the handling of the pandemic. He keeps on saying that **"now is not the time".** However in a report in *The Guardian* yesterday The Institute for Government (IfG), whose leadership includes the former Conservative cabinet minister David Lidington and the former Labour science minister Lord Sainsbury, will call on the prime minister to set up a statutory public inquiry in May, with hearings to start in September.

At the same time the respected healthcare thinktank, the King's Fund, which is chaired by Lord Kakkar, a government adviser on race and professor of surgery at University College London, will tell Downing Street: **"Now IS the time."**

Also the accusations (which he denies) about the PM shouting "no more fucking lockdowns – let the bodies pile high in their thousands" late last year, have reignited calls from the bereaved for an inquiry.

In its 33-page case for an urgent investigation into a pandemic that has claimed more than 150,000 lives according to death certificates, the IfG will say an inquiry could provide "a focus for collective grief" and deliver "some form of justice for the victims and their families". The King's Fund said: "The suggestion that everyone in government is too busy for an inquiry is a poor excuse."

****

The Covid bereaved group has threatened to take the prime minister and the health secretary, Matt Hancock, to court to challenge their refusal so far to trigger a public inquiry, arguing that the scale of deaths requires it. Johnson has repeatedly refused to meet them. **The list of bodies and public figures now demanding an inquiry** includes the British Medical Association, the Trades Union Congress, the Archbishop of Canterbury, the Labour leader Keir Starmer, the government scientific adviser Prof John Edmunds, the Muslim Council of Britain and the Covid-19 Bereaved Families for Justice group which represents more than 3,000 families who lost their loved ones to the virus.

The Royal College of Nursing (RCN) also repeated its commitment to an inquiry on Thursday, saying: "Justice delayed will be justice denied." **Last year the deaths of 256 nurses, nursing auxiliaries and assistants in England and Wales involved Covid, according to the Office for National Statistics.**

****

MAY 16TH

About 25 members of the All-Party Parliamentary Group on Coronavirus have written a letter to the Prime Minister warning him that the current timetable which is saying that the inquiry will not begin until next spring will mean that **vital lessons will go unlearned** ahead of a potential third wave. They also say that it is really important that the inquiry **is fully independent with the chair and panel being decided on a cross-party basis**.

****

How many times do people have to ask for this inquiry? Of course Boris Johnson does not want one because he will be found out to have been the wrong person at the wrong time to be the leader of this once great country of ours. One of the first sentences in this book described how Johnson achieved his life-long ambition of becoming Prime Minister. Someone recently said to me that an acquaintance who had met him said he was actually very charming. Well he possibly is, but as a leader of a once great country he is a complete and abject failure.

****

LOCAL ELECTIONS

2021

MAY 19TH

So, a huge shock for Labour today with the Conservative win in Hartlepool. The Tories are also making gains in the council elections. So why are the inadequacies of this government not getting through to the voters? And why is Keir Starmer not making sufficient inroads to even just hold on to what were safe Labour seats? Well, you can be sure they are asking themselves such questions today!

I actually think that both the fact that we are coming out of lockdown and that the vaccination rollout is going so well must have played a part. But also, it has been difficult for the Labour leader to speak to a crowd of people or to even shake someone's hand during the pandemic and that can't have helped. And of course, he has had no live backup from his MPs in the Commons as they are all on Zoom.

But enough of excuses. Labour has to remember that the only time they have been in power over the last 40 years was when Tony Blair was their leader, won three general elections and was Prime Minister from 1997 to 2007. We do not want a right, right party or a left, left party, we want a centre left party with empathy and support for the vulnerable. (Well, that is what I want!) Starmer needs to have the courage of his convictions and stop worrying about whom he might offend. He also needs to get some dynamic people on to his front bench. Where are Harriet Harman, Yvette Cooper, Hilary Benn, Jess Phillips etc.? He should also go and talk to Mr Blair and stop treating him, their most successful political leader ever, as an embarrassment.

****

MAY 21ST

Bu after a couple of days I have further thoughts.

Starmer: Actually in the circumstances I think he has done quite well. (I honestly do not mean to sound patronising!) It is only a year since Corbyn, the pandemic has meant that he has had no physical back-up in PMQs, no conferences or any talks to crowded rooms, and no shaking of hands or proper meetings with the general public. He does come across as a serious and articulate guy who could be a Prime Minister, although maybe needing more of a 'personality'.

However: The labour Party is at a crossroads and I don't think it can hark back to years ago when it stood for the 'working class' any more. Starmer was too focused on the 'wallpaper' fiasco and Johnson's lies in Parliament, which actually the ordinary man or woman in the street is really not bothered about. Harking back to 'Tory sleaze' did not resonate with the public. Apparently, it was thought that Starmer would turn up in Hartlepool surrounded by nurses which might have caused some pause for thought. Starmer had so much else which he should have focused on.

I have also come to realise that most people, but especially those who are struggling just to survive, are not interested in others who are struggling too. That is not criticism – it is an observation. The inhumane treatment of asylum seekers, the locking up of women and young children, the abject poverty of some in society, the decimation of our fishing industry, the cuts in foreign aid which affects women and children disproportionately, the funding cuts in music and the arts, the lack of any plan for social care, the gross mishandling of the pandemic resulting in so many unnecessary deaths, the enormous waste of money and so many well-documented lies in parliament told by the Prime Minister are possibly not even noticed by the general electorate.

But they are by me!! And I am in the lucky position of having the time and the inclination to record it all! And when the amazing promises given to the people of Hartlepool by Boris Johnson do not come to fruition as they won't (believe me), maybe things will change. Today they have been furloughed, they are being vaccinated and they are coming out of lockdown. They could even be booking up summer holidays. And Boris Johnson can charm and wiggle and bluster and persuade people that he can deliver, as he did of course with Brexit. But the dreadful results of Brexit are still being felt.

The one phrase that I keep hearing again and again about this government is "We feel let down. They have not kept their side of the bargain". Boris Johnson can talk the talk but he absolutely does not deliver.

But his day of reckoning will come, there **will** be a public inquiry and hopefully there will be someone with compassion, fight, personality and morality to take his place. And the one name being bandied about is Andy Burnham, Mayor of Manchester.

****

Now there are many promises about 'levelling up' and improving our infra-structure. And indeed structural repairs on hospitals do appear to be on-going, but so much is needed elsewhere.

****

INFRASTRUCTURE

2021

APRIL 3RD

London Bridges Falling Down? Tomorrow sees the annual **Oxford and Cambridge boat race**. This is usually watched by around 200,000 spectators on the banks of the Thames. However, this year there will be no spectators because of the coronavirus and it will not be taking place on the Thames because of **Hammersmith Bridge**. Just in case you are not aware of the problems of the bridge, I will enlighten you.

As serious cracks appeared in the bridge, Hammersmith Bridge was closed to motor traffic on **April 10th, 2019** leaving it accessible only to pedestrians and cyclists. On **13th August 2020** the bridge was closed completely, following an increase in size of the cracks in the North-East pedestal due to the hot weather. Boats are prevented from passing under the bridge for safety reasons, and the pedestrian underpasses on each side are closed. The engineers have advised it will cost £46million to stabilise Hammersmith Bridge and make it safe for pedestrians, cyclists and river traffic; up to £141million to fully restore the bridge so it can be reopened to buses and motor vehicles; or £163million if they were to reduce the three-year timescale by as much as 12 months. However, they are now saying that Hammersmith Bridge will not fully reopen to traffic for about six and a half years, that is until **2027**. Hammersmith and Fulham Council says it can't afford it.

Elsewhere TfL owns seven bridges, all of them showing varying signs of deterioration. Documents show Chiswick and Westminster bridges are defined as being in a "good" condition but that still means there are early signs of deterioration and some minor treatments "may be merited".

Four bridges – Twickenham, Kew, Battersea and Lambeth – are classed as "fair". That means "more extensive interventions may be required within 10 years".

Vauxhall Bridge is rated as "poor". It is already getting extensive renovations and the Rotherhithe Tunnel will need repairing at an estimated cost of between £116m and £178m.

The other issue is that there isn't one over-arching strategic body in charge of London's bridges. **Twenty years ago, a letter to the *Evening Standard* stated that London's bridges ought to be London's treasure and are now London's disgrace.**

There were calls in Parliament for a "strong, co-ordinated body responsible for the planning and financing" of all London's bridges.

But not much has happened since then. It **is** a disgrace and an ongoing and increasing problem, and hugely worrying that no-one seems remotely concerned.

Because of all this incompetence the boat race will be held on the River Ouse in Cambridgeshire. Roads have been closed and people have been told to watch it on the television. However...why is there always a 'however'? Janet and Robin Edwards have **a back garden that leads down to the river.** They have invited two friends to join them to watch, socially distanced of course, from their garden and their neighbours will also watch it live. But they have both received letters telling them they must watch it on television and if they go into their garden and other people come to watch with them **there will be consequences.** You really couldn't make it up and of course they are taking no notice whatsoever of these stupid letters.

****

MAY 4TH

After a 16-month freedom of information battle by *The Times* they report today on the **state of our crumbling prisons**. They say there are more than a thousand fire hazards going months and sometimes years without being fixed. **Fire doors, fire alarms and fire extinguishers** are either missing or in need of repair. Steve Gillan, general secretary of the Prison Officer's association, said: "This needs to be remedied as quickly as possible if anything is to be learnt from **the Grenfell disaster**." The National Audit Office said last year that 41 % of prison buildings required significant repairs, some were at risk of breakdown and an estimated 500 prison places had to be taken out of use. Assaults on prison officers rose 110% as inmates were given crowded and degrading cells. The Ministry of Justice refused to disclose details until the Information Commissioner's Office intervened.

****

MAY 11TH

Apparently, the department for education has reported that schools repair work could amount to £11 billion.

****

And in the Queen's Speech today, we hope to hear about the promises to work on infrastructure. I hope it includes **bridges and prisons and schools**.

****

THE QUEEN'S SPEECH AND BEYOND

2021

11TH MAY

Well, what a banal speech that was. A record length of only nine minutes. The Queen looked amazing at 95, in a smart coat, dress and hat, so not in robes today, but my word absolutely not worth it for a speech such as this one.

So on the topics already covered in this book we had what we expected:

Social care

Precisely eight words on social care as he said that "Proposals for social care will be brought forward".

Photos and ID cards for voting

Plans will be put in place for it to be mandatory for all voters to have photo ID cards in order to be able to vote. Some people think this is an excellent idea. However, this could cost £20 million per general election to sort out a problem that doesn't exist. There is hardly any fraud in British elections. And it will stop many people from voting at all.

The Employment Bill

This has been dropped after the furore over whether the worker's rights would be torn up after Brexit. The government still says it will bring in the bill "when the time is right".

The Erasmus scheme

You could be forgiven for missing this one. The Turing scheme which has replaced the Erasmus scheme since Brexit will be less generous to non-disadvantaged students who will now get £335 instead of £445 in living costs per month.

Levelling-up

This is one of the phrases you will hear again and again from this Prime Minister, but there are no details about what it actually means. However, there will be a 'white paper' later in the year.

Building planning law

There are new planning laws being introduced to make the laws "simpler, faster and more modern". But they have already been dismissed as a "complete disaster in the making". Darren Rodwell, London Council's executive member for housing and planning, said: "Our concern is that ripping up planning regulations will only lead to more slum housing built to maximise profits rather than address Londoners' needs." Theresa May said that this Bill will put the "wrong homes in the wrong places" and countryside campaigners said that the reforms would mean "open season for developers" in rural areas. I admit it is very complicated but important just to keep track of what the actual outcome really means.

Asylum seekers

Plans will be brought forward to reduce access to the legal system for refugees, making it easier for the Home Office to deport them. As many as half of immigration and asylum decisions are overturned when challenged in court. However, in the speech yesterday the Prime Minister set out plans to remove this barrier by overturning a decade of legal precedent and will remove the right to have a High Court judge review their case. And also further new legislation in the Queen's Speech aims to deter desperate people from crossing the Channel by banning people from claiming asylum in the UK if they have already travelled through safe countries like France and Belgium.

Contracts

A procurement bill will remove many of the legal mechanisms around awarding government contracts. The process will be "simplified". Always a worry. It will give ministers more flexibility to "consider wider social value when picking suppliers". But people are worried about what this means exactly when so many contracts have been given to allies of the government. Will this now become even easier?

Northern Ireland

There is no Bill to end prosecutions for historic crimes in Northern Ireland as had previously been promised.

The Public Inquiry

There **will** be a Public Inquiry the PM has announced today in this Parliament. No confirmed date as yet but probably next spring. So more disappointment that it isn't much sooner. A cartoon in *The Times* this morning (May13th) by Peter Brookes puts it very eloquently when he shows Boris Johnson kicking the inquiry ball into the long grass.

Fixed term parliaments

Buried away under the word 'democracy' was the announcement that the Fixed Term Parliament Bill will be repealed. This means that Boris Johnson could call a general election in 2023. But he also announced legislation to "restore the balance of power between the executive, legislature and the courts". What exactly does this mean? Why is everything so vague in this speech? **I certainly am worried about this one.**

****

MAY 20TH

Well, I think **I am right to be worried**. Last July Robert Buckland QC, the Justice Secretary, announced a six-month independent review of administrative law to consider options for **reforming judicial review**, the process by which government decisions are challenged in the courts. We are seeing quite a lot of these at the moment.

Lord Faulks, the former Conservative justice minister and now a crossbench peer, was charged with carrying out this review. During the House of Lords debate on the proposed bills which took place earlier this week he said: "The terms of reference were broad; The timescale short." The 195-page report submitted in January and published in March did not give ministers the conclusions they might have wanted. Contrary to government assertions of a rise in judicial review, it said that cases stood at the same level as in the 1990s and found claims were actually decreasing. Neither did they find that judges were meddling inappropriately in political matters. He said that "Having received an enormous amount of material of a very high quality **the panel were not ultimately convinced that judicial review needed radical reform**".

Apparently, they think that Boris Johnson was so cross when the Supreme Court ruled that he had acted unlawfully when he **suspended parliament in 2019** that it was this ruling that precipitated the government's desire to limit judicial review. As it is being said, **"Nobody likes being told they are wrong"**. Well, that could be a problem because I am afraid Boris Johnson is going to be told that again and again and again.

The review concluded that ministers could be "confident that the courts will respect institutional boundaries in exercising their inherent powers to review the legality of government action", and said that **"politicians should in turn afford the judiciary the respect which it is undoubtedly due when it exercise these powers"**.

****

So as Sir Keir Starmer said in his response to the Speech, there was "no new funding, no details, no timescale". He added that "failure to act for a decade was bad enough but failure to act after the pandemic is nothing short of an insult".

****

SO WHAT OF THE FUTURE?

JUNE 2021

These are two reports just out which paint a picture of Britain today.

They make dismal reading and any government is in for a hard time over the next decade. But in order to progress at all we need transparency and honesty, commitment and certainty. If you have read the entirety of this book, you will understand that I do not think we have the appropriate government for the task ahead. It is being said that the Labour Party has a mountain to climb, but I think that the Conservative Party has, as well.

MAY 17TH
A report by the **Resolution Foundation** written with the London School of Economics Centre for Economic Performance has said that Britain's economy will fall further behind other nations like Germany unless "seismic" shifts including climate change, an ageing population, Brexit and the Covid aftermath are addressed.

"The UK faces a 'decisive decade' and is neither prepared for, nor used to, change on this scale," it says. "The UK is more unequal than any EU country apart from Bulgaria and has just gone through its slowest decade of productivity growth in 120 years. This makes a new economic approach desirable," the report said. "What makes it essential is the scale of coming challenges. If the UK continues on its current path of relative underperformance, income levels will be closer to those in Italy than Germany by 2030. Italy's economy has stagnated for the past 20 years."

To avert this outcome, the report's authors are calling for a new strategy to tackle a number of economic challenges that will have broad societal impact.

"Slow growth, high inequality and badly-handled economic disruption undermine wellbeing, intensify social divisions and create political problems all with enduring effects," the researchers wrote.

While Boris Johnson has committed to "build back better" after the pandemic, the government has yet to set out a plan for achieving its objective.

"Any such strategy was notably absent from last week's Queen's Speech," the Resolution Foundation said.

****

MAY 19TH

And here is yet another report highlighting the divisions in our society.

A report by the **National Audit Office** has said that Coronavirus has exposed decades-long weaknesses in government and divisions in wider society, including neglect of social care and chronic underfunding in local government.

In their report released today, the NAO said **the virus "laid bare existing fault lines within society, such as the risk of widening inequalities, and within public service delivery and government itself".**

273

It highlighted the need for **long-term solutions** across areas including the disconnect between adult social care and the NHS, failings in data and IT systems, workforce shortages and ongoing monetary shortfalls, with a warning that already-struggling local government finances had been "scarred by the pandemic".

Jonathan Ashworth, the shadow heath secretary, said Covid had "exposed the NHS and social care to extreme pressure like never before".

He said: "We entered the pandemic with a weakened NHS, with growing waiting lists, fewer beds and desperately short of staff. We cannot afford to repeat the same mistakes. We need both an NHS rescue plan to bring waiting lists down and a plan for social care reform. Our NHS and care system cannot be left exposed in the same way again."

****

But in all fairness, we must give the **reply from the government**. A government spokesperson said: "Throughout the pandemic, our approach has been guided by data and the advice of scientific and medical experts. As new evidence emerged, **we acted quickly and decisively to protect lives and livelihoods**. We have committed to a full public independent inquiry to look at what lessons we can learn from our response to this unprecedented global challenge."

****

Obviously it is up to you as to who, or what, you believe.

EYES AND EARS

JUNE 2021

As I bring this book to a close we hear about the shock resignation of our health secretary, Matt Hancock. Photographs of him were published in *The Sun* on Friday 25th June showing him in an amorous clinch with one of his personal aides, Gina Coladangelo. Apparently, this photo was taken last May when he was telling us all not to hug. We were not allowed to hug our elderly relatives or even hold their hands as they were dying in care homes. Young singletons were not allowed to hug each other, you couldn't hug people at a funeral, or dance at a wedding. We were even told not to hug our young grandchildren.

So, he apologised profusely for his mistake and for his breach of the rules. The PM stood by him, accepted the apology and said the matter is closed.

But people were furious. MPs were flooded with emails from their constituents and there was a deafening silence from his colleagues. By late Saturday he had tendered his resignation. Boris Johnson, however, was being accused of a lack of leadership as it was being said that he should have sacked Mr Hancock immediately. But as he resigned, his colleagues started to say how good he had been and don't worry, he is a young man and he will soon be back. Boris Johnson said that he should be proud of what he has achieved both during and before the pandemic. I find it very difficult to get my head around this, actually.

And indeed many people are citing the debacle over test and trace, over the care home scandal and over the PPE inefficiencies, all of which have been well documented in this book. Also, there is a further dimension to this story. Questions are being asked about how this aide, an old university friend of Hancock, was appointed in the first place. And apparently Hancock faces a fresh allegation about the fact that he has been using his own personal email account to conduct vital Department of Health business instead of the official government email account. This is in complete contravention of official guidelines and will make it more difficult for any independent inquiry to access all records.

But I will tell you what disgusts me the most. On Thursday evening, as soon as he hears that the story is about to break, he rushes home to tell his wife that he is leaving her and he wakes up his eight year old child to tell him and his other two children that he is going as well.

****

But just now I think I can feel a very slight seismic shock happening beneath my feet! I believe that things are beginning to add up with the general public at last. They remember Cummings, G7, the Uefa VIPs, the Grand Prix at Silverstone, and now this very minute, Michael Gove. The phrase I am hearing over and over again is that there is one law for them and another for the rest of us.

Could this just be the beginning of the end for Boris Johnson and his inadequate cabinet, I wonder?

Well, we are locked down until the 19th July and the scientists are still full of doom and gloom, but I am bringing this tale of woe to an end – although I don't rule out a volume two! However I do ask you to please keep your eyes and ears open for news of asylum seekers, Brexit traders, Universal benefit, foreign aid cuts, NHS funding, the locking up of women, Nazanin Zaghari-Ratcliffe, the funding of science, the immigration procedures at our borders, or U turns, resignations, weasel words and lies by this government, improper uses of our taxes, the extent of poverty in the UK, and the proper and lawful use of parliament. In other words, watch out for new laws being passed without being voted on and for the breaking of the Ministerial Code.

But more important than any of all of that, please, please, please keep a sharp look out for **our children**. From birth to students in further education, they must be everyone's top priority. Wraparound affordable childcare from birth, an extended curriculum which involves music, sport, drama, creative arts, outdoors adventure, a curriculum of excellence, free of paranoid testing and unnecessary exams, but an array of subjects taught by dedicated teachers who love the children they teach and who are respected and properly paid. It is a sad reflection on our present education system that a large proportion of children move up from year 6 to secondary school without being able to read well. In spite of SATs tests, 47% of primary school children fell below official standards this year. So, abolish SATs and encourage the talk of abolishing GCSEs. But watch out for the locking up of young children, for the abolition of free school meals, for the low maintenance of playgrounds, for mental health concerns and for the lies and misinformation that I know you will hear.

However, I am determined to end on a positive note. I put my faith in **the ordinary person** who crowd-funds for good causes, who takes care of their neighbours, who goes the extra mile to help someone who needs their help, who have continued to work throughout the pandemic as key workers putting their own lives and those of their families at risk and often not getting any recognition, and all those of course who work in the NHS. In fact, nearly all of us have tried to do our best to get through these past 21 months or so.

But we remember, too, all those who have suffered such huge loss. Loss of life, loss of health and loss of livelihoods. Not only due to the pandemic, but also of course due to Brexit.

I applaud the Good Law Project and Open Democracy who try so hard to bring this government to account. We need transparency

and honesty, cool heads, wise council, willingness to learn, analytical brains, vision and strong leadership. Never afraid to make the tough and unpopular decisions. To put country before personal ambition. Is that really too much to ask?

I leave it...all of it...with you.

****

ACKNOWLEDGEMENTS

I want to say a huge thank you to all our brilliant journalists. The accurate reporting of news is something that we all need to fight for, now more than ever.

My thanks go to:

The Times	The Sun
The Sunday Times	The Yorkshire Post
The Guardian	The Financial Times
The Observer	LBC
The Independent	BBC
The Evening Standard	ITV
The Mirror	Sky News
The Daily Mail	Centre for Crime and
The i	Justice Studies
PoliticsHome	The Howard League
HuffPost	for Penal Reform
The Express	

Many, many people, charities and protest groups have been credited throughout this text and if I have left anyone out, I apologise. But without all of you this book would never have been written.

****

ABOUT THE AUTHOR

Sue Wood was born and brought up in a medical family in Coventry. She was educated in Leamington Spa and Maria Grey Froebel College in Twickenham. She worked as a Primary school teacher in Coventry and Cambridge and then took a break from teaching and worked as Director of Public Relations at Coventry Cathedral. After her wedding there she moved with her husband, first to Abu Dhabi and then to Aberdeen. She is now settled in Hertfordshire with her husband, and has two children and two grand-children.

On retiring from teaching she became a Speaker for Save the Children. She has always been concerned about those whom she feels are being treated unjustly and she has been a member of The Howard League for Penal Reform for over 25 years.